HALO®

ESCALATION

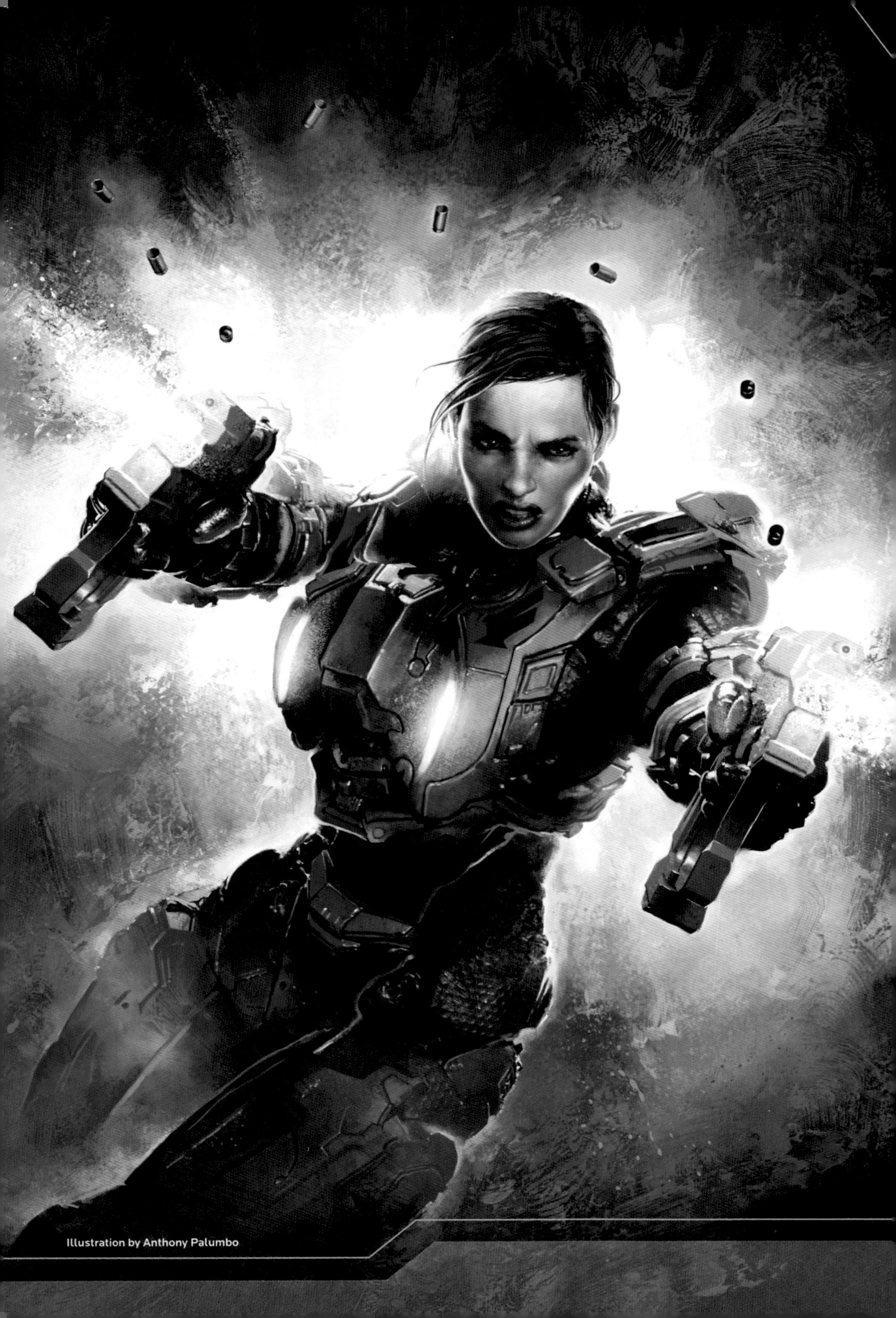

Illustration by Anthony Palumbo

ESCALATION

VOLUME 1

SCRIPT
CHRIS SCHLERF

PENCILS
SERGIO ARIÑO
RICARDO SÁNCHEZ

INKS
JUAN CASTRO
ROB LEAN
JASON GORDER

COLORS
MICHAEL ATIYEH

LETTERING
MICHAEL HEISLER

COVER ART
ANTHONY PALUMBO

DARK HORSE BOOKS

PUBLISHER
MIKE RICHARDSON

COLLECTION DESIGNER
SANDY TANAKA

ASSISTANT EDITORS
SHANTEL LAROCQUE
ROXY POLK
IAN TUCKER
AARON WALKER

EDITOR
DAVE MARSHALL

This volume collects issues #1–#6 of the Dark Horse comic-book series *Halo: Escalation*.

Special thanks to Nicolas Bouvier, Mike Gonzales, Kevin Grace, Tyler Jeffers, Carlos Naranjo, Tiffany O'Brien, Frank O'Connor, Jeremy Patenaude, Brian Reed, and Kiki Wolfkill at Microsoft.

Published by
Dark Horse Books
A division of Dark Horse Comics, Inc.
10956 SE Main Street
Milwaukie, OR 97222

DarkHorse.com
HaloWaypoint.com

First edition: October 2014
ISBN 978-1-61655-456-9

1 3 5 7 9 10 8 6 4 2
Printed in China

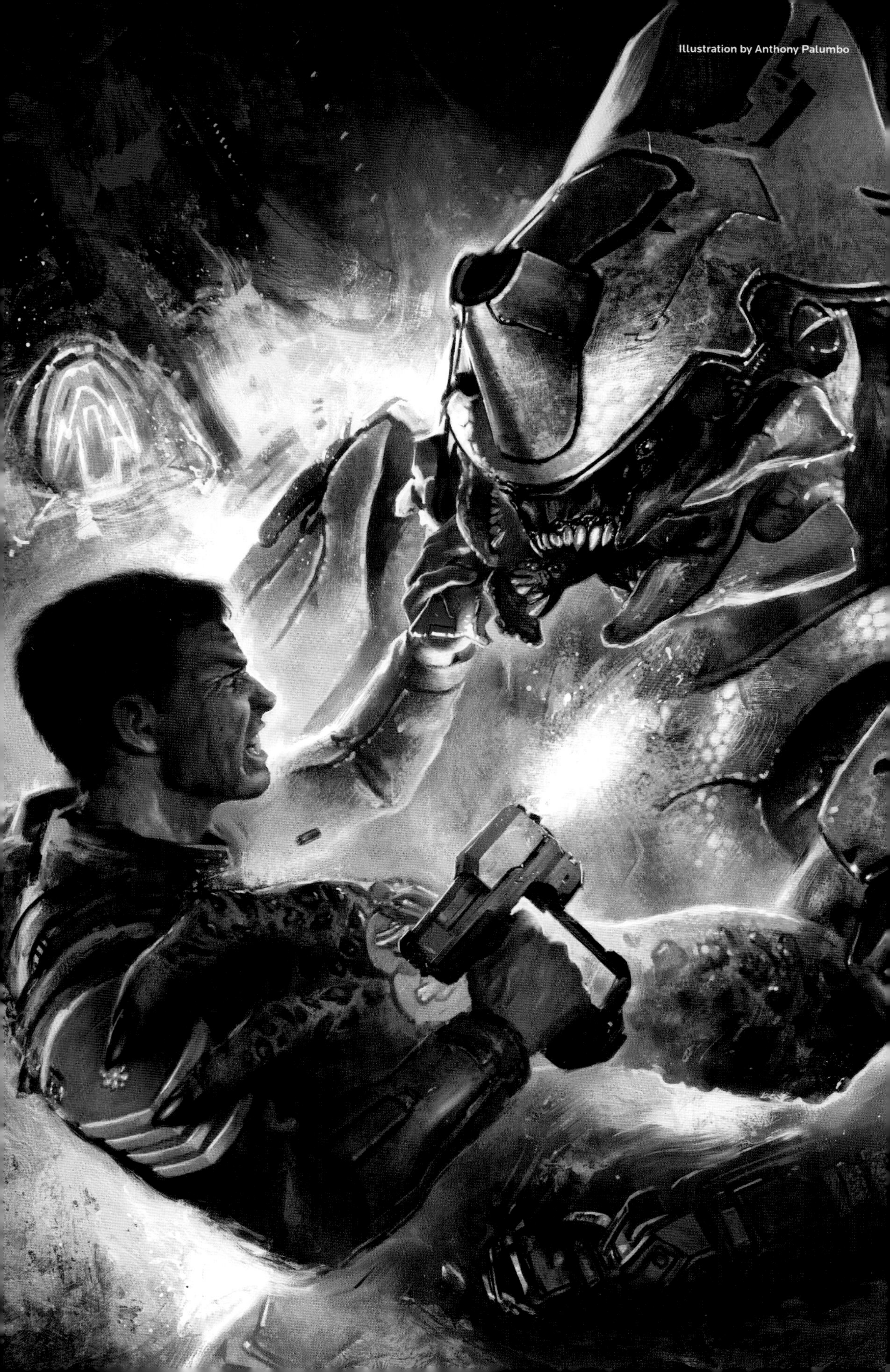
Illustration by Anthony Palumbo

Five years after the Human-Covenant War, long-lost Spartan John-117—the Master Chief—has been rescued off a Forerunner shield world, Requiem. Pursuing an awakened Forerunner known as the Didact, the Master Chief defeats the ancient warrior above Earth, but at a terrible cost—the death of the Chief's AI, Cortana.

The attack on Earth opens the door to an emergent threat in the form of Jul 'Mdama, a Covenant renegade who takes command of the Didact's Promethean army. The UNSC *Infinity*, led by Captain Thomas Lasky, is deployed to prevent 'Mdama from gaining control of Requiem, with the help of a new generation of Spartans led by Commander Sarah Palmer.

Infinity drives 'Mdama's forces into retreat, but the victory proves to be a temporary one . . .

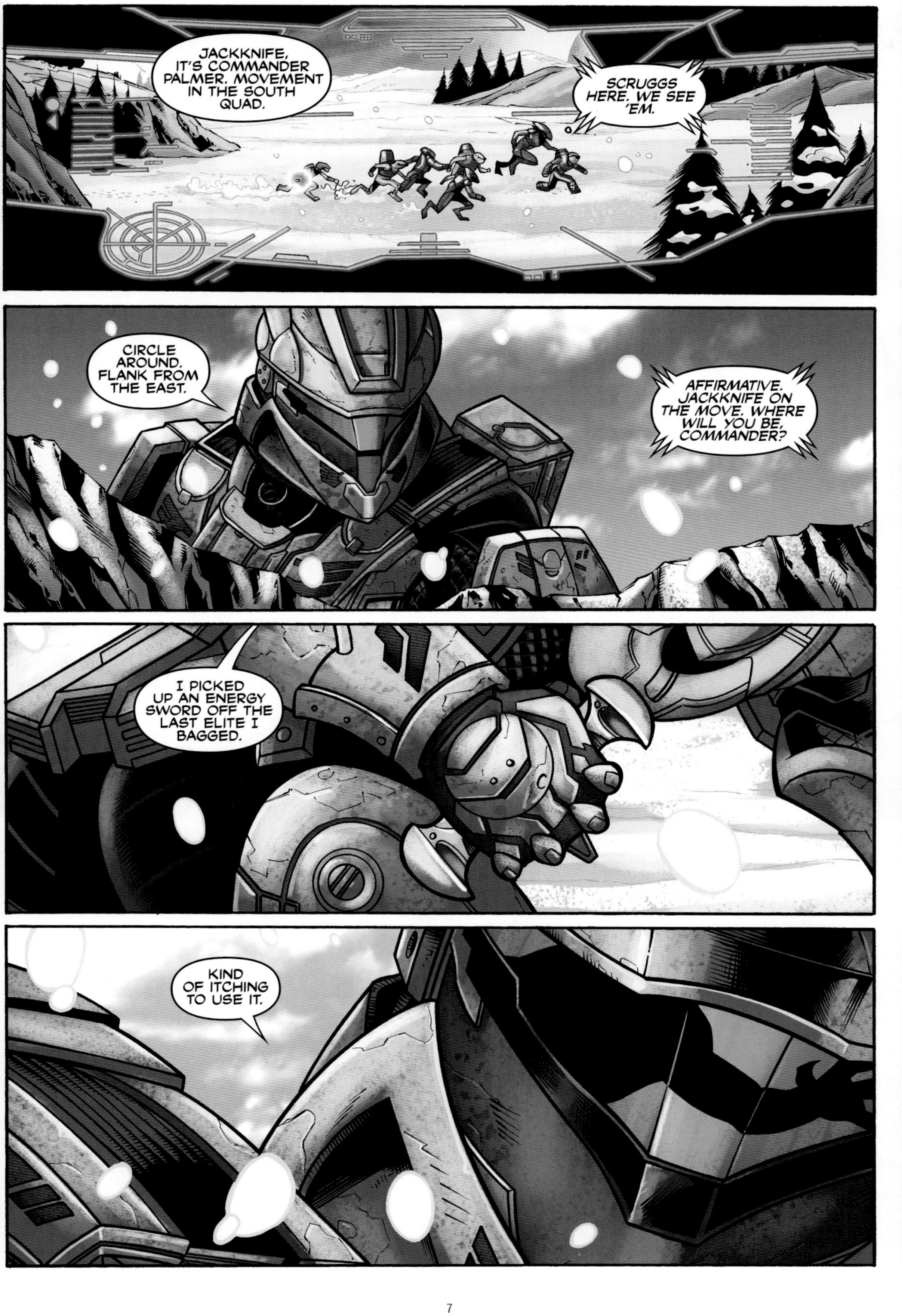
JACKKNIFE, IT'S COMMANDER PALMER. MOVEMENT IN THE SOUTH QUAD.
SCRUGGS HERE. WE SEE 'EM.
CIRCLE AROUND. FLANK FROM THE EAST.
AFFIRMATIVE. JACKKNIFE ON THE MOVE. WHERE WILL YOU BE, COMMANDER?
I PICKED UP AN ENERGY SWORD OFF THE LAST ELITE I BAGGED.
KIND OF ITCHING TO USE IT.

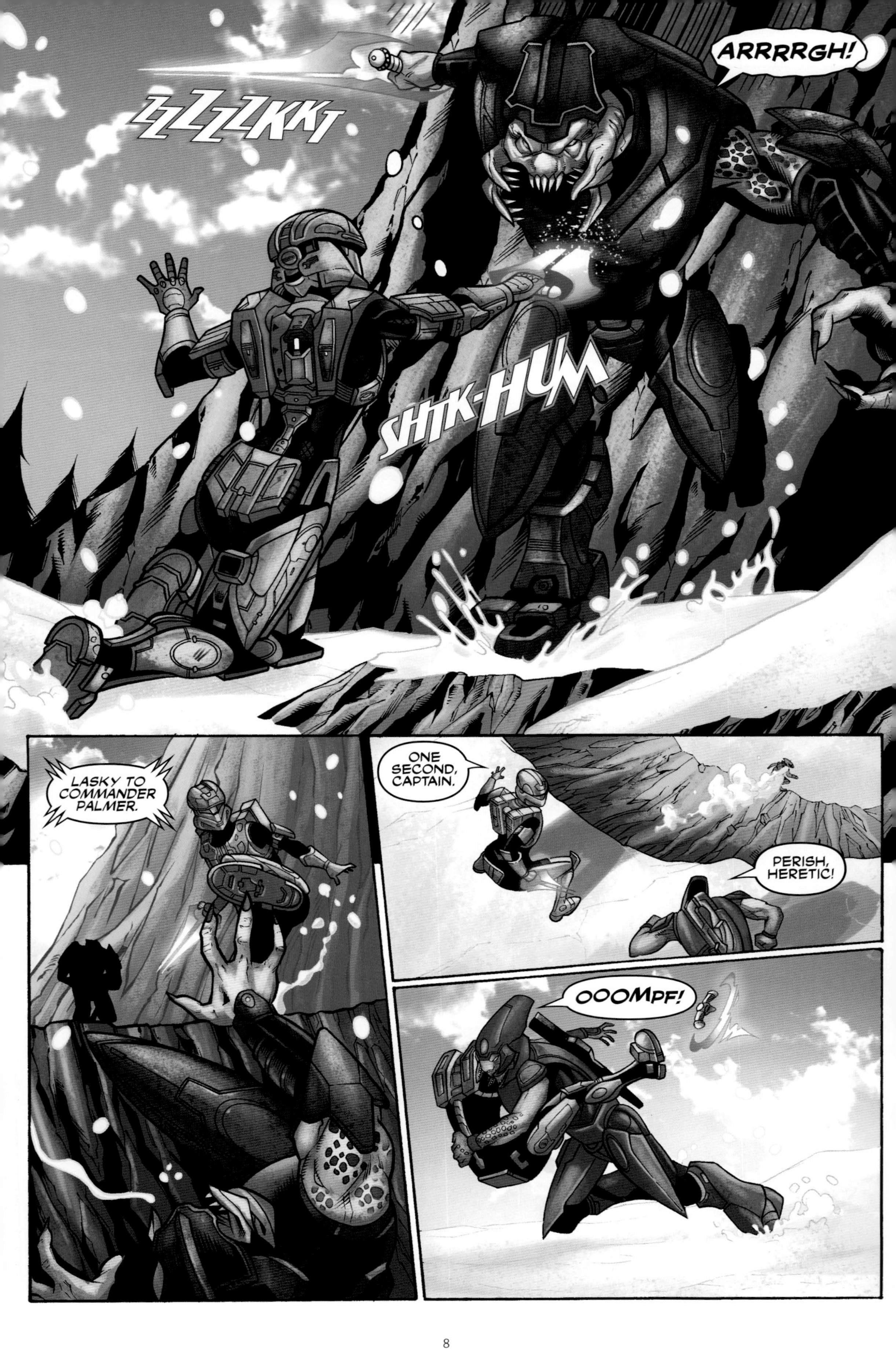
ZZZZZKKT
ARRRRGH!
SHTK-HUM
LASKY TO COMMANDER PALMER.
ONE SECOND, CAPTAIN.
PERISH, HERETIC!
OOOMPF!

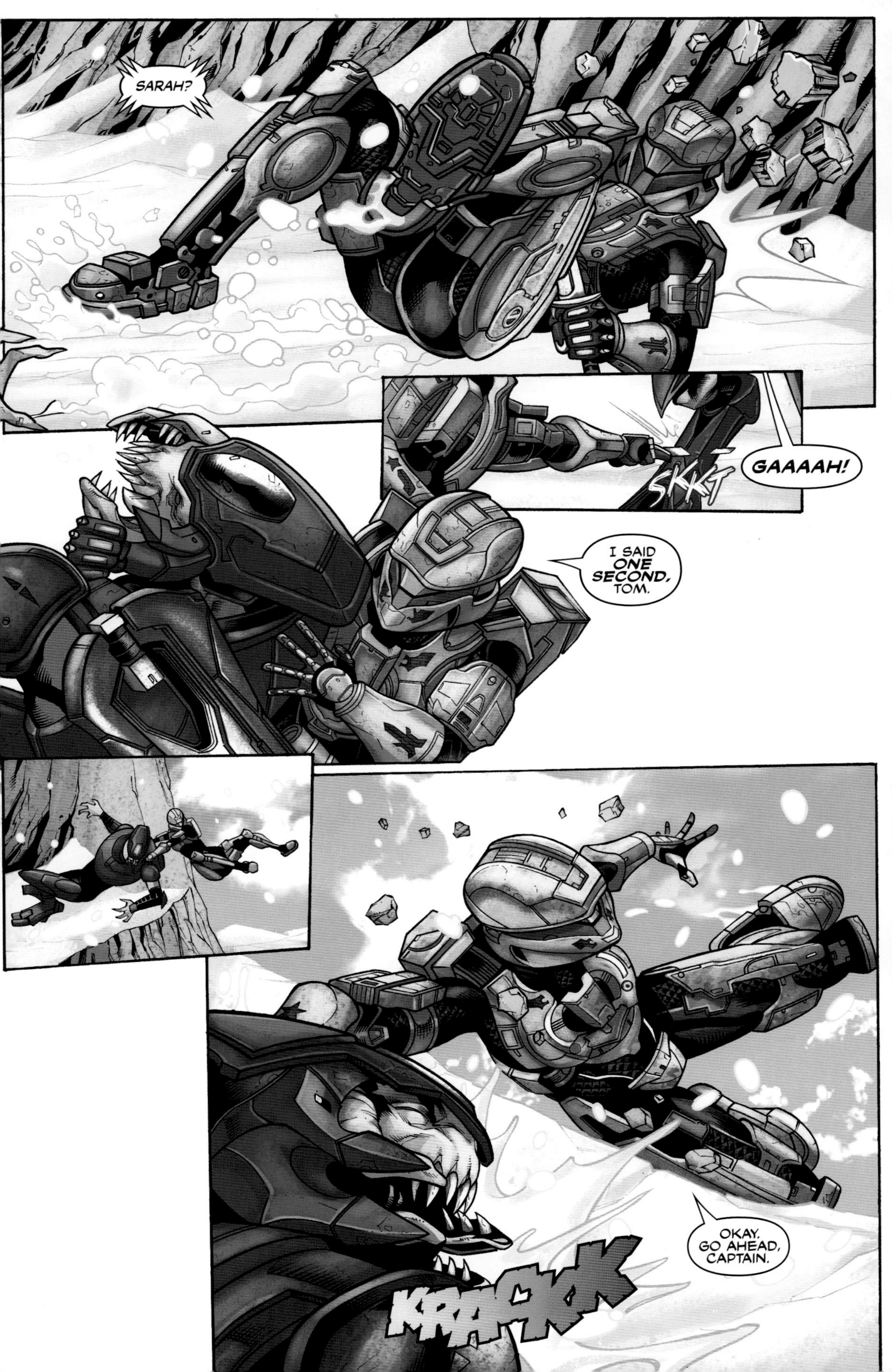
SARAH?
SKKT
GAAAAH!
I SAID ONE SECOND, TOM.
OKAY. GO AHEAD, CAPTAIN.
KRACKK

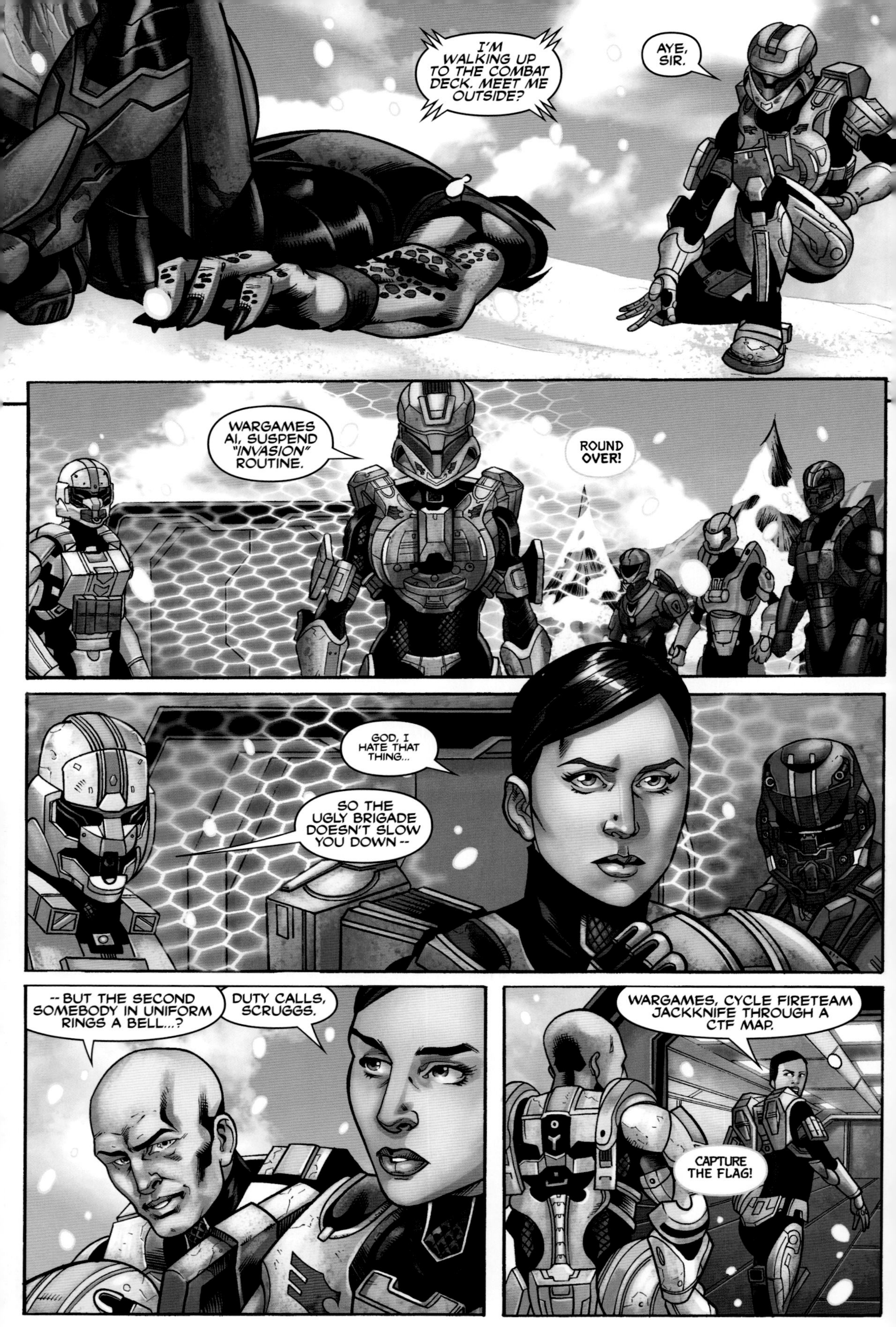
I'M WALKING UP TO THE COMBAT DECK. MEET ME OUTSIDE?
AYE, SIR.
WARGAMES AI, SUSPEND "INVASION" ROUTINE.
ROUND OVER!
GOD, I HATE THAT THING...
SO THE UGLY BRIGADE DOESN'T SLOW YOU DOWN --
-- BUT THE SECOND SOMEBODY IN UNIFORM RINGS A BELL...?
DUTY CALLS, SCRUGGS.
WARGAMES, CYCLE FIRETEAM JACKKNIFE THROUGH A CTF MAP.
CAPTURE THE FLAG!

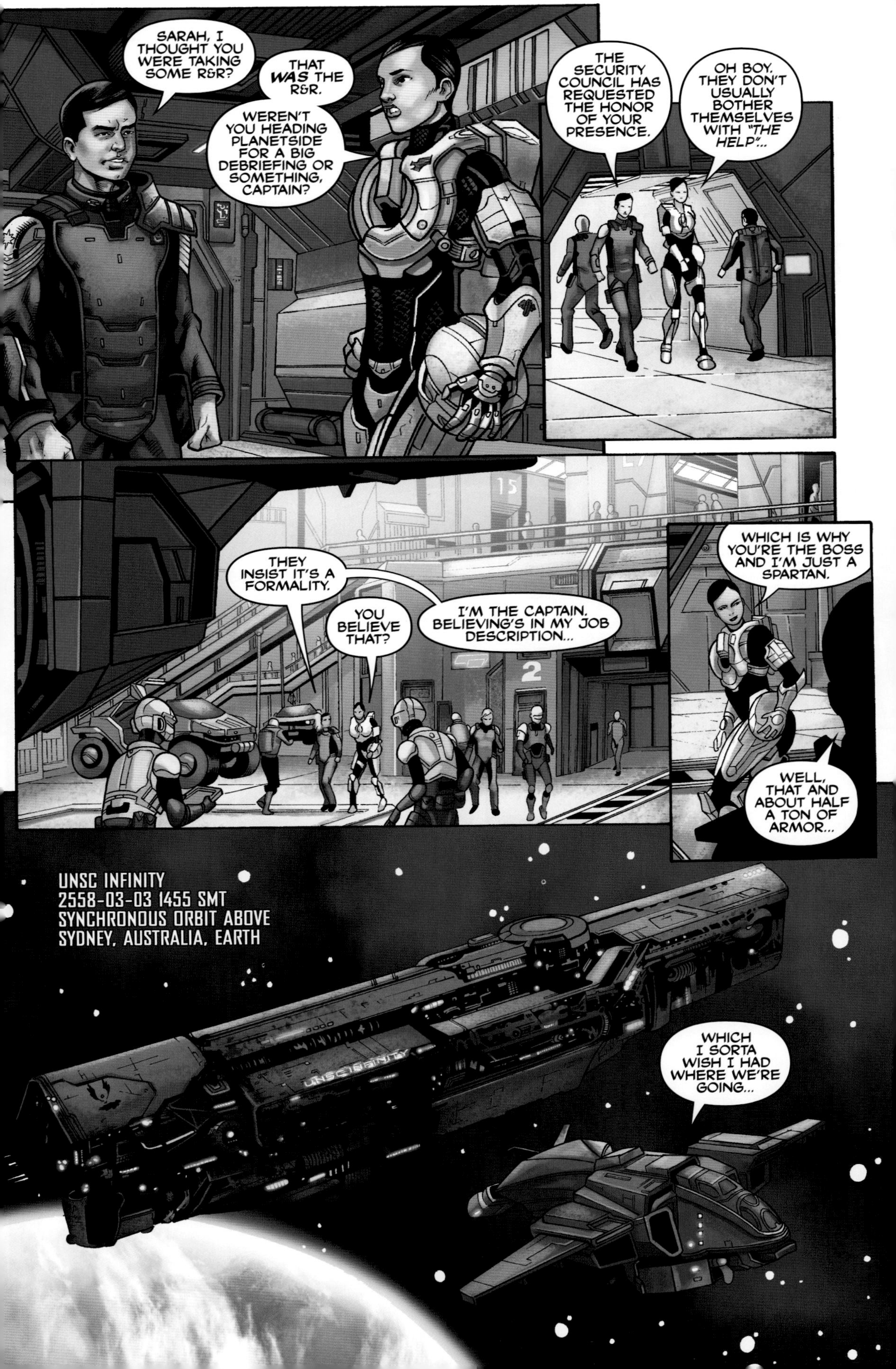
SARAH, I THOUGHT YOU WERE TAKING SOME R&R?
THAT ***WAS*** THE R&R.
WEREN'T YOU HEADING PLANETSIDE FOR A BIG DEBRIEFING OR SOMETHING, CAPTAIN?
THE SECURITY COUNCIL HAS REQUESTED THE HONOR OF YOUR PRESENCE.
OH BOY. THEY DON'T USUALLY BOTHER THEMSELVES WITH *"THE HELP"*...
THEY INSIST IT'S A FORMALITY.
YOU BELIEVE THAT?
I'M THE CAPTAIN. BELIEVING'S IN MY JOB DESCRIPTION...
WHICH IS WHY YOU'RE THE BOSS AND I'M JUST A SPARTAN.
WELL, THAT AND ABOUT HALF A TON OF ARMOR...
UNSC INFINITY
2558-03-03 1455 SMT
SYNCHRONOUS ORBIT ABOVE
SYDNEY, AUSTRALIA, EARTH
WHICH I SORTA WISH I HAD WHERE WE'RE GOING...

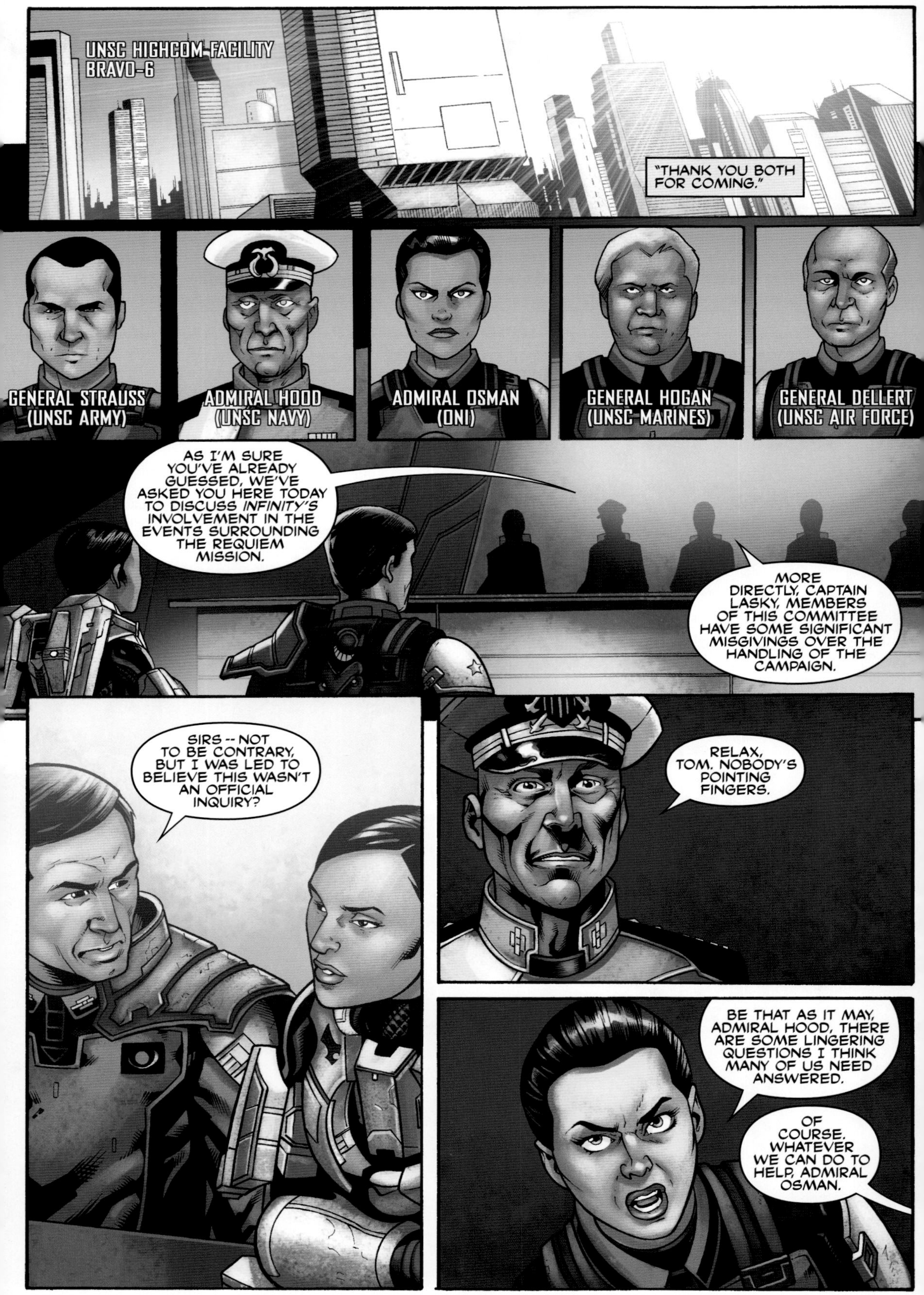
UNSC HIGHCOM FACILITY
BRAVO-6
"THANK YOU BOTH FOR COMING."
GENERAL STRAUSS (UNSC ARMY)
ADMIRAL HOOD (UNSC NAVY)
ADMIRAL OSMAN (ONI)
GENERAL HOGAN (UNSC MARINES)
GENERAL DELLERT (UNSC AIR FORCE)
AS I'M SURE YOU'VE ALREADY GUESSED, WE'VE ASKED YOU HERE TODAY TO DISCUSS *INFINITY'S* INVOLVEMENT IN THE EVENTS SURROUNDING THE REQUIEM MISSION.
MORE DIRECTLY, CAPTAIN LASKY, MEMBERS OF THIS COMMITTEE HAVE SOME SIGNIFICANT MISGIVINGS OVER THE HANDLING OF THE CAMPAIGN.
SIRS -- NOT TO BE CONTRARY, BUT I WAS LED TO BELIEVE THIS WASN'T AN OFFICIAL INQUIRY?
RELAX, TOM. NOBODY'S POINTING FINGERS.
BE THAT AS IT MAY, ADMIRAL HOOD, THERE ARE SOME LINGERING QUESTIONS I THINK MANY OF US NEED ANSWERED.
OF COURSE. WHATEVER WE CAN DO TO HELP, ADMIRAL OSMAN.

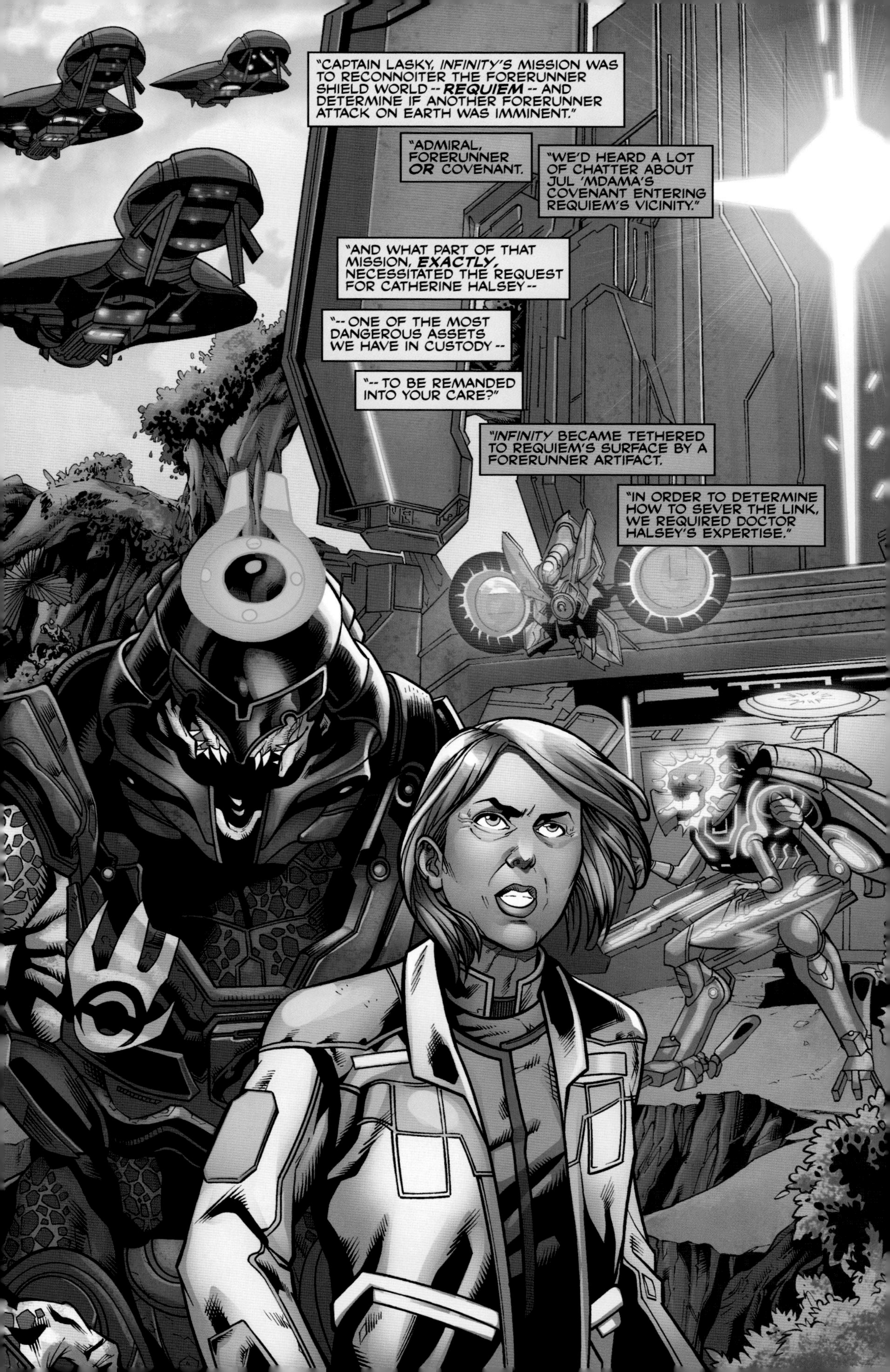
"CAPTAIN LASKY, INFINITY'S MISSION WAS TO RECONNOITER THE FORERUNNER SHIELD WORLD -- REQUIEM -- AND DETERMINE IF ANOTHER FORERUNNER ATTACK ON EARTH WAS IMMINENT."
"ADMIRAL, FORERUNNER OR COVENANT.
"WE'D HEARD A LOT OF CHATTER ABOUT JUL 'MDAMA'S COVENANT ENTERING REQUIEM'S VICINITY."
"AND WHAT PART OF THAT MISSION, EXACTLY, NECESSITATED THE REQUEST FOR CATHERINE HALSEY --
"-- ONE OF THE MOST DANGEROUS ASSETS WE HAVE IN CUSTODY --
"-- TO BE REMANDED INTO YOUR CARE?"
"INFINITY BECAME TETHERED TO REQUIEM'S SURFACE BY A FORERUNNER ARTIFACT.
"IN ORDER TO DETERMINE HOW TO SEVER THE LINK, WE REQUIRED DOCTOR HALSEY'S EXPERTISE."

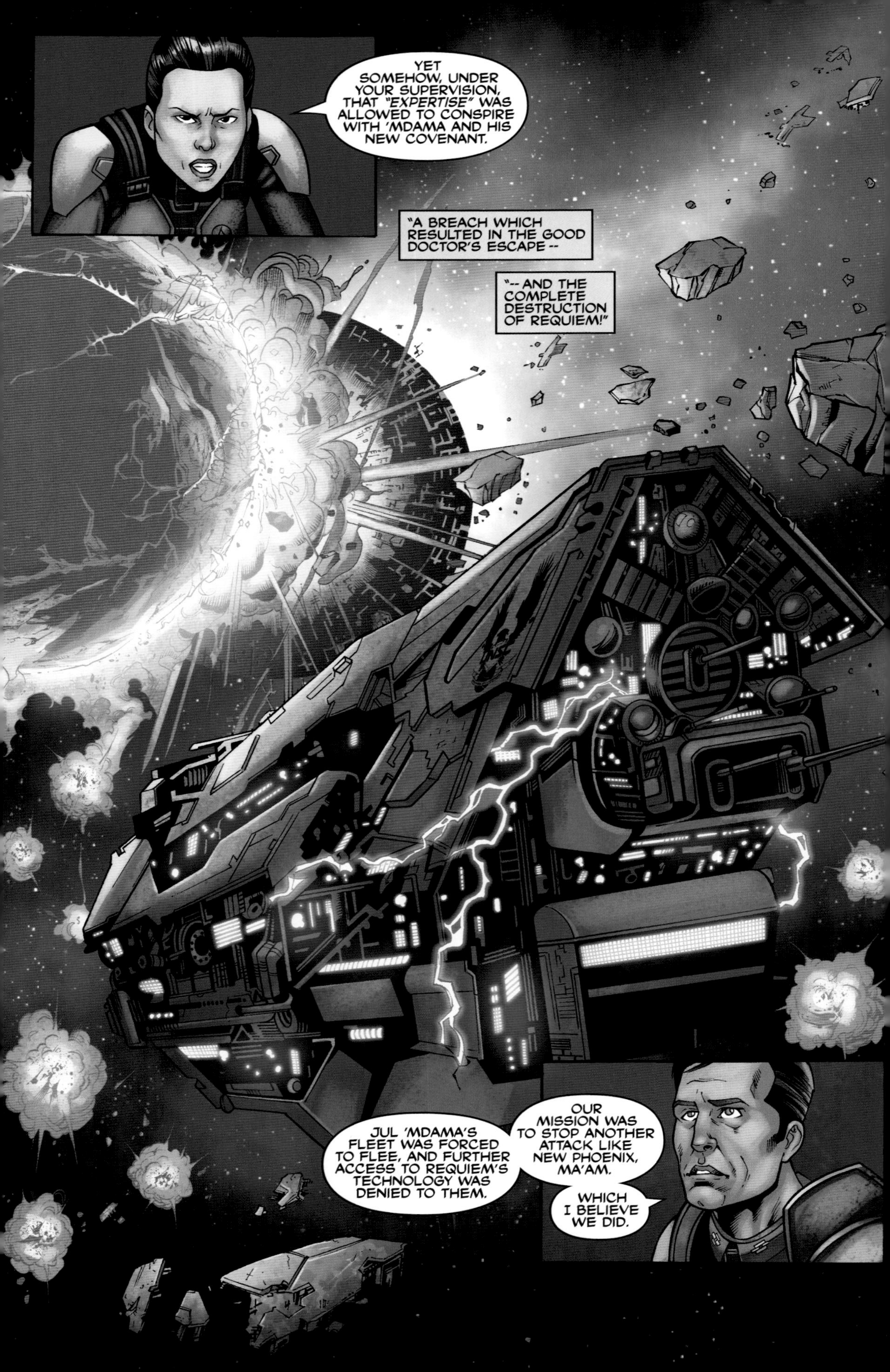
YET SOMEHOW, UNDER YOUR SUPERVISION, THAT "EXPERTISE" WAS ALLOWED TO CONSPIRE WITH 'MDAMA AND HIS NEW COVENANT.
"A BREACH WHICH RESULTED IN THE GOOD DOCTOR'S ESCAPE --
"-- AND THE COMPLETE DESTRUCTION OF REQUIEM!"
JUL 'MDAMA'S FLEET WAS FORCED TO FLEE, AND FURTHER ACCESS TO REQUIEM'S TECHNOLOGY WAS DENIED TO THEM.
OUR MISSION WAS TO STOP ANOTHER ATTACK LIKE NEW PHOENIX, MA'AM.
WHICH I BELIEVE WE DID.

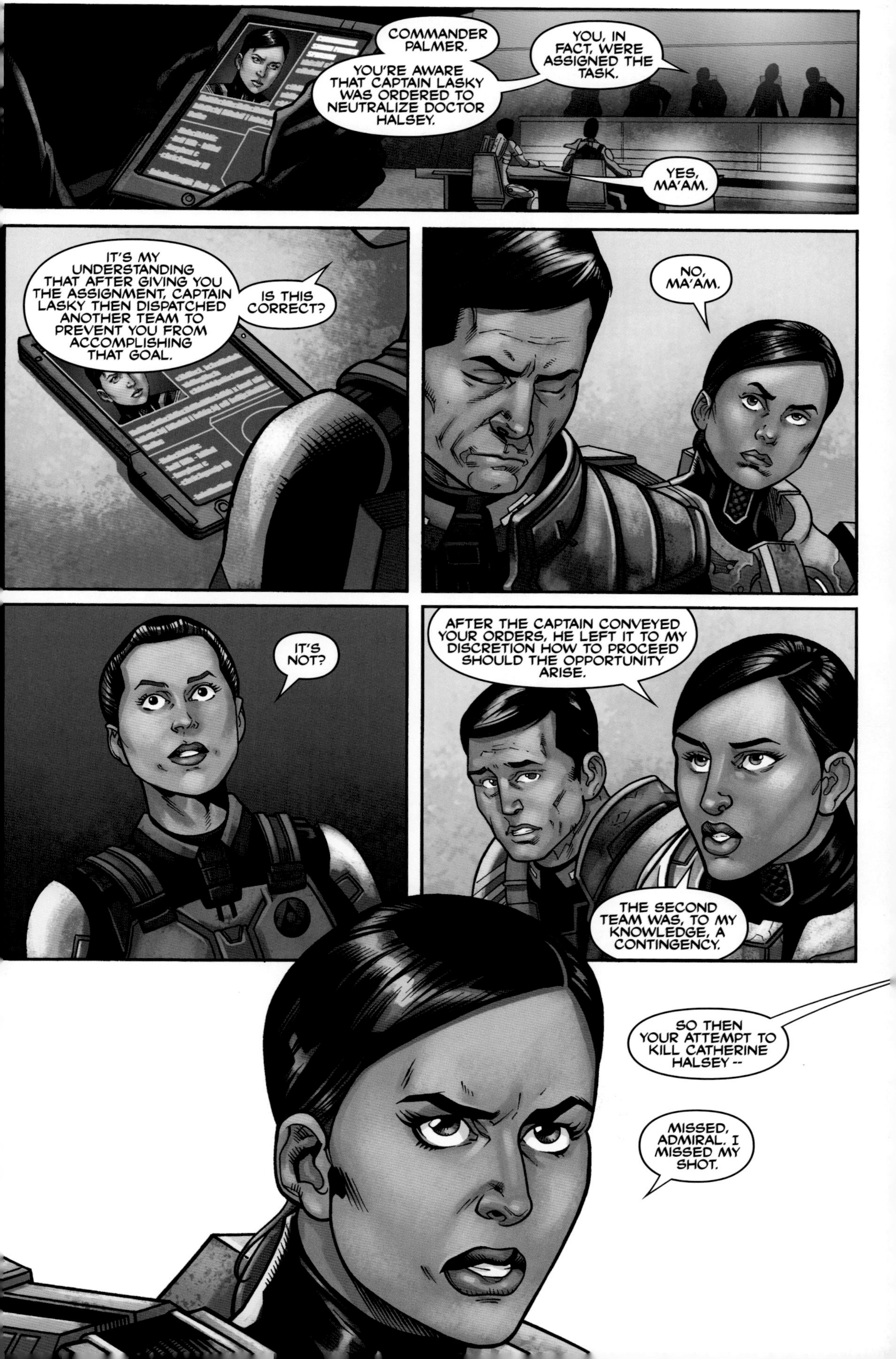
COMMANDER PALMER.
YOU'RE AWARE THAT CAPTAIN LASKY WAS ORDERED TO NEUTRALIZE DOCTOR HALSEY.
YOU, IN FACT, WERE ASSIGNED THE TASK.
YES, MA'AM.
IT'S MY UNDERSTANDING THAT AFTER GIVING YOU THE ASSIGNMENT, CAPTAIN LASKY THEN DISPATCHED ANOTHER TEAM TO PREVENT YOU FROM ACCOMPLISHING THAT GOAL.
IS THIS CORRECT?
NO, MA'AM.
IT'S NOT?
AFTER THE CAPTAIN CONVEYED YOUR ORDERS, HE LEFT IT TO MY DISCRETION HOW TO PROCEED SHOULD THE OPPORTUNITY ARISE.
THE SECOND TEAM WAS, TO MY KNOWLEDGE, A CONTINGENCY.
SO THEN YOUR ATTEMPT TO KILL CATHERINE HALSEY --
MISSED, ADMIRAL. I MISSED MY SHOT.

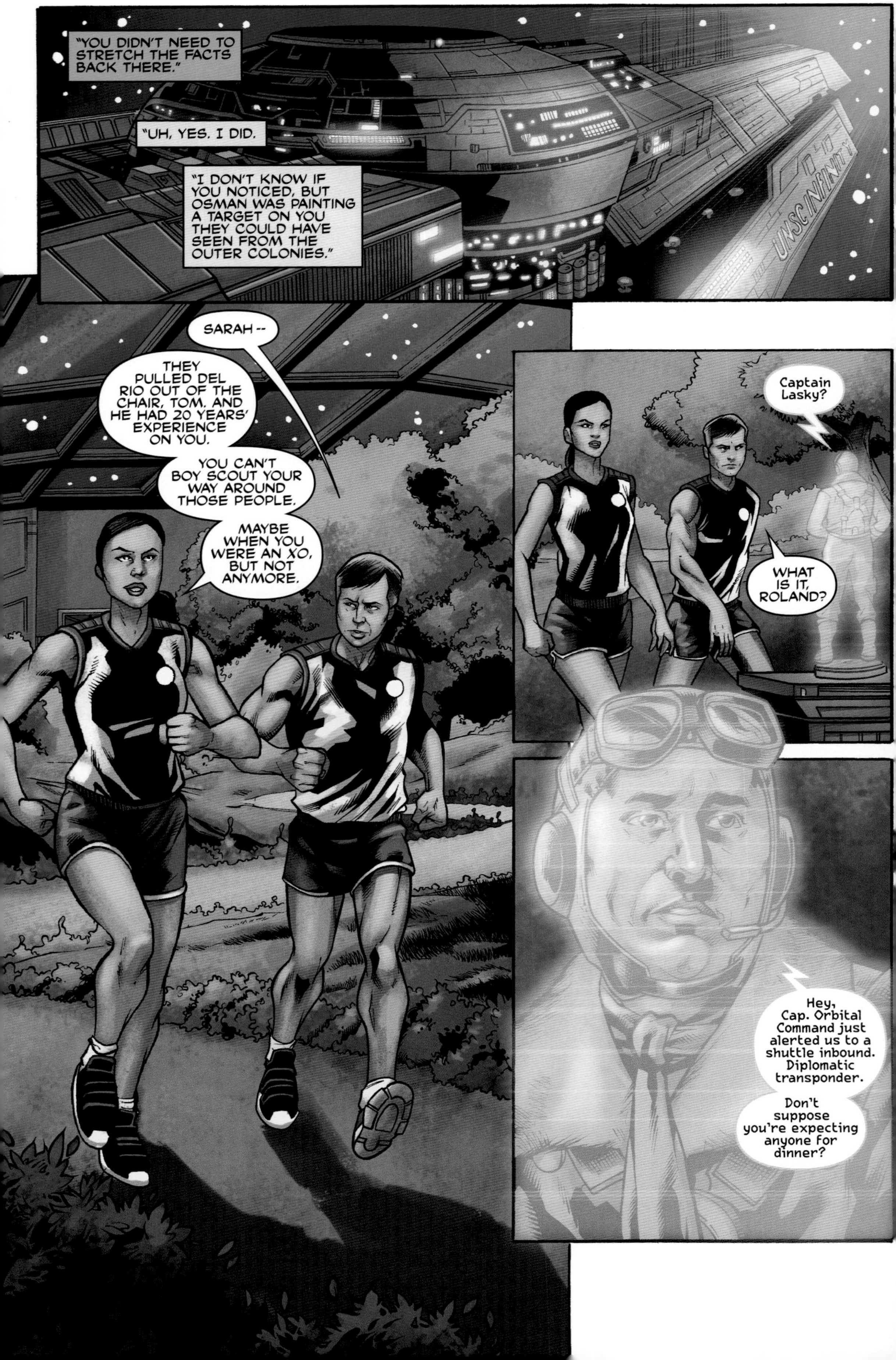
"YOU DIDN'T NEED TO STRETCH THE FACTS BACK THERE."
"UH, YES. I DID.
"I DON'T KNOW IF YOU NOTICED, BUT OSMAN WAS PAINTING A TARGET ON YOU THEY COULD HAVE SEEN FROM THE OUTER COLONIES."
UNSC INFINITY
SARAH --
THEY PULLED DEL RIO OUT OF THE CHAIR, TOM. AND HE HAD 20 YEARS' EXPERIENCE ON YOU.
YOU CAN'T BOY SCOUT YOUR WAY AROUND THOSE PEOPLE.
MAYBE WHEN YOU WERE AN XO, BUT NOT ANYMORE.
Captain Lasky?
WHAT IS IT, ROLAND?
Hey, Cap. Orbital Command just alerted us to a shuttle inbound. Diplomatic transponder.
Don't suppose you're expecting anyone for dinner?

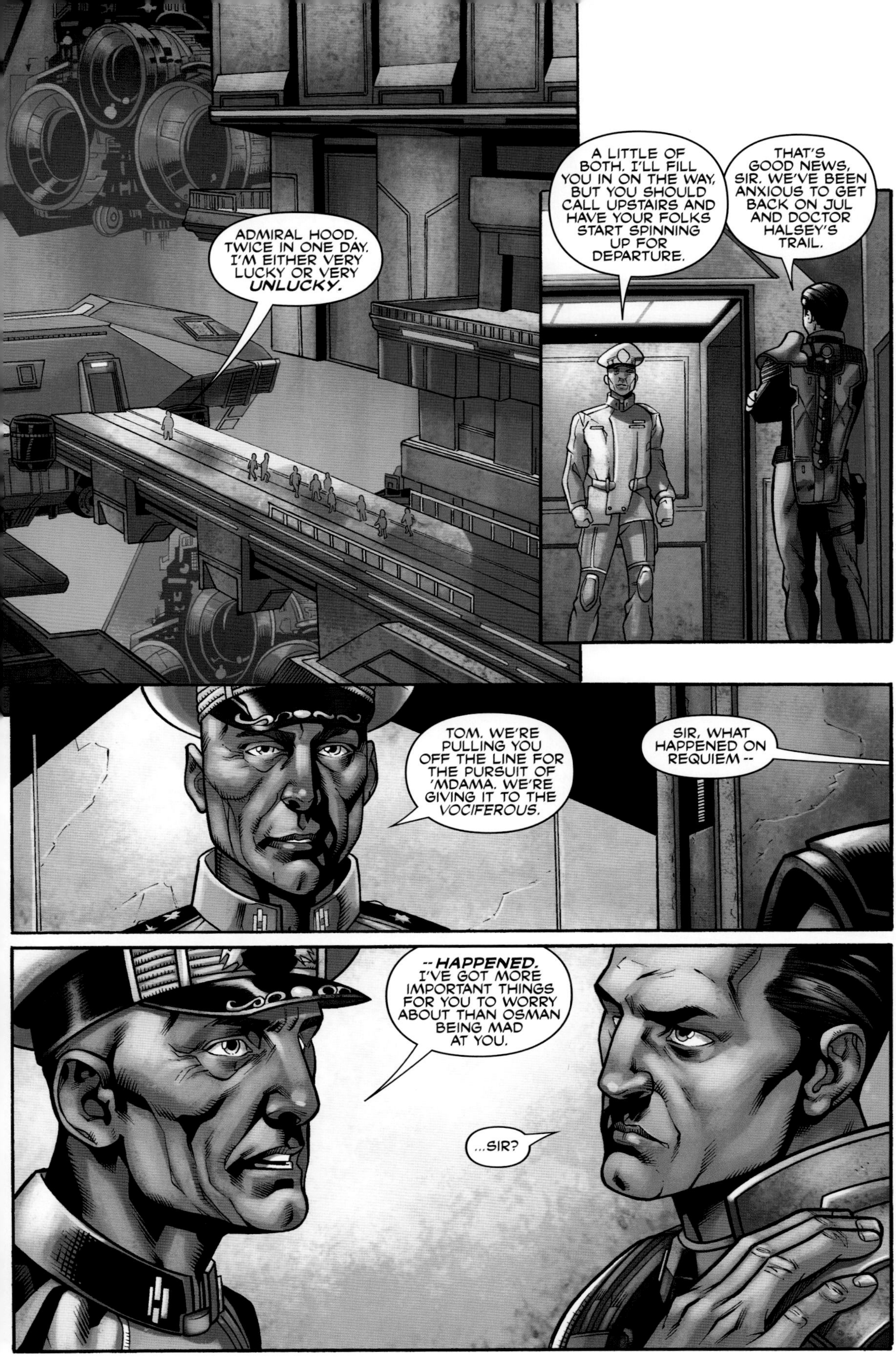
ADMIRAL HOOD. TWICE IN ONE DAY. I'M EITHER VERY LUCKY OR VERY UNLUCKY.
A LITTLE OF BOTH. I'LL FILL YOU IN ON THE WAY, BUT YOU SHOULD CALL UPSTAIRS AND HAVE YOUR FOLKS START SPINNING UP FOR DEPARTURE.
THAT'S GOOD NEWS, SIR. WE'VE BEEN ANXIOUS TO GET BACK ON JUL AND DOCTOR HALSEY'S TRAIL.
TOM, WE'RE PULLING YOU OFF THE LINE FOR THE PURSUIT OF 'MDAMA. WE'RE GIVING IT TO THE VOCIFEROUS.
SIR, WHAT HAPPENED ON REQUIEM --
-- HAPPENED. I'VE GOT MORE IMPORTANT THINGS FOR YOU TO WORRY ABOUT THAN OSMAN BEING MAD AT YOU.
...SIR?

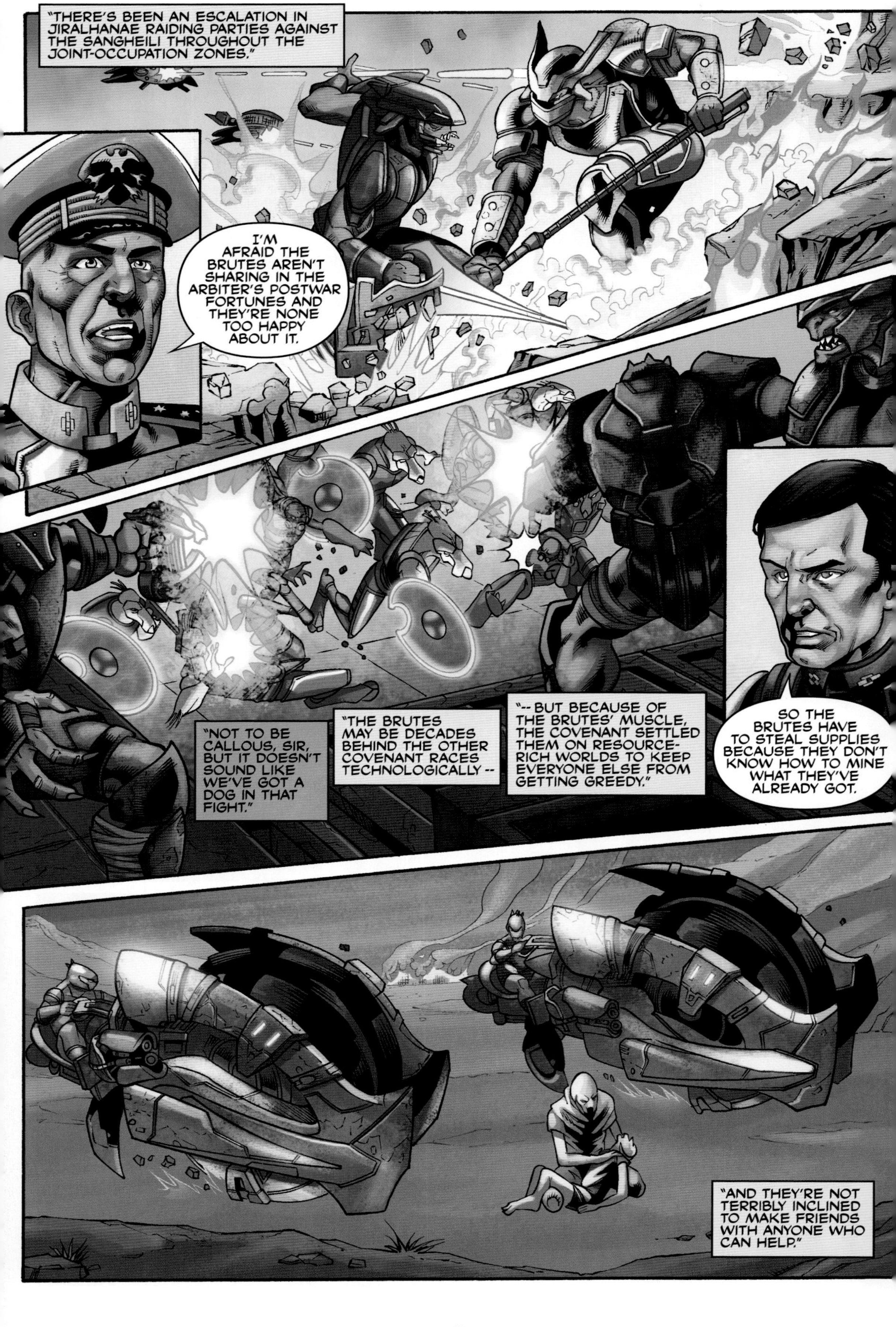
"THERE'S BEEN AN ESCALATION IN JIRALHANAE RAIDING PARTIES AGAINST THE SANGHEILI THROUGHOUT THE JOINT-OCCUPATION ZONES."
I'M AFRAID THE BRUTES AREN'T SHARING IN THE ARBITER'S POSTWAR FORTUNES AND THEY'RE NONE TOO HAPPY ABOUT IT.
"NOT TO BE CALLOUS, SIR, BUT IT DOESN'T SOUND LIKE WE'VE GOT A DOG IN THAT FIGHT."
"THE BRUTES MAY BE DECADES BEHIND THE OTHER COVENANT RACES TECHNOLOGICALLY --
"-- BUT BECAUSE OF THE BRUTES' MUSCLE, THE COVENANT SETTLED THEM ON RESOURCE-RICH WORLDS TO KEEP EVERYONE ELSE FROM GETTING GREEDY."
SO THE BRUTES HAVE TO STEAL SUPPLIES BECAUSE THEY DON'T KNOW HOW TO MINE WHAT THEY'VE ALREADY GOT.
"AND THEY'RE NOT TERRIBLY INCLINED TO MAKE FRIENDS WITH ANYONE WHO CAN HELP."

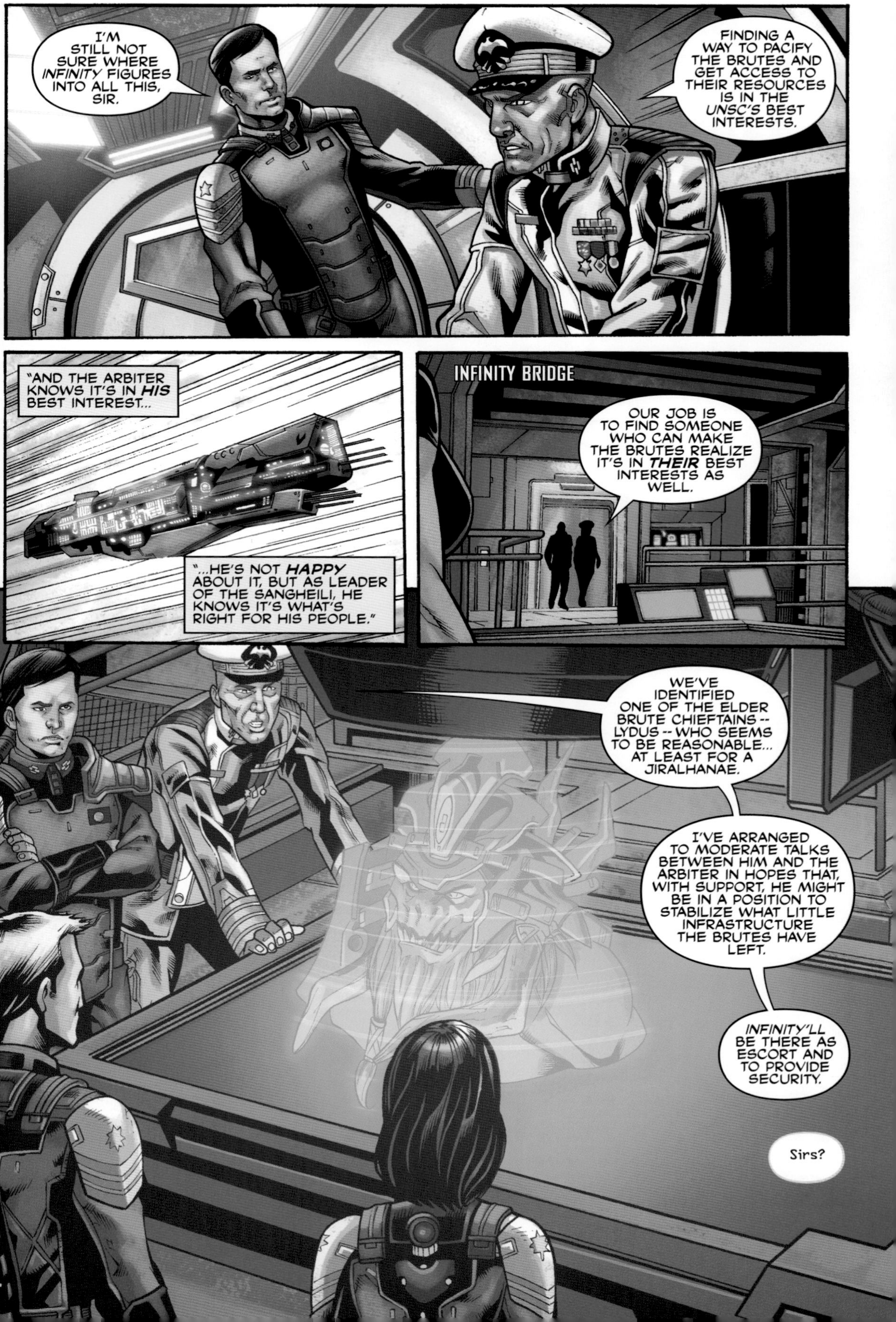

I'M STILL NOT SURE WHERE INFINITY FIGURES INTO ALL THIS, SIR.
FINDING A WAY TO PACIFY THE BRUTES AND GET ACCESS TO THEIR RESOURCES IS IN THE UNSC'S BEST INTERESTS.
"AND THE ARBITER KNOWS IT'S IN HIS BEST INTEREST...
"...HE'S NOT HAPPY ABOUT IT, BUT AS LEADER OF THE SANGHEILI, HE KNOWS IT'S WHAT'S RIGHT FOR HIS PEOPLE."
INFINITY BRIDGE
OUR JOB IS TO FIND SOMEONE WHO CAN MAKE THE BRUTES REALIZE IT'S IN THEIR BEST INTERESTS AS WELL.
WE'VE IDENTIFIED ONE OF THE ELDER BRUTE CHIEFTAINS -- LYDUS -- WHO SEEMS TO BE REASONABLE... AT LEAST FOR A JIRALHANAE.
I'VE ARRANGED TO MODERATE TALKS BETWEEN HIM AND THE ARBITER IN HOPES THAT, WITH SUPPORT, HE MIGHT BE IN A POSITION TO STABILIZE WHAT LITTLE INFRASTRUCTURE THE BRUTES HAVE LEFT.
INFINITY'LL BE THERE AS ESCORT AND TO PROVIDE SECURITY.
Sirs?

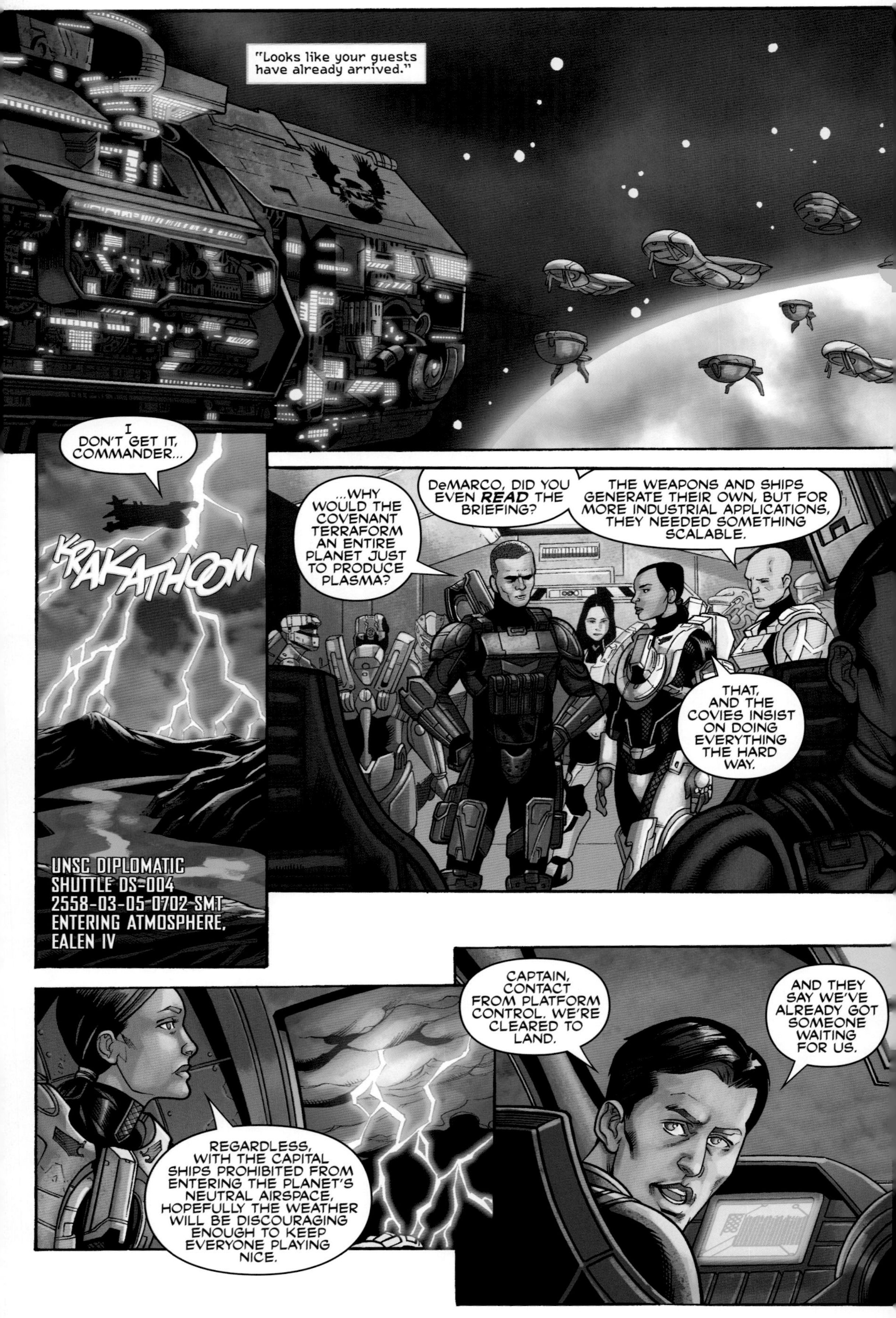
"Looks like your guests have already arrived."
I DON'T GET IT, COMMANDER...
KRAKATHOOM
UNSC DIPLOMATIC SHUTTLE DS-004
2558-03-05-0702 SMT
ENTERING ATMOSPHERE, EALEN IV
...WHY WOULD THE COVENANT TERRAFORM AN ENTIRE PLANET JUST TO PRODUCE PLASMA?
DeMARCO, DID YOU EVEN READ THE BRIEFING?
THE WEAPONS AND SHIPS GENERATE THEIR OWN, BUT FOR MORE INDUSTRIAL APPLICATIONS, THEY NEEDED SOMETHING SCALABLE.
THAT, AND THE COVIES INSIST ON DOING EVERYTHING THE HARD WAY.
REGARDLESS, WITH THE CAPITAL SHIPS PROHIBITED FROM ENTERING THE PLANET'S NEUTRAL AIRSPACE, HOPEFULLY THE WEATHER WILL BE DISCOURAGING ENOUGH TO KEEP EVERYONE PLAYING NICE.
CAPTAIN, CONTACT FROM PLATFORM CONTROL. WE'RE CLEARED TO LAND.
AND THEY SAY WE'VE ALREADY GOT SOMEONE WAITING FOR US.

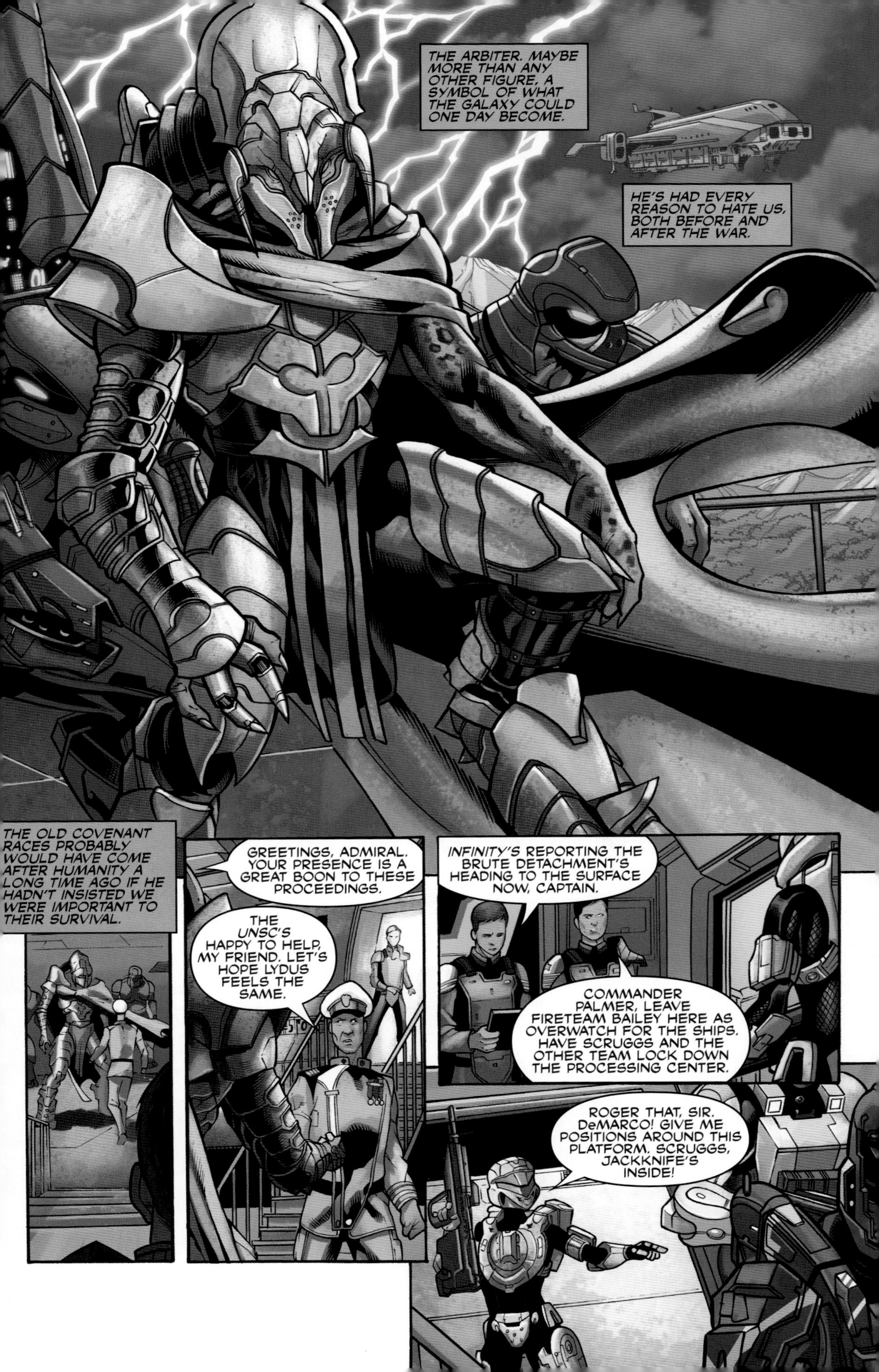
THE ARBITER. MAYBE MORE THAN ANY OTHER FIGURE, A SYMBOL OF WHAT THE GALAXY COULD ONE DAY BECOME.
HE'S HAD EVERY REASON TO HATE US, BOTH BEFORE AND AFTER THE WAR.
THE OLD COVENANT RACES PROBABLY WOULD HAVE COME AFTER HUMANITY A LONG TIME AGO IF HE HADN'T INSISTED WE WERE IMPORTANT TO THEIR SURVIVAL.
GREETINGS, ADMIRAL. YOUR PRESENCE IS A GREAT BOON TO THESE PROCEEDINGS.
THE *UNSC'S* HAPPY TO HELP, MY FRIEND. LET'S HOPE LYDUS FEELS THE SAME.
INFINITY'S REPORTING THE BRUTE DETACHMENT'S HEADING TO THE SURFACE NOW, CAPTAIN.
COMMANDER PALMER, LEAVE FIRETEAM BAILEY HERE AS OVERWATCH FOR THE SHIPS. HAVE SCRUGGS AND THE OTHER TEAM LOCK DOWN THE PROCESSING CENTER.
ROGER THAT, SIR. DeMARCO! GIVE ME POSITIONS AROUND THIS PLATFORM. SCRUGGS, JACKKNIFE'S INSIDE!

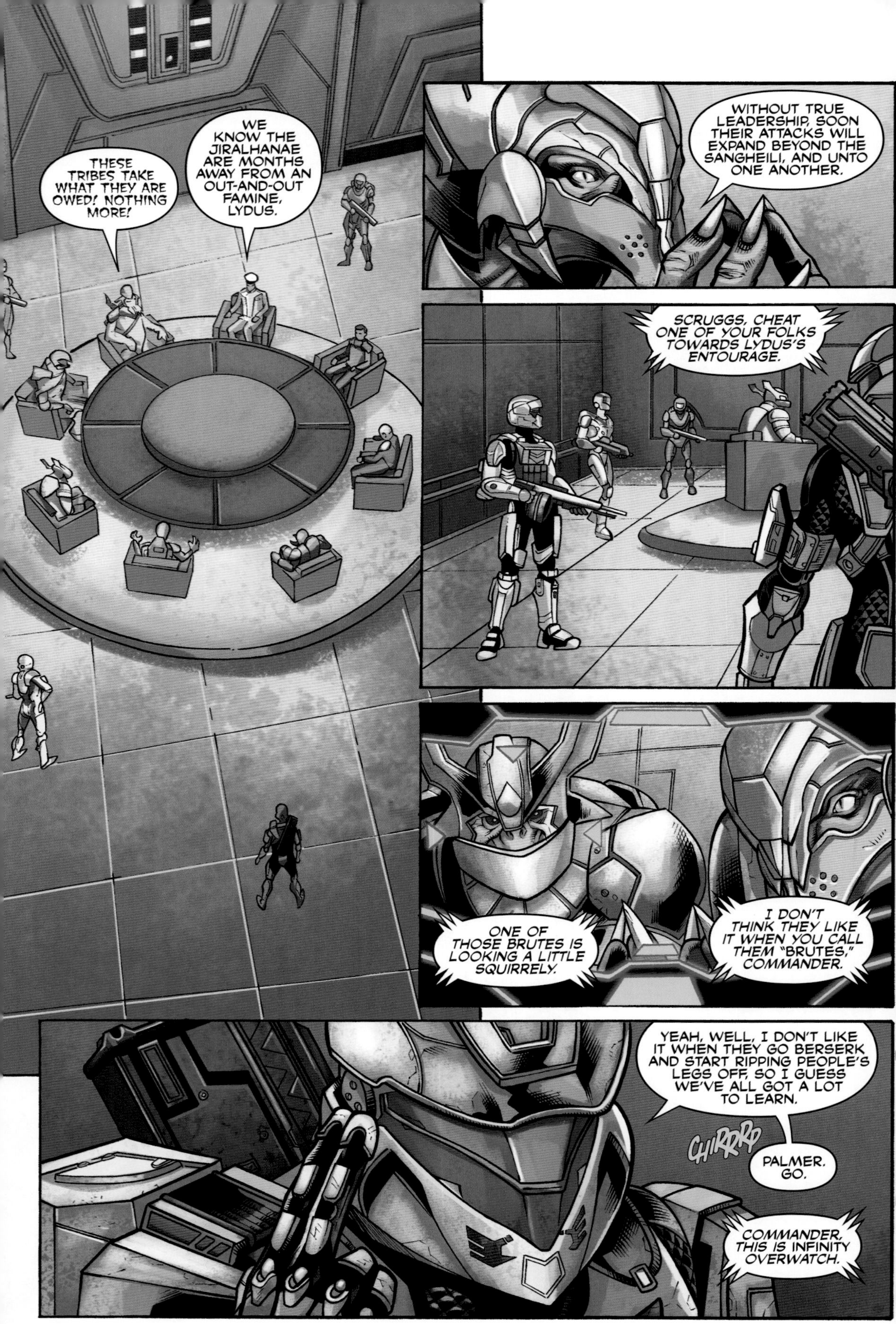
THESE TRIBES TAKE WHAT THEY ARE OWED! NOTHING MORE!
WE KNOW THE JIRALHANAE ARE MONTHS AWAY FROM AN OUT-AND-OUT FAMINE, LYDUS.
WITHOUT TRUE LEADERSHIP, SOON THEIR ATTACKS WILL EXPAND BEYOND THE SANGHEILI, AND UNTO ONE ANOTHER.
SCRUGGS, CHEAT ONE OF YOUR FOLKS TOWARDS LYDUS'S ENTOURAGE.
ONE OF THOSE BRUTES IS LOOKING A LITTLE SQUIRRELY.
I DON'T THINK THEY LIKE IT WHEN YOU CALL THEM "BRUTES," COMMANDER.
YEAH, WELL, I DON'T LIKE IT WHEN THEY GO BERSERK AND START RIPPING PEOPLE'S LEGS OFF, SO I GUESS WE'VE ALL GOT A LOT TO LEARN.
CHIRRRP
PALMER. GO.
COMMANDER, THIS IS INFINITY OVERWATCH.

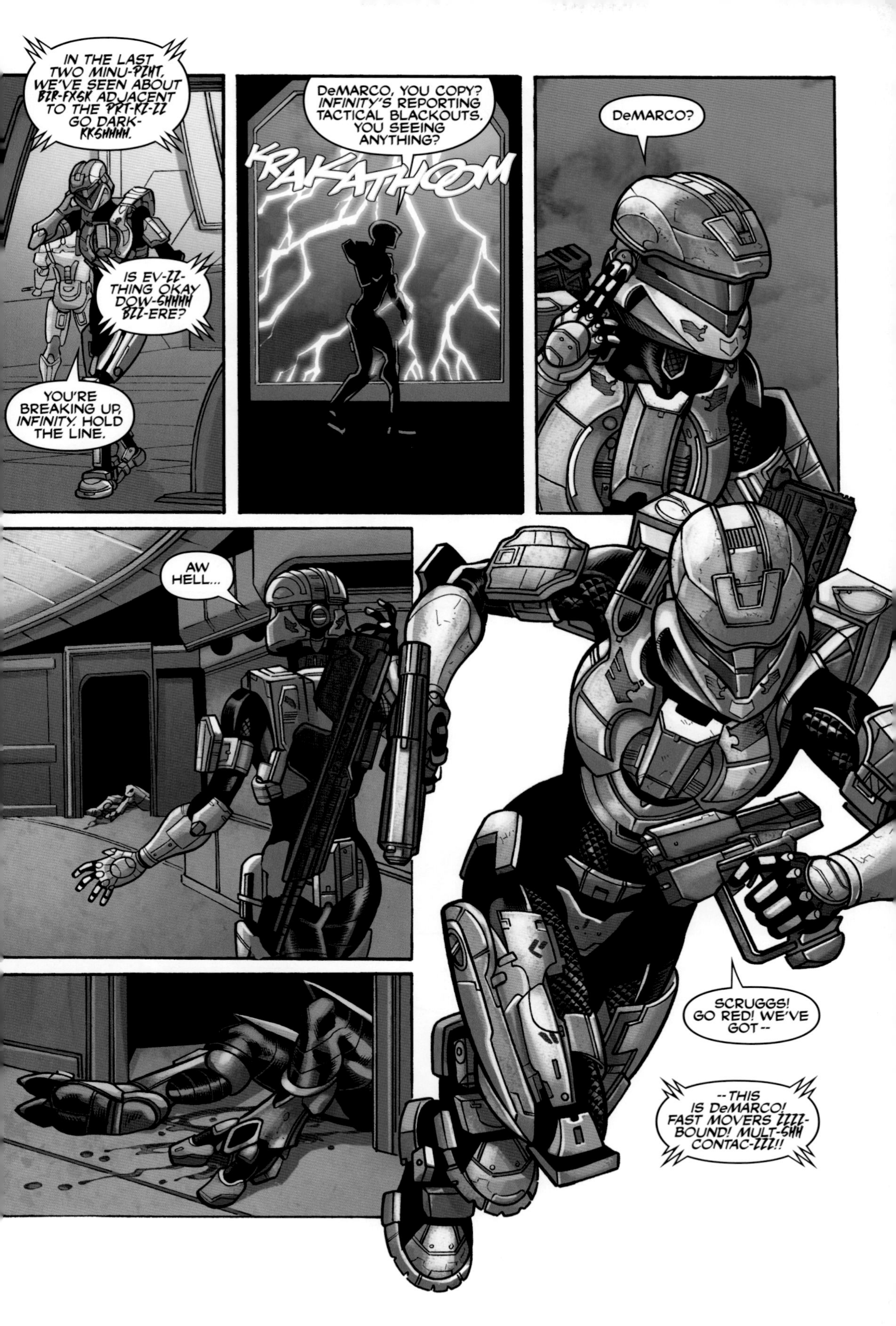
IN THE LAST TWO MINU-PZHT, WE'VE SEEN ABOUT BZR-FXSK ADJACENT TO THE PRT-KZ-ZZ GO DARK-KKSHHHH.
IS EV-ZZ-THING OKAY DOW-SHHHH BZZ-ERE?
YOU'RE BREAKING UP, INFINITY. HOLD THE LINE.
DeMARCO, YOU COPY? INFINITY'S REPORTING TACTICAL BLACKOUTS. YOU SEEING ANYTHING?
KRAKATHOOM
DeMARCO?
AW HELL...
SCRUGGS! GO RED! WE'VE GOT --
--THIS IS DeMARCO! FAST MOVERS ZZZZ-BOUND! MULT-SHH CONTAC-ZZZ!!

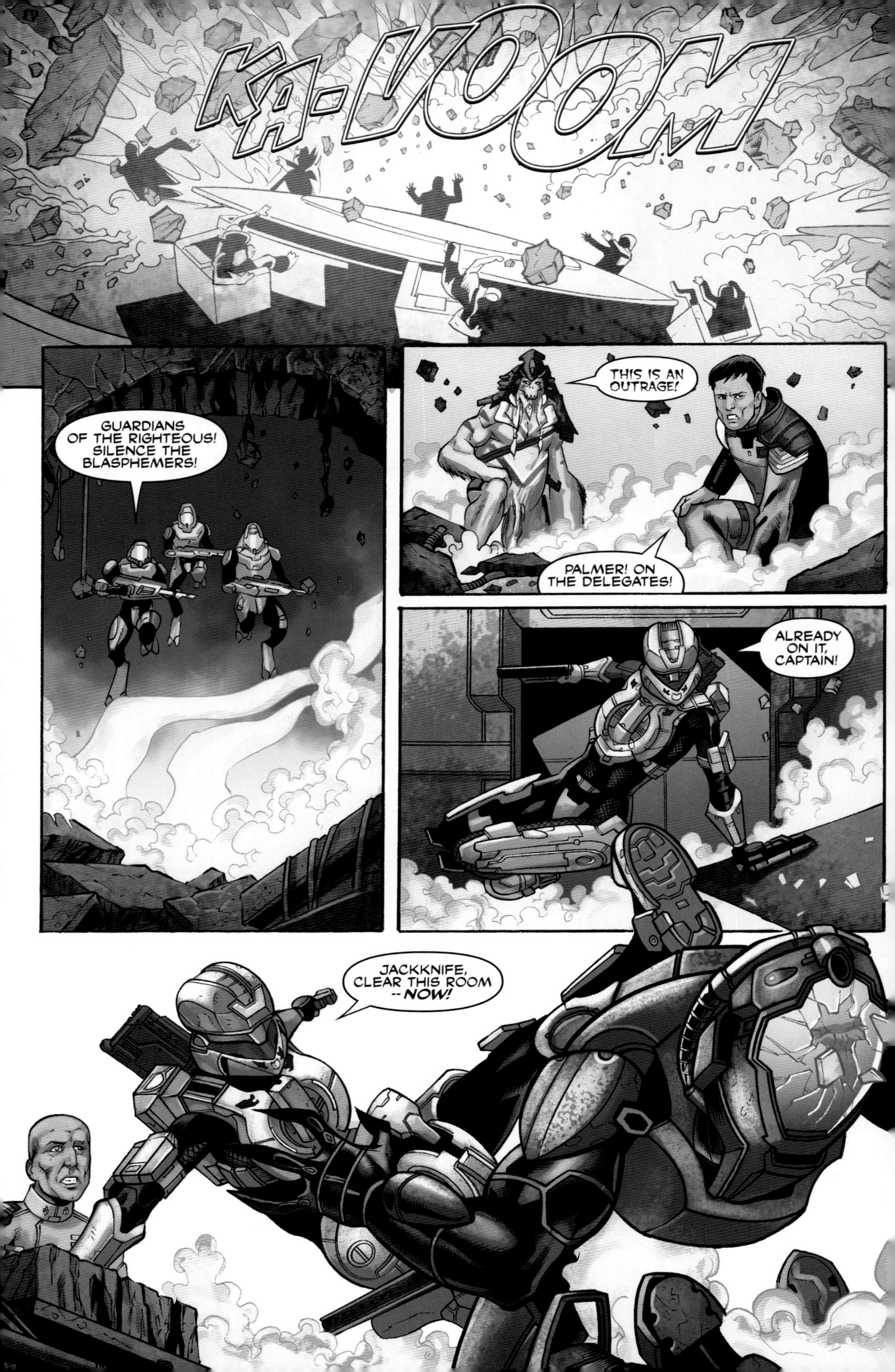
KA-VOOM
GUARDIANS OF THE RIGHTEOUS! SILENCE THE BLASPHEMERS!
THIS IS AN OUTRAGE!
PALMER! ON THE DELEGATES!
ALREADY ON IT, CAPTAIN!
JACKKNIFE, CLEAR THIS ROOM --NOW!

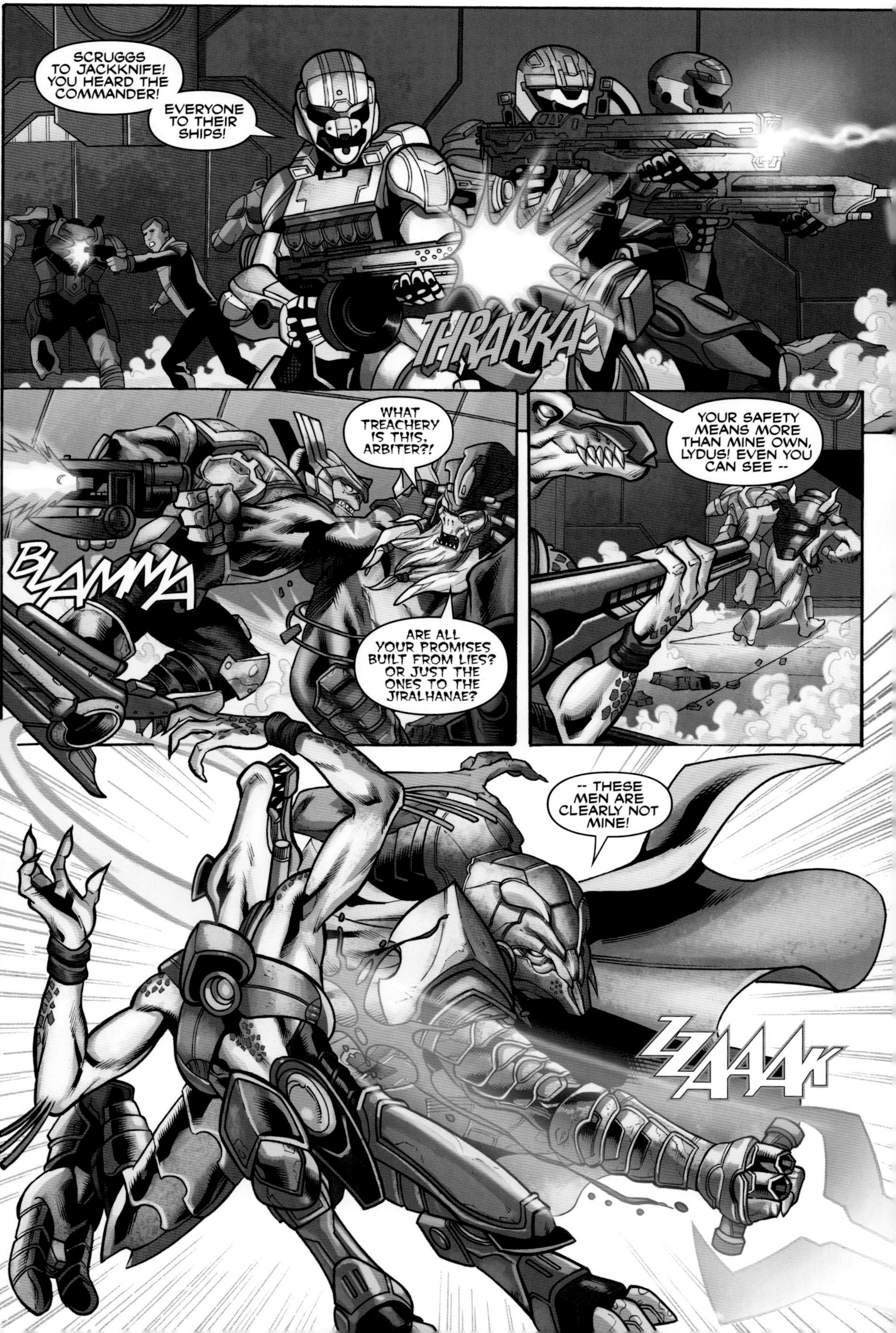
SCRUGGS TO JACKKNIFE! YOU HEARD THE COMMANDER!
EVERYONE TO THEIR SHIPS!
THRAKKA
WHAT TREACHERY IS THIS, ARBITER?!
BLAMMA
ARE ALL YOUR PROMISES BUILT FROM LIES? OR JUST THE ONES TO THE JIRALHANAE?
YOUR SAFETY MEANS MORE THAN MINE OWN, LYDUS! EVEN YOU CAN SEE --
-- THESE MEN ARE CLEARLY NOT MINE!
ZZAAAK

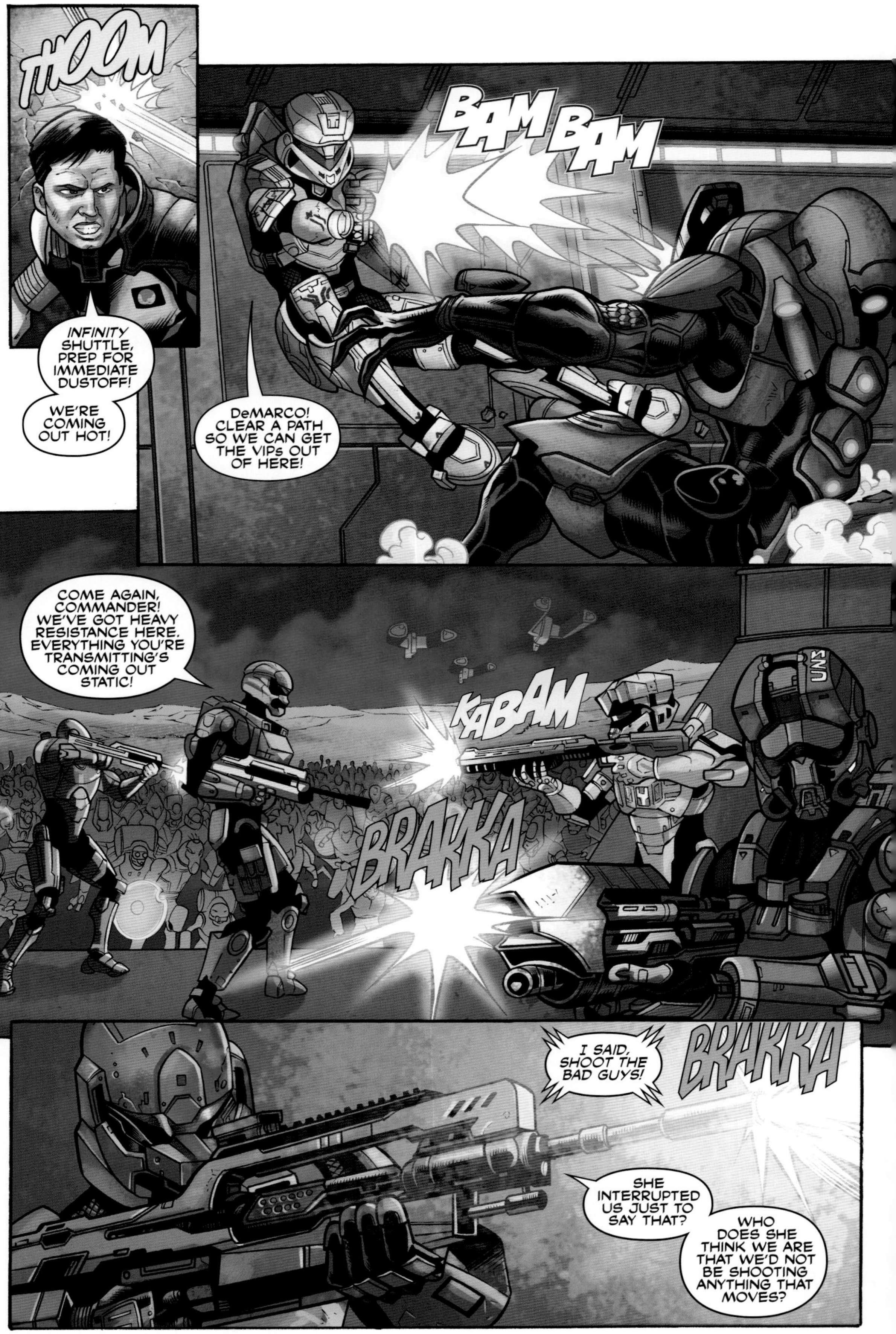
THOOM
INFINITY SHUTTLE, PREP FOR IMMEDIATE DUSTOFF!
WE'RE COMING OUT HOT!
BAM BAM
DeMARCO! CLEAR A PATH SO WE CAN GET THE VIPs OUT OF HERE!
COME AGAIN, COMMANDER! WE'VE GOT HEAVY RESISTANCE HERE. EVERYTHING YOU'RE TRANSMITTING'S COMING OUT STATIC!
KABAM
BRAKKA
UNS
I SAID, SHOOT THE BAD GUYS!
BRAKKA
SHE INTERRUPTED US JUST TO SAY THAT?
WHO DOES SHE THINK WE ARE THAT WE'D NOT BE SHOOTING ANYTHING THAT MOVES?

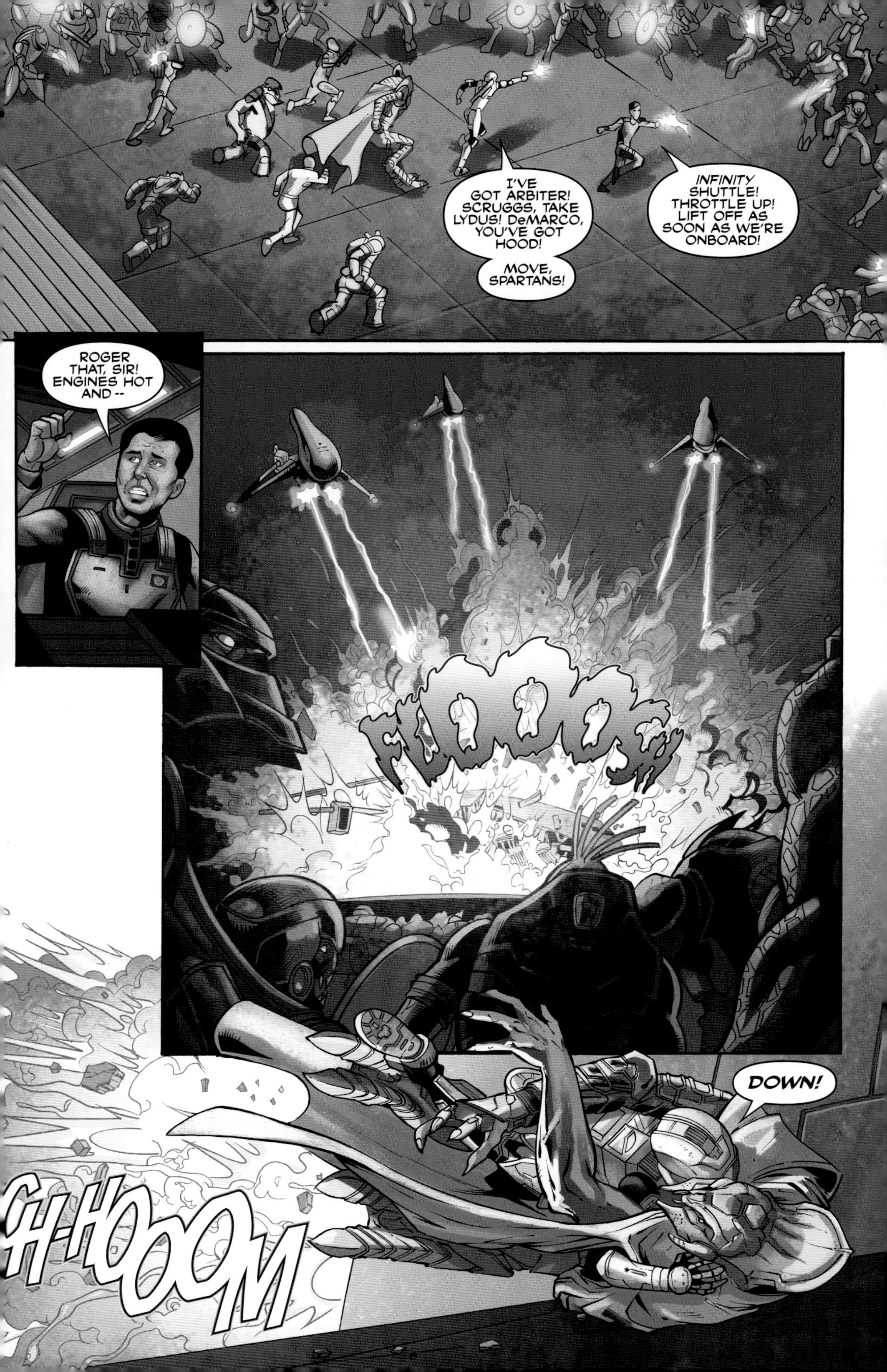
I'VE GOT ARBITER! SCRUGGS, TAKE LYDUS! DeMARCO, YOU'VE GOT HOOD!
MOVE, SPARTANS!
INFINITY SHUTTLE! THROTTLE UP! LIFT OFF AS SOON AS WE'RE ONBOARD!
ROGER THAT, SIR! ENGINES HOT AND --
DOWN!
CH-HOOOM

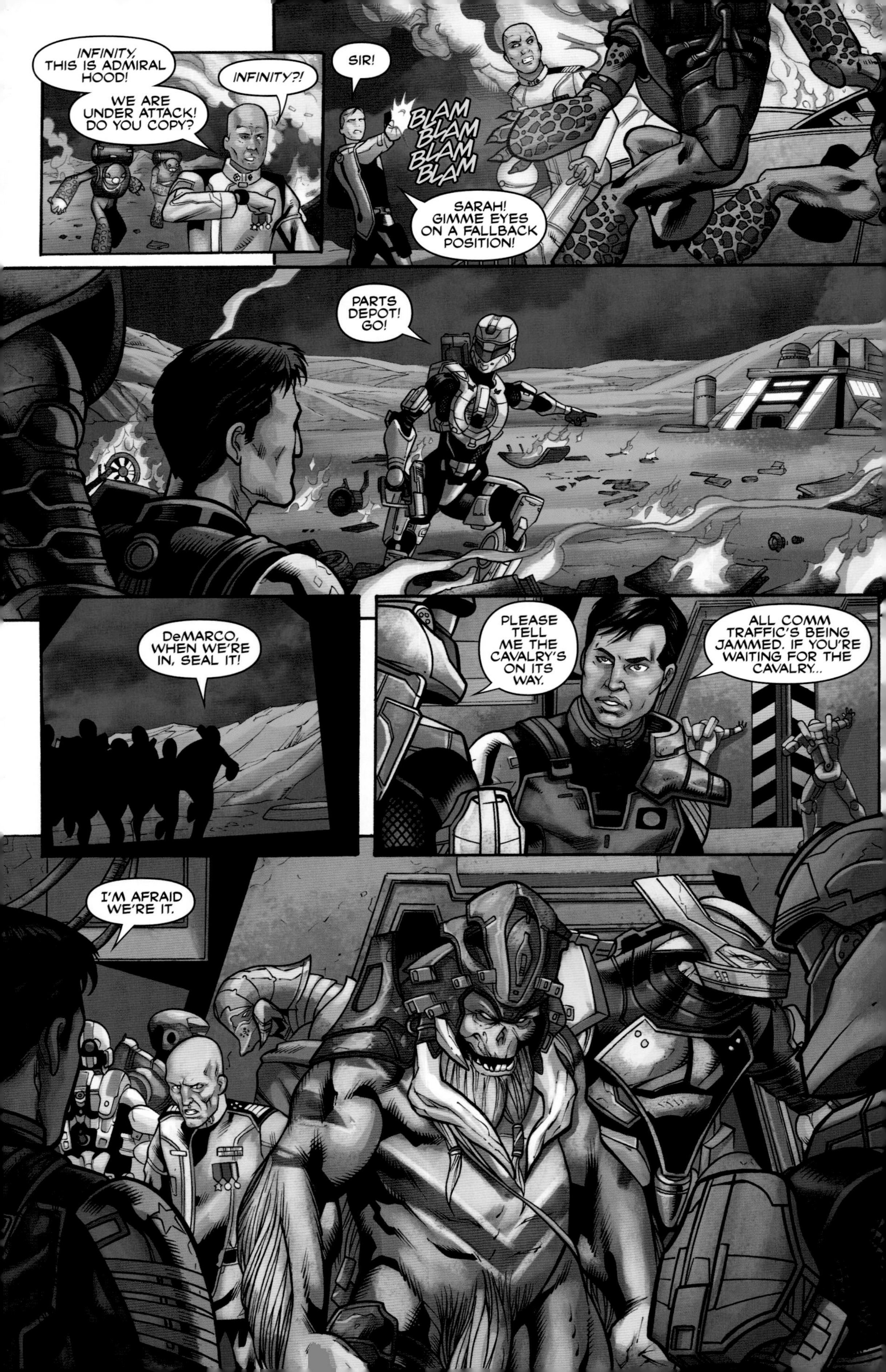

INFINITY, THIS IS ADMIRAL HOOD!
WE ARE UNDER ATTACK! DO YOU COPY?
INFINITY?!
SIR!
BLAM BLAM BLAM BLAM
SARAH! GIMME EYES ON A FALLBACK POSITION!
PARTS DEPOT! GO!
DeMARCO, WHEN WE'RE IN, SEAL IT!
PLEASE TELL ME THE CAVALRY'S ON ITS WAY.
ALL COMM TRAFFIC'S BEING JAMMED. IF YOU'RE WAITING FOR THE CAVALRY...
I'M AFRAID WE'RE IT.

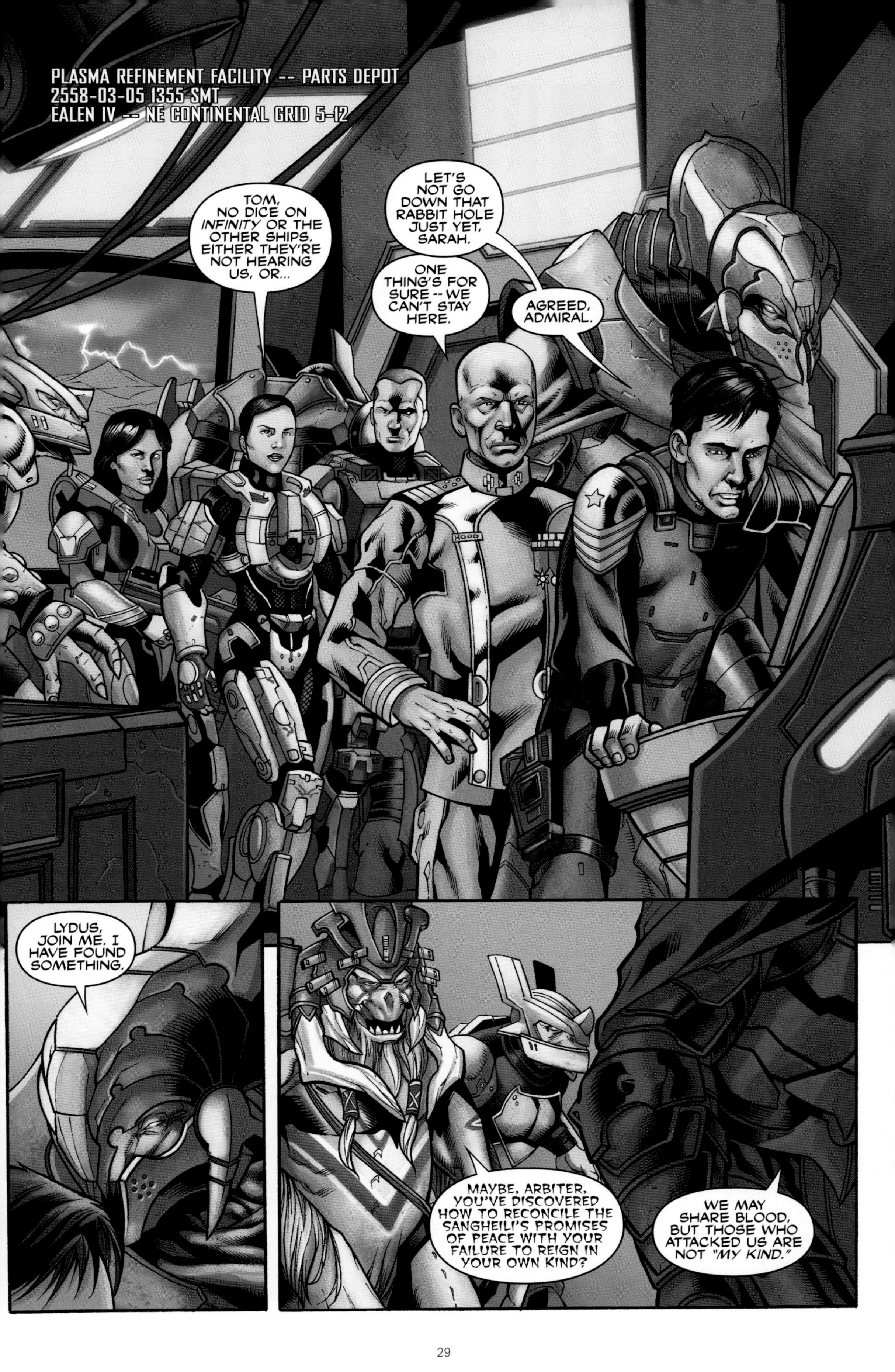
PLASMA REFINEMENT FACILITY -- PARTS DEPOT
2558-03-05 1355 SMT
EALEN IV -- NE CONTINENTAL GRID 5-12
TOM, NO DICE ON *INFINITY* OR THE OTHER SHIPS. EITHER THEY'RE NOT HEARING US, OR...
LET'S NOT GO DOWN THAT RABBIT HOLE JUST YET, SARAH.
ONE THING'S FOR SURE -- WE CAN'T STAY HERE.
AGREED, ADMIRAL.
LYDUS, JOIN ME. I HAVE FOUND SOMETHING.
MAYBE, ARBITER, YOU'VE DISCOVERED HOW TO RECONCILE THE SANGHEILI'S PROMISES OF PEACE WITH YOUR FAILURE TO REIGN IN YOUR OWN KIND?
WE MAY SHARE BLOOD, BUT THOSE WHO ATTACKED US ARE NOT *"MY KIND."*

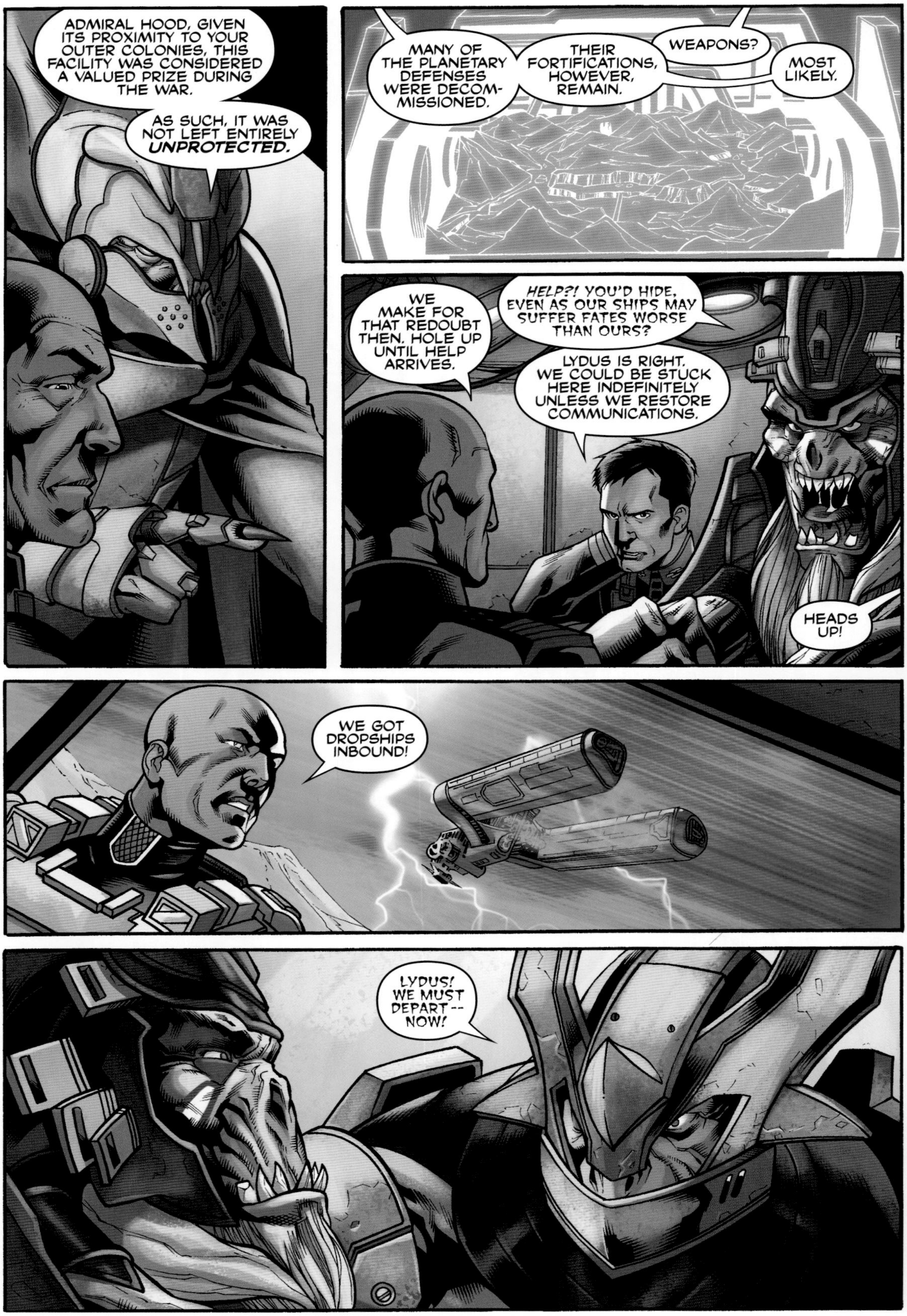
ADMIRAL HOOD, GIVEN ITS PROXIMITY TO YOUR OUTER COLONIES, THIS FACILITY WAS CONSIDERED A VALUED PRIZE DURING THE WAR.
AS SUCH, IT WAS NOT LEFT ENTIRELY *UNPROTECTED.*
MANY OF THE PLANETARY DEFENSES WERE DECOM-MISSIONED.
THEIR FORTIFICATIONS, HOWEVER, REMAIN.
WEAPONS?
MOST LIKELY.
WE MAKE FOR THAT REDOUBT THEN. HOLE UP UNTIL HELP ARRIVES.
HELP?! YOU'D HIDE, EVEN AS OUR SHIPS MAY SUFFER FATES WORSE THAN OURS?
LYDUS IS RIGHT. WE COULD BE STUCK HERE INDEFINITELY UNLESS WE RESTORE COMMUNICATIONS.
HEADS UP!
WE GOT DROPSHIPS INBOUND!
LYDUS! WE MUST DEPART-- NOW!

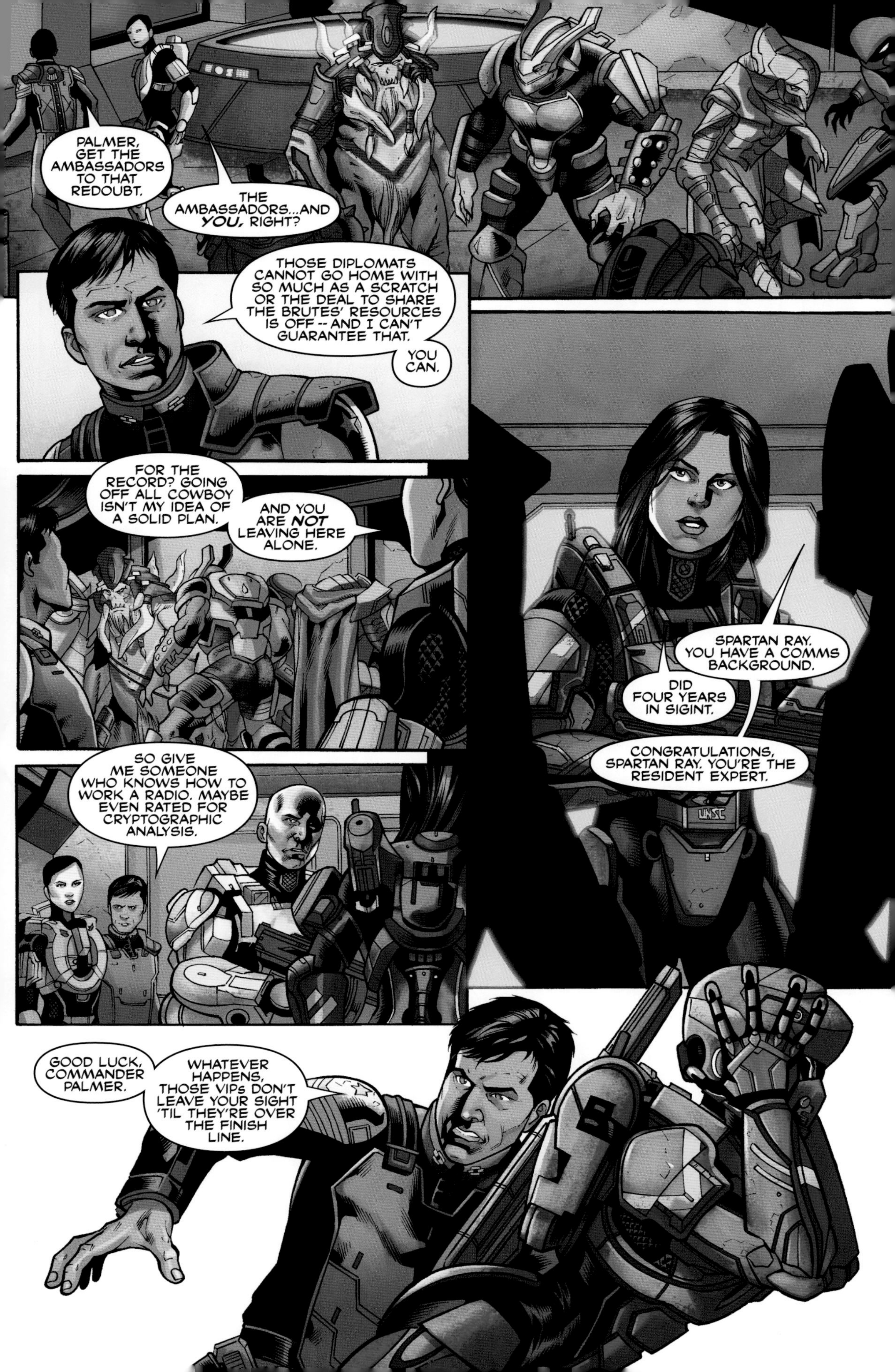
PALMER, GET THE AMBASSADORS TO THAT REDOUBT.
THE AMBASSADORS...AND *YOU,* RIGHT?
THOSE DIPLOMATS CANNOT GO HOME WITH SO MUCH AS A SCRATCH OR THE DEAL TO SHARE THE BRUTES' RESOURCES IS OFF -- AND I CAN'T GUARANTEE THAT.
YOU CAN.
FOR THE RECORD? GOING OFF ALL COWBOY ISN'T MY IDEA OF A SOLID PLAN.
AND YOU ARE ***NOT*** LEAVING HERE ALONE.
SO GIVE ME SOMEONE WHO KNOWS HOW TO WORK A RADIO. MAYBE EVEN RATED FOR CRYPTOGRAPHIC ANALYSIS.
SPARTAN RAY. YOU HAVE A COMMS BACKGROUND.
DID FOUR YEARS IN SIGINT.
CONGRATULATIONS, SPARTAN RAY. YOU'RE THE RESIDENT EXPERT.
UNSC
GOOD LUCK, COMMANDER PALMER.
WHATEVER HAPPENS, THOSE VIPs DON'T LEAVE YOUR SIGHT 'TIL THEY'RE OVER THE FINISH LINE.

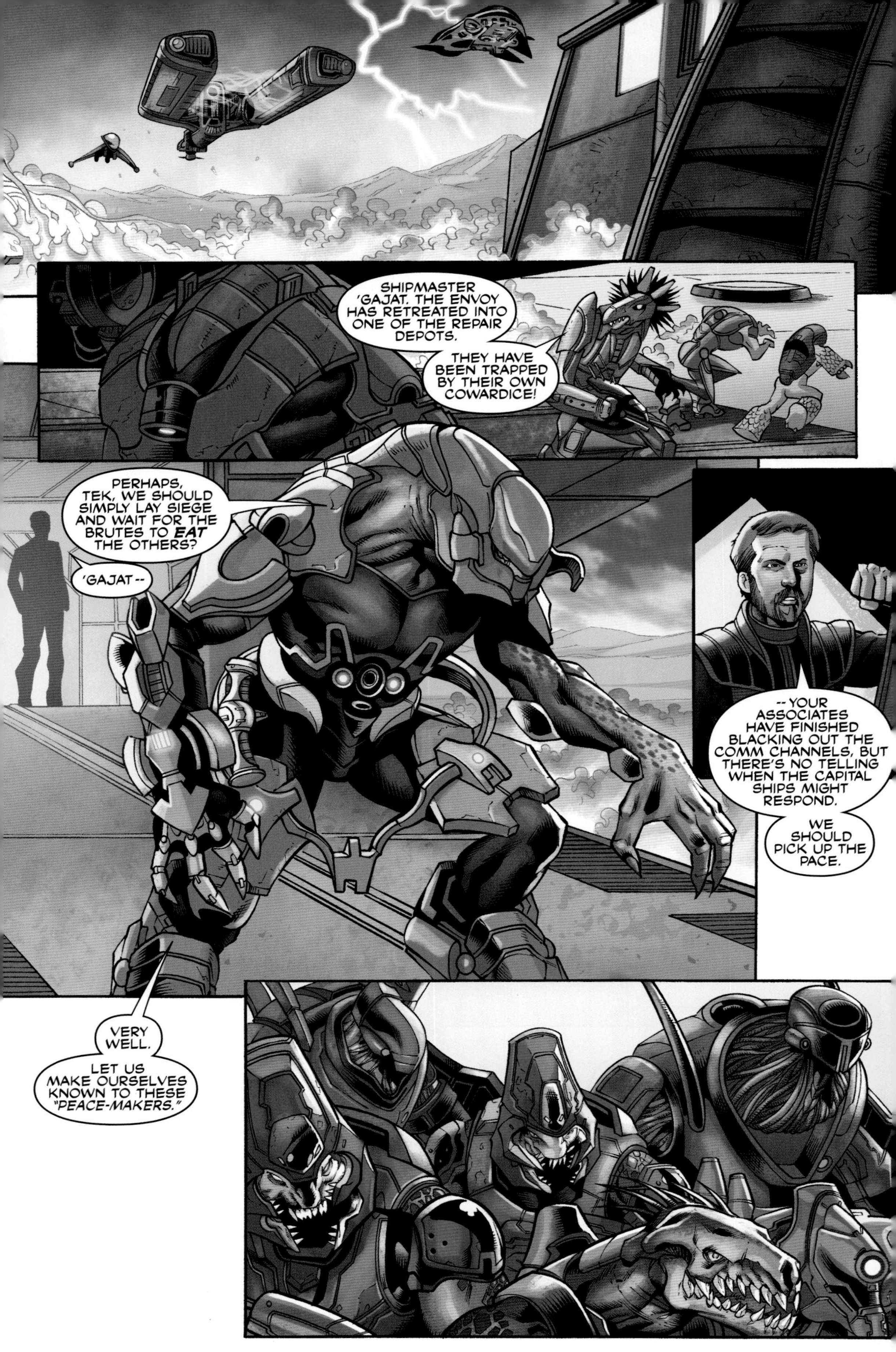
SHIPMASTER 'GAJAT. THE ENVOY HAS RETREATED INTO ONE OF THE REPAIR DEPOTS.
THEY HAVE BEEN TRAPPED BY THEIR OWN COWARDICE!
PERHAPS, TEK, WE SHOULD SIMPLY LAY SIEGE AND WAIT FOR THE BRUTES TO *EAT* THE OTHERS?
'GAJAT --
-- YOUR ASSOCIATES HAVE FINISHED BLACKING OUT THE COMM CHANNELS, BUT THERE'S NO TELLING WHEN THE CAPITAL SHIPS MIGHT RESPOND.
WE SHOULD PICK UP THE PACE.
VERY WELL.
LET US MAKE OURSELVES KNOWN TO THESE *"PEACE-MAKERS."*

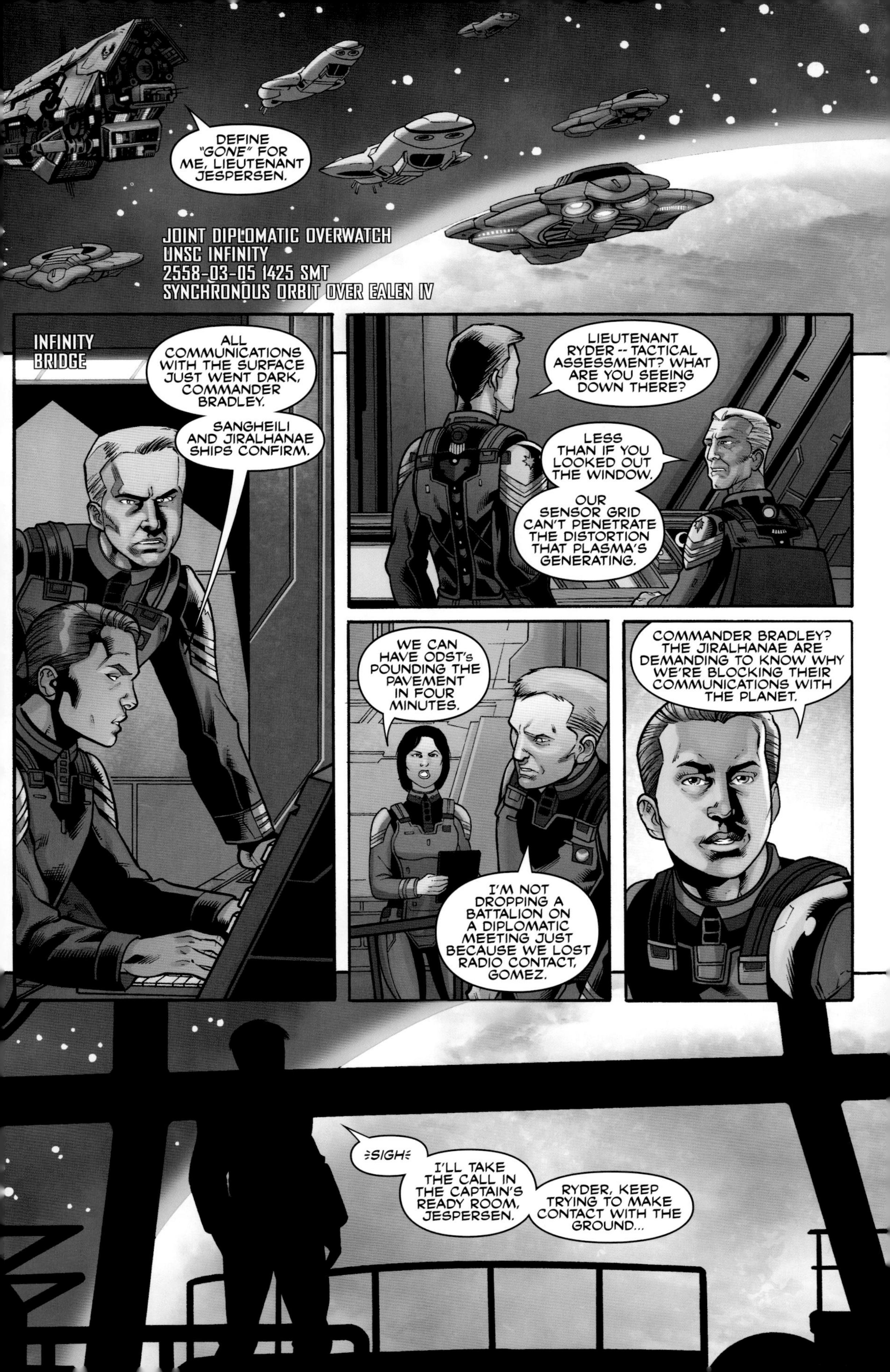
DEFINE "GONE" FOR ME, LIEUTENANT JESPERSEN.
JOINT DIPLOMATIC OVERWATCH
UNSC INFINITY
2558-03-05 1425 SMT
SYNCHRONOUS ORBIT OVER EALEN IV
INFINITY BRIDGE
ALL COMMUNICATIONS WITH THE SURFACE JUST WENT DARK, COMMANDER BRADLEY.
SANGHEILI AND JIRALHANAE SHIPS CONFIRM.
LIEUTENANT RYDER -- TACTICAL ASSESSMENT? WHAT ARE YOU SEEING DOWN THERE?
LESS THAN IF YOU LOOKED OUT THE WINDOW.
OUR SENSOR GRID CAN'T PENETRATE THE DISTORTION THAT PLASMA'S GENERATING.
WE CAN HAVE ODST's POUNDING THE PAVEMENT IN FOUR MINUTES.
I'M NOT DROPPING A BATTALION ON A DIPLOMATIC MEETING JUST BECAUSE WE LOST RADIO CONTACT, GOMEZ.
COMMANDER BRADLEY? THE JIRALHANAE ARE DEMANDING TO KNOW WHY WE'RE BLOCKING THEIR COMMUNICATIONS WITH THE PLANET.
SIGH
I'LL TAKE THE CALL IN THE CAPTAIN'S READY ROOM, JESPERSEN.
RYDER, KEEP TRYING TO MAKE CONTACT WITH THE GROUND...

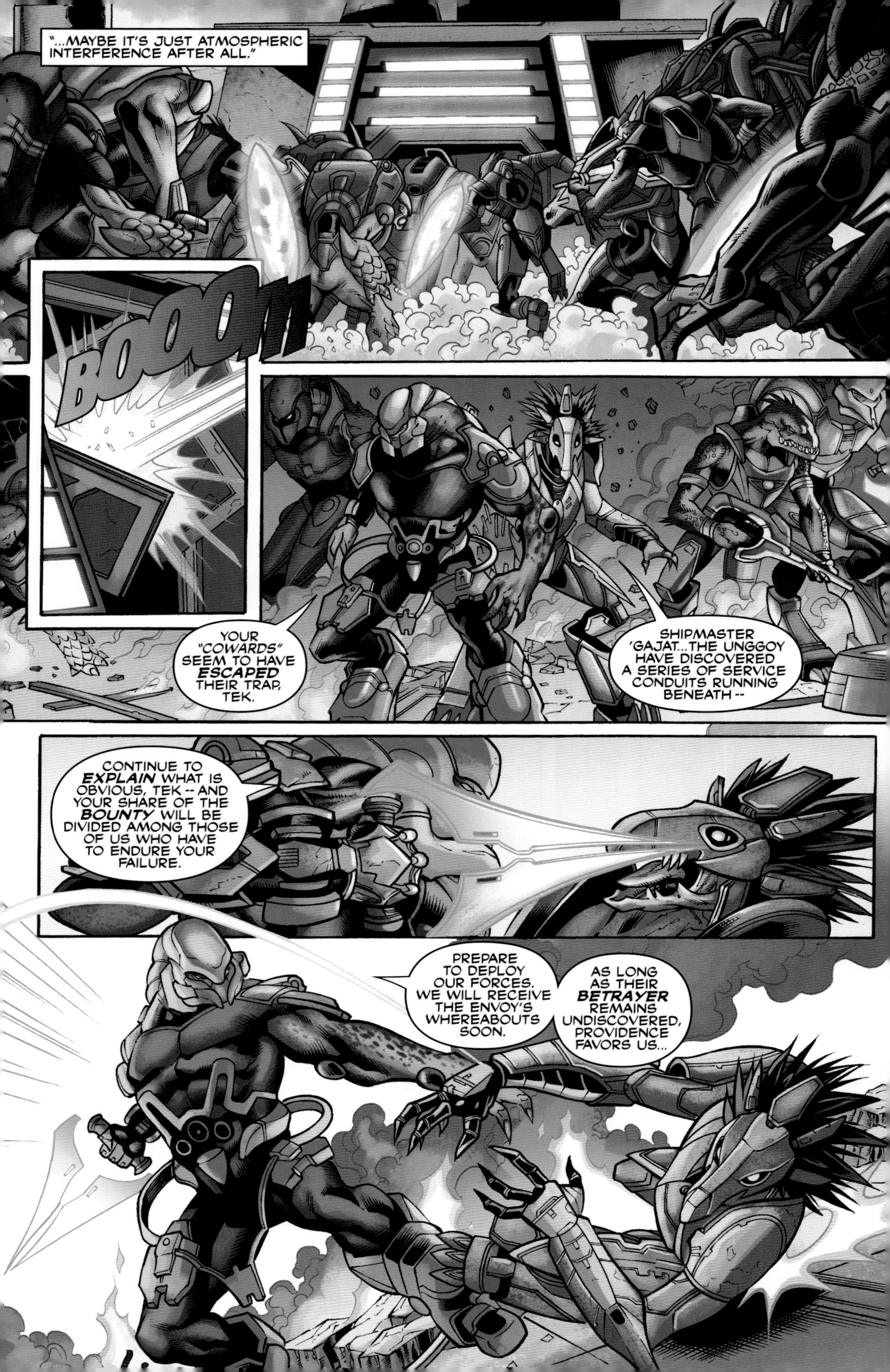
"...MAYBE IT'S JUST ATMOSPHERIC INTERFERENCE AFTER ALL."
BOOOM
YOUR "COWARDS" SEEM TO HAVE ESCAPED THEIR TRAP, TEK.
SHIPMASTER 'GAJAT...THE UNGGOY HAVE DISCOVERED A SERIES OF SERVICE CONDUITS RUNNING BENEATH --
CONTINUE TO EXPLAIN WHAT IS OBVIOUS, TEK -- AND YOUR SHARE OF THE BOUNTY WILL BE DIVIDED AMONG THOSE OF US WHO HAVE TO ENDURE YOUR FAILURE.
PREPARE TO DEPLOY OUR FORCES. WE WILL RECEIVE THE ENVOY'S WHEREABOUTS SOON.
AS LONG AS THEIR BETRAYER REMAINS UNDISCOVERED, PROVIDENCE FAVORS US...

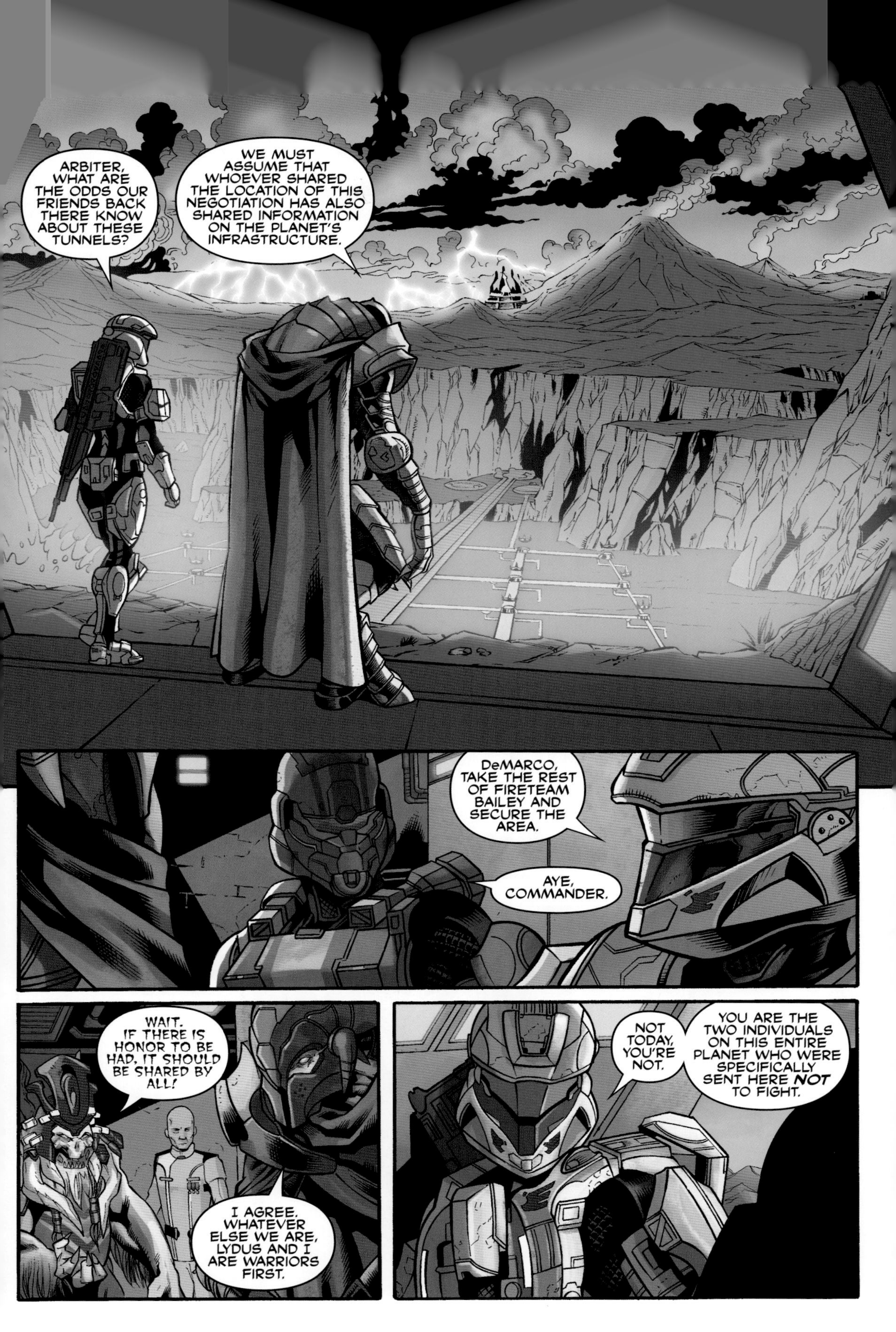
ARBITER, WHAT ARE THE ODDS OUR FRIENDS BACK THERE KNOW ABOUT THESE TUNNELS?
WE MUST ASSUME THAT WHOEVER SHARED THE LOCATION OF THIS NEGOTIATION HAS ALSO SHARED INFORMATION ON THE PLANET'S INFRASTRUCTURE.
DeMARCO, TAKE THE REST OF FIRETEAM BAILEY AND SECURE THE AREA.
AYE, COMMANDER.
WAIT. IF THERE IS HONOR TO BE HAD, IT SHOULD BE SHARED BY ALL!
I AGREE. WHATEVER ELSE WE ARE, LYDUS AND I ARE WARRIORS FIRST.
NOT TODAY, YOU'RE NOT.
YOU ARE THE TWO INDIVIDUALS ON THIS ENTIRE PLANET WHO WERE SPECIFICALLY SENT HERE ***NOT*** TO FIGHT.

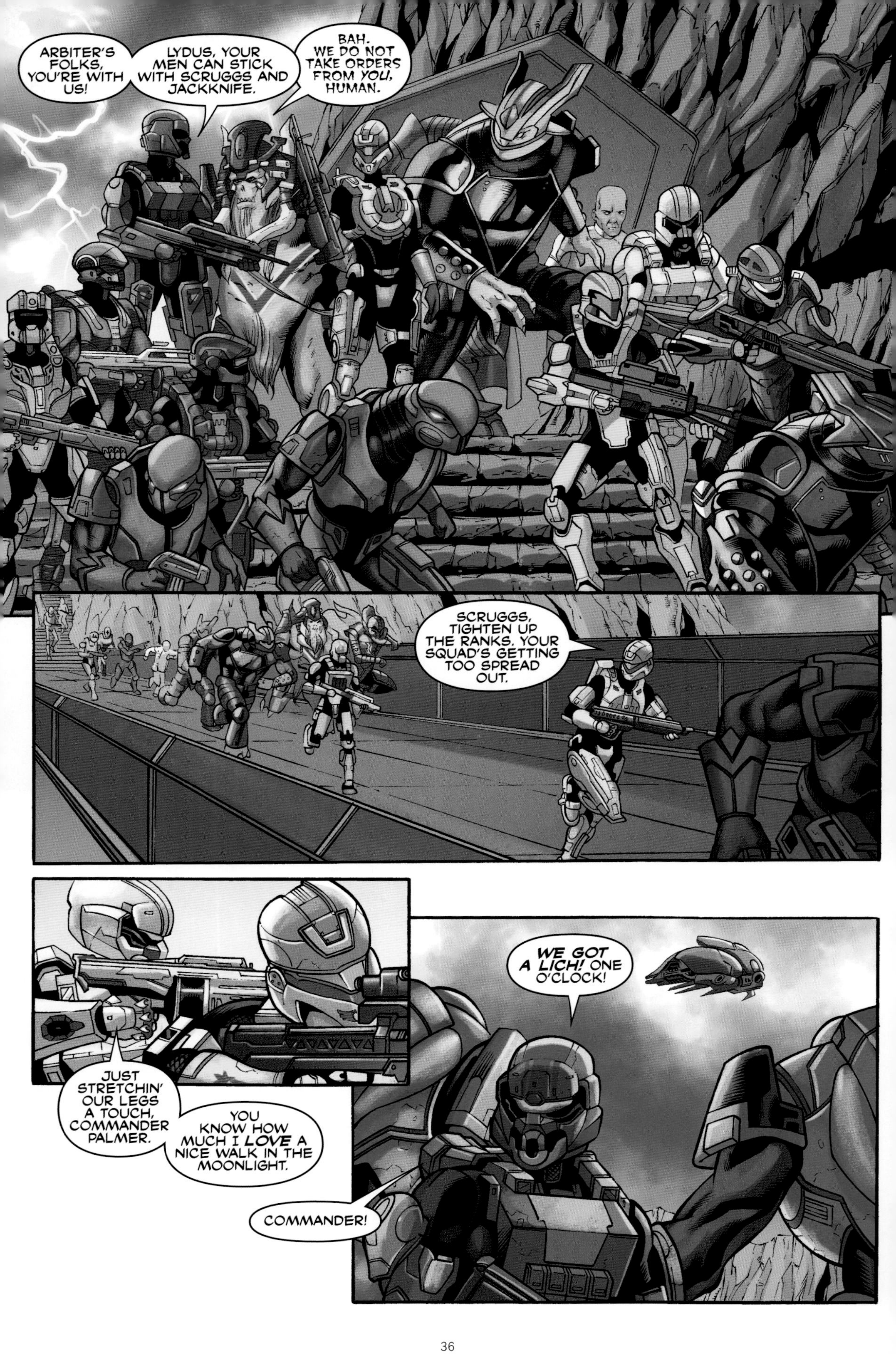
ARBITER'S FOLKS, YOU'RE WITH US!
LYDUS, YOUR MEN CAN STICK WITH SCRUGGS AND JACKKNIFE.
BAH. WE DO NOT TAKE ORDERS FROM *YOU*, HUMAN.
SCRUGGS, TIGHTEN UP THE RANKS. YOUR SQUAD'S GETTING TOO SPREAD OUT.
JUST STRETCHIN' OUR LEGS A TOUCH, COMMANDER PALMER.
YOU KNOW HOW MUCH I ***LOVE*** A NICE WALK IN THE MOONLIGHT.
WE GOT A LICH! ONE O'CLOCK!
COMMANDER!

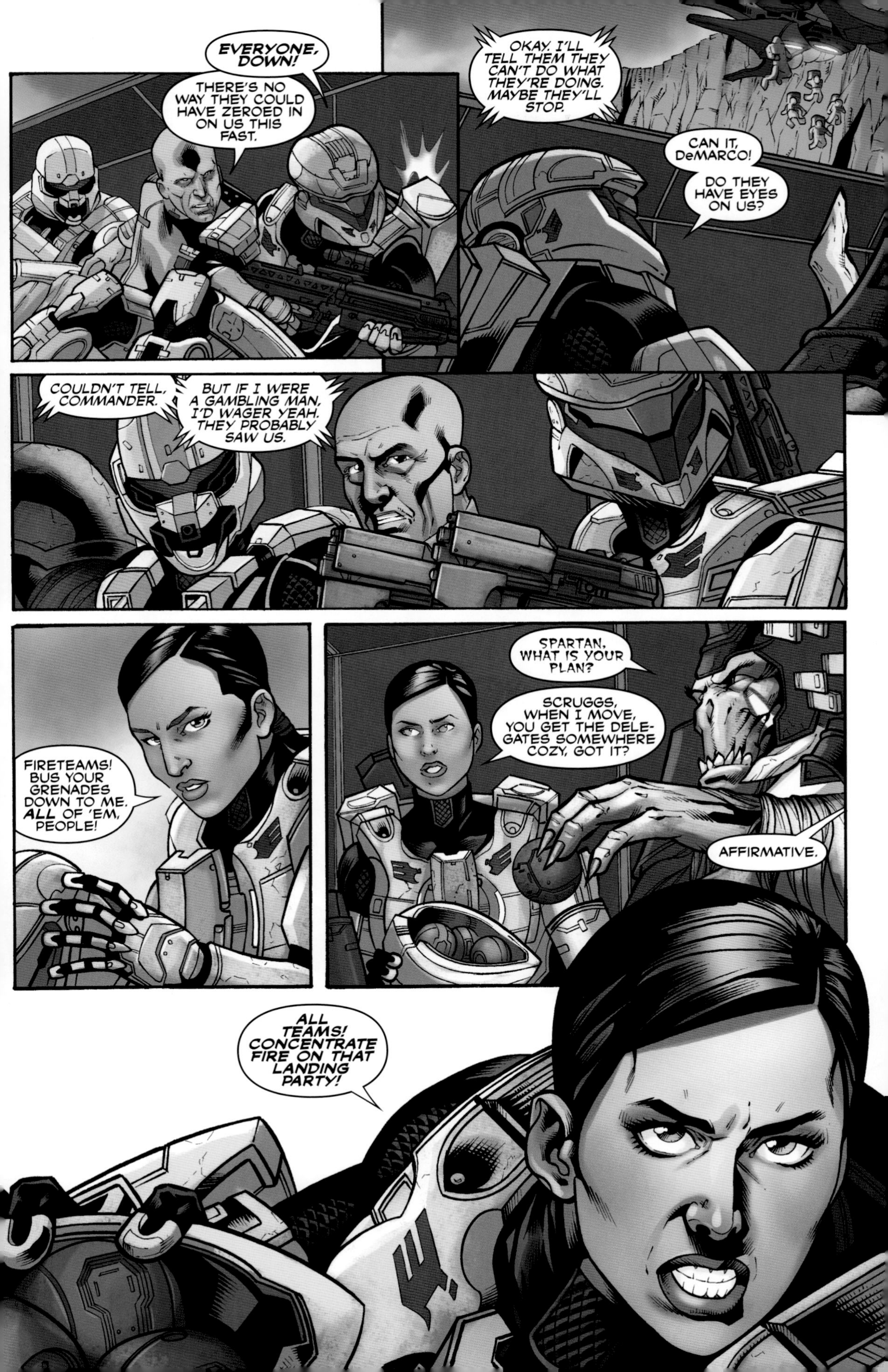
EVERYONE, DOWN!
THERE'S NO WAY THEY COULD HAVE ZEROED IN ON US THIS FAST.
OKAY. I'LL TELL THEM THEY CAN'T DO WHAT THEY'RE DOING. MAYBE THEY'LL STOP.
CAN IT, DeMARCO!
DO THEY HAVE EYES ON US?
COULDN'T TELL, COMMANDER.
BUT IF I WERE A GAMBLING MAN, I'D WAGER YEAH. THEY PROBABLY SAW US.
FIRETEAMS! BUS YOUR GRENADES DOWN TO ME. ALL OF 'EM, PEOPLE!
SPARTAN, WHAT IS YOUR PLAN?
SCRUGGS, WHEN I MOVE, YOU GET THE DELEGATES SOMEWHERE COZY, GOT IT?
AFFIRMATIVE.
ALL TEAMS! CONCENTRATE FIRE ON THAT LANDING PARTY!

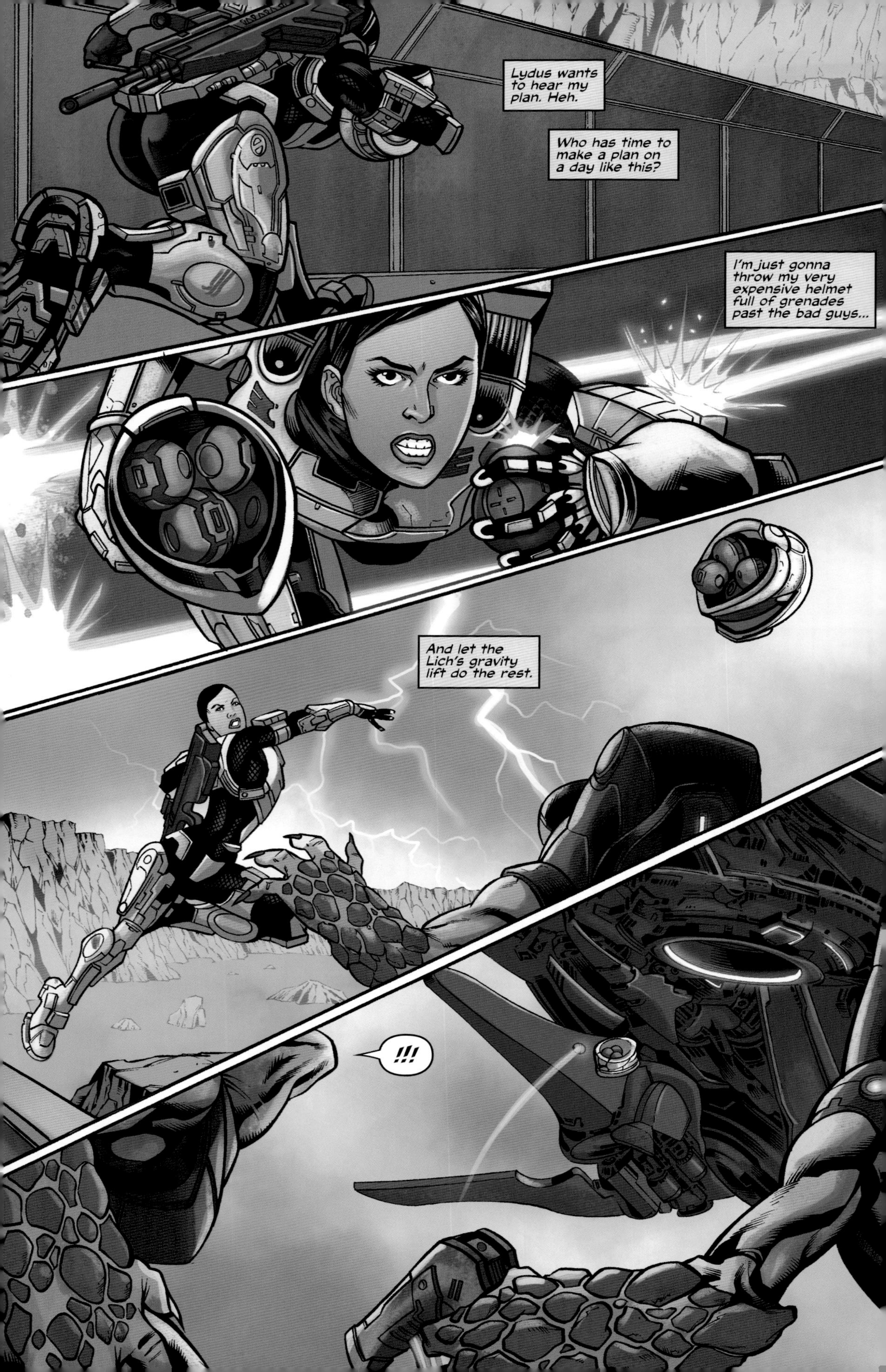
Lydus wants to hear my plan. Heh.
Who has time to make a plan on a day like this?
I'm just gonna throw my very expensive helmet full of grenades past the bad guys...
And let the Lich's gravity lift do the rest.
!!!

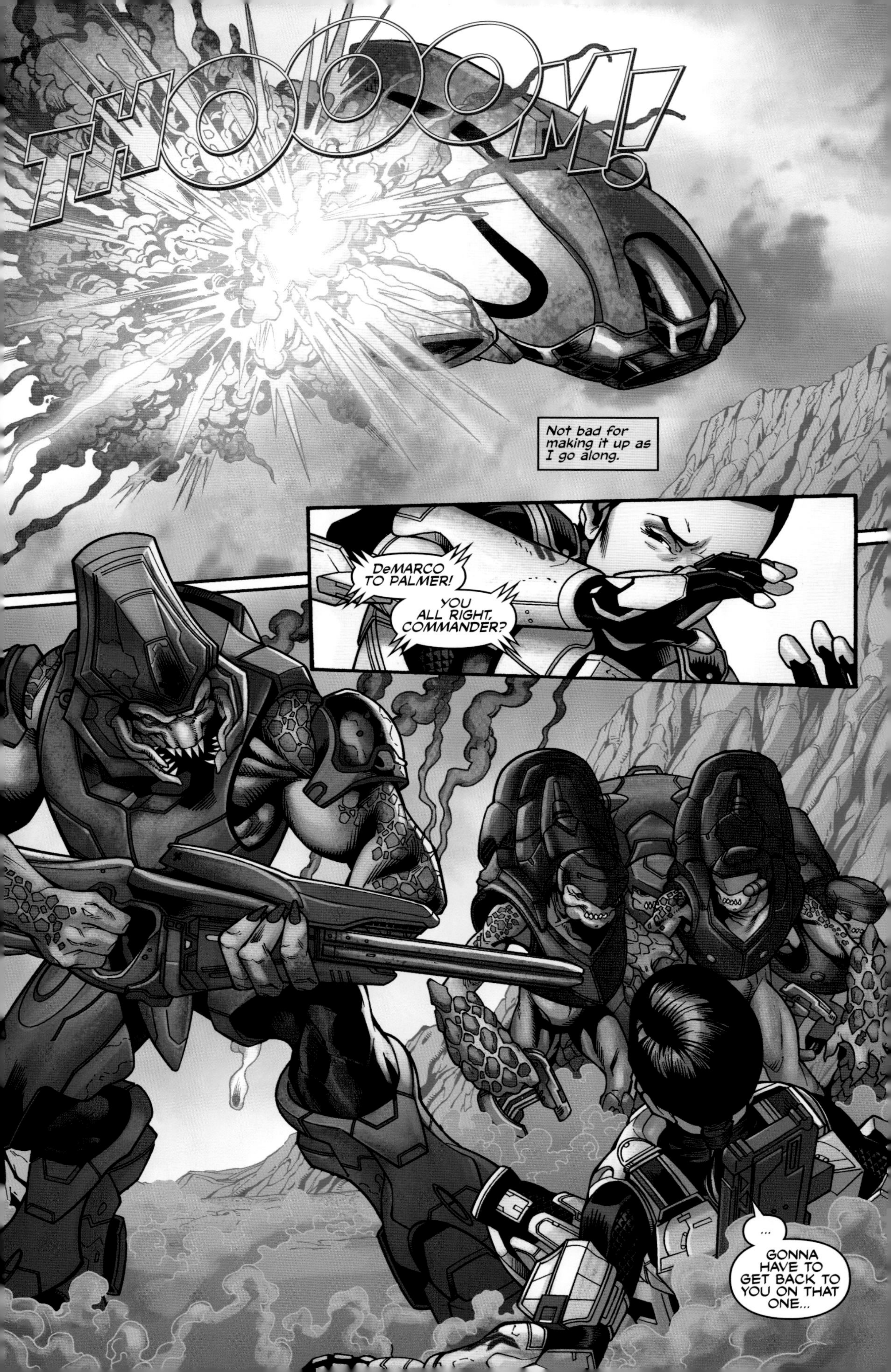
THOOOOM!
Not bad for making it up as I go along.
DeMARCO TO PALMER!
YOU ALL RIGHT, COMMANDER?
...
GONNA HAVE TO GET BACK TO YOU ON THAT ONE...

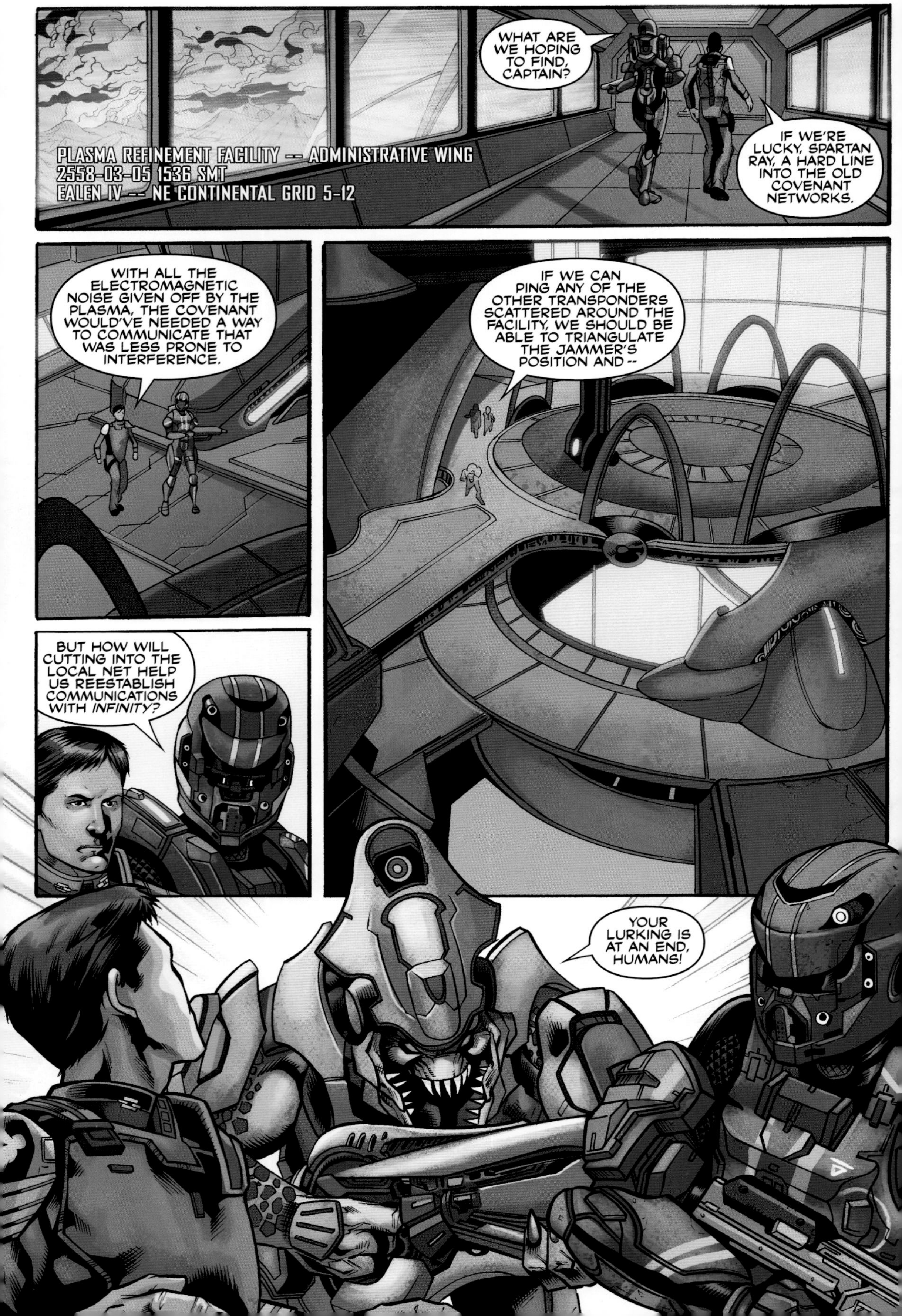
PLASMA REFINEMENT FACILITY -- ADMINISTRATIVE WING
2558-03-05 1536 SMT
EALEN IV -- NE CONTINENTAL GRID 5-12
WHAT ARE WE HOPING TO FIND, CAPTAIN?
IF WE'RE LUCKY, SPARTAN RAY, A HARD LINE INTO THE OLD COVENANT NETWORKS.
WITH ALL THE ELECTROMAGNETIC NOISE GIVEN OFF BY THE PLASMA, THE COVENANT WOULD'VE NEEDED A WAY TO COMMUNICATE THAT WAS LESS PRONE TO INTERFERENCE.
IF WE CAN PING ANY OF THE OTHER TRANSPONDERS SCATTERED AROUND THE FACILITY, WE SHOULD BE ABLE TO TRIANGULATE THE JAMMER'S POSITION AND --
BUT HOW WILL CUTTING INTO THE LOCAL NET HELP US REESTABLISH COMMUNICATIONS WITH INFINITY?
YOUR LURKING IS AT AN END, HUMANS!

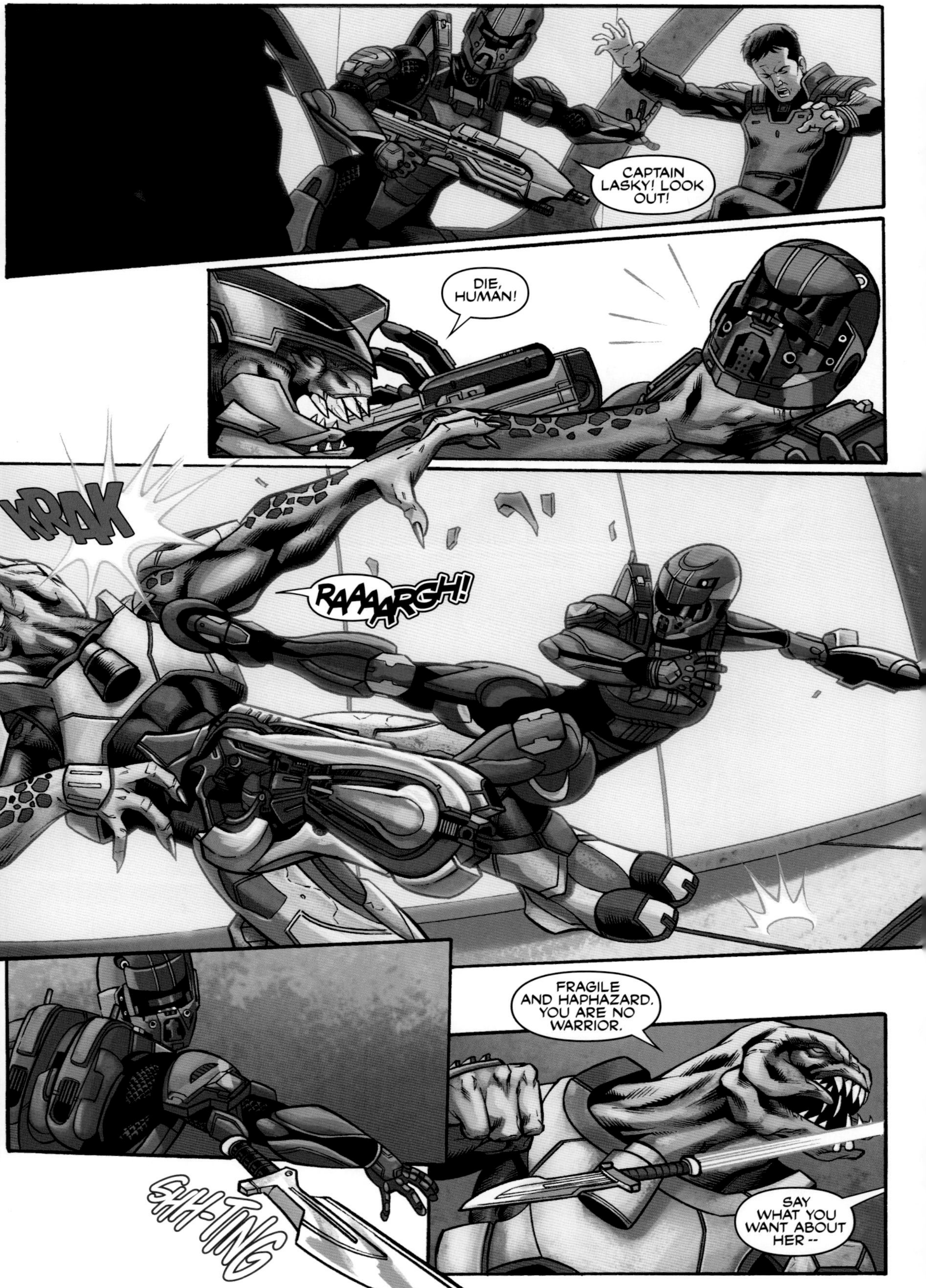
CAPTAIN LASKY! LOOK OUT!
DIE, HUMAN!
KRAK
RAAAARGH!
FRAGILE AND HAPHAZARD. YOU ARE NO WARRIOR.
SHH-TING
SAY WHAT YOU WANT ABOUT HER --

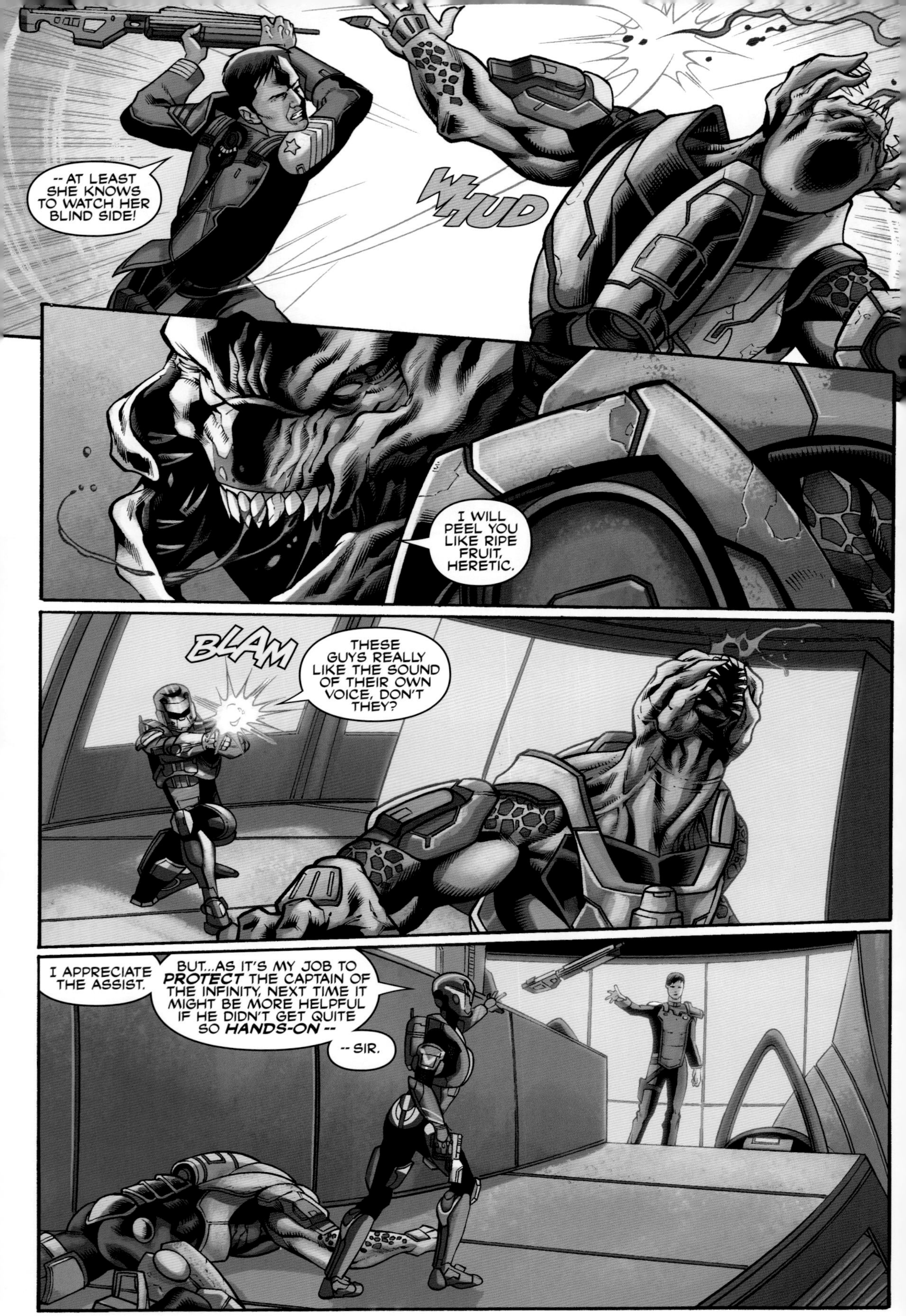
-- AT LEAST SHE KNOWS TO WATCH HER BLIND SIDE!
WHUD
I WILL PEEL YOU LIKE RIPE FRUIT, HERETIC.
BLAM
THESE GUYS REALLY LIKE THE SOUND OF THEIR OWN VOICE, DON'T THEY?
I APPRECIATE THE ASSIST.
BUT...AS IT'S MY JOB TO PROTECT THE CAPTAIN OF THE INFINITY, NEXT TIME IT MIGHT BE MORE HELPFUL IF HE DIDN'T GET QUITE SO HANDS-ON --
-- SIR.

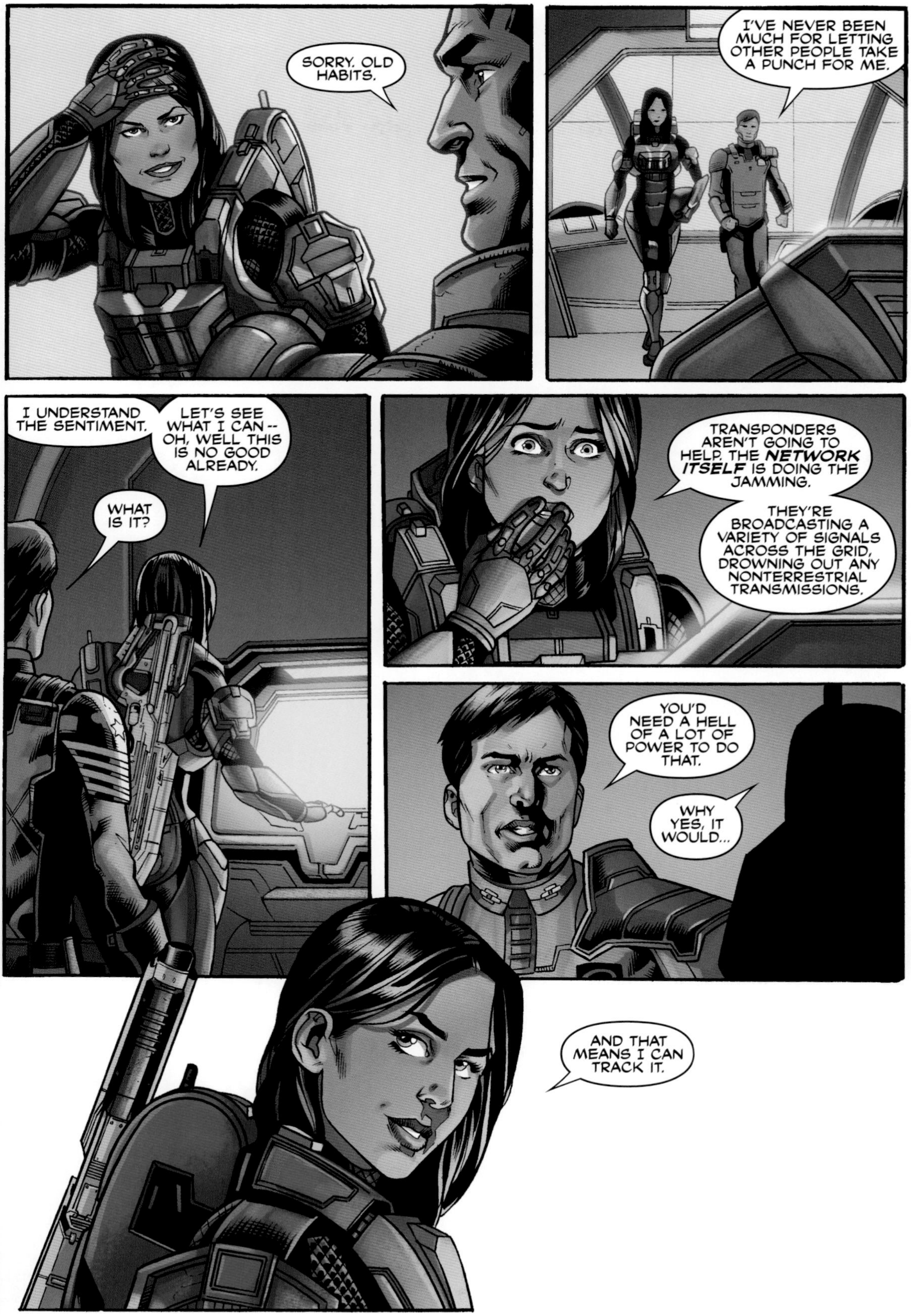
SORRY. OLD HABITS.
I'VE NEVER BEEN MUCH FOR LETTING OTHER PEOPLE TAKE A PUNCH FOR ME.
I UNDERSTAND THE SENTIMENT.
LET'S SEE WHAT I CAN -- OH, WELL THIS IS NO GOOD ALREADY.
WHAT IS IT?
TRANSPONDERS AREN'T GOING TO HELP. THE NETWORK ITSELF IS DOING THE JAMMING.
THEY'RE BROADCASTING A VARIETY OF SIGNALS ACROSS THE GRID, DROWNING OUT ANY NONTERRESTRIAL TRANSMISSIONS.
YOU'D NEED A HELL OF A LOT OF POWER TO DO THAT.
WHY YES, IT WOULD...
AND THAT MEANS I CAN TRACK IT.

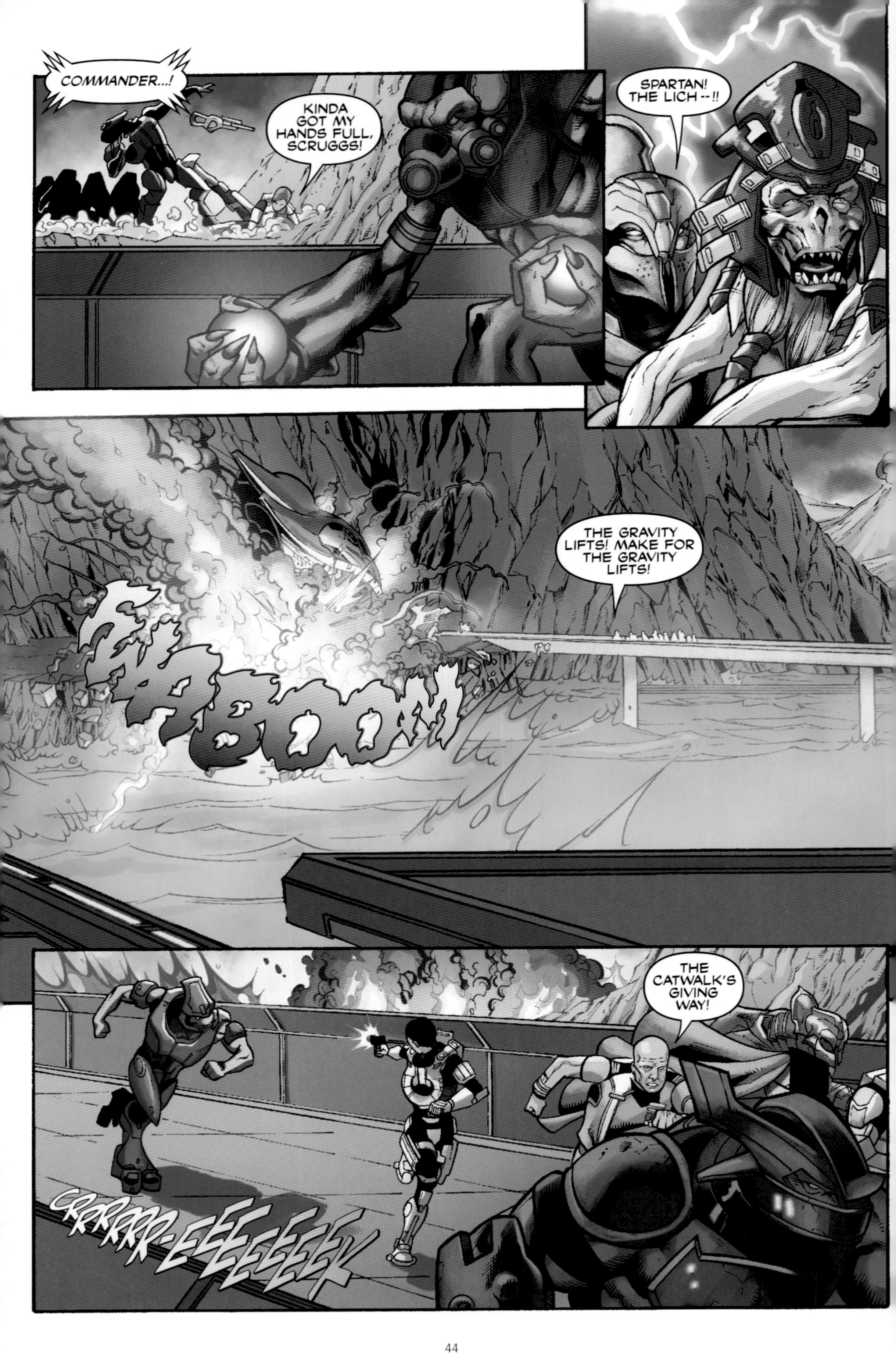
COMMANDER...!
KINDA GOT MY HANDS FULL, SCRUGGS!
SPARTAN! THE LICH--!!
THE GRAVITY LIFTS! MAKE FOR THE GRAVITY LIFTS!
KA-BOOM
THE CATWALK'S GIVING WAY!
CRRRRRR-EEEEEEEEK

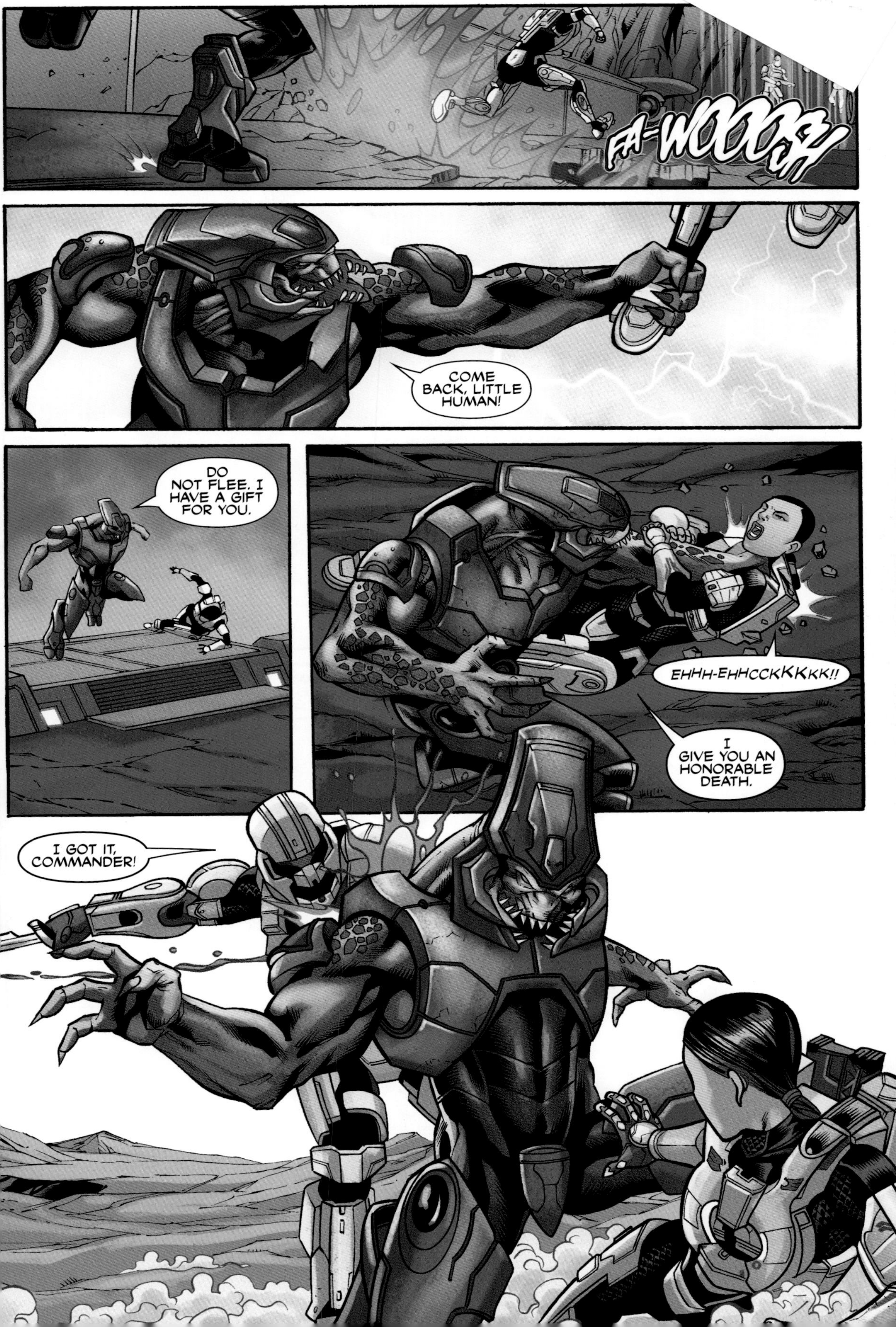
FA-WOOOSH
COME BACK, LITTLE HUMAN!
DO NOT FLEE. I HAVE A GIFT FOR YOU.
EHHH-EHHCCKKKKK!!
I GIVE YOU AN HONORABLE DEATH.
I GOT IT, COMMANDER!

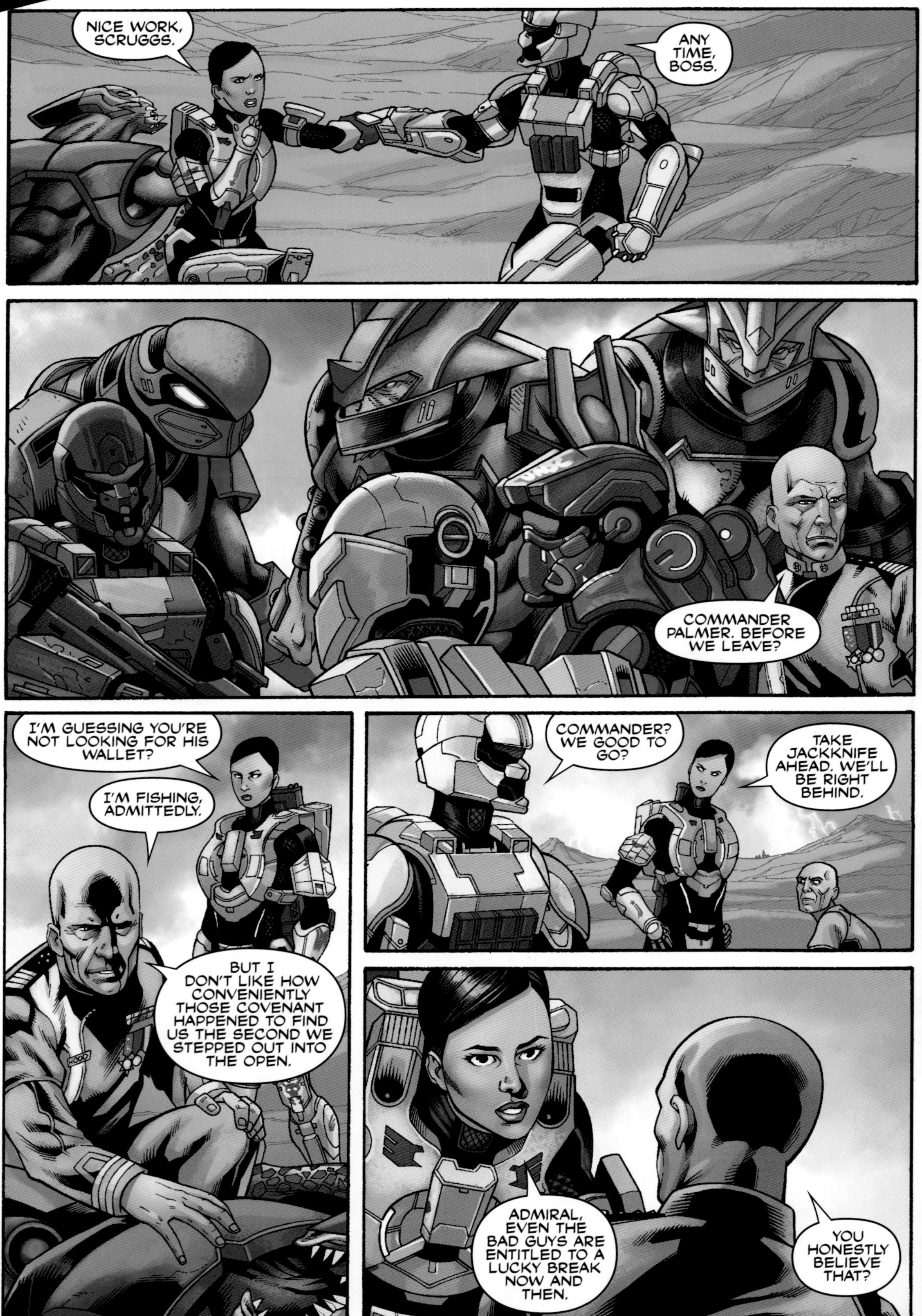
NICE WORK, SCRUGGS.
ANY TIME, BOSS.
COMMANDER PALMER. BEFORE WE LEAVE?
I'M GUESSING YOU'RE NOT LOOKING FOR HIS WALLET?
I'M FISHING, ADMITTEDLY.
BUT I DON'T LIKE HOW CONVENIENTLY THOSE COVENANT HAPPENED TO FIND US THE SECOND WE STEPPED OUT INTO THE OPEN.
COMMANDER? WE GOOD TO GO?
TAKE JACKKNIFE AHEAD. WE'LL BE RIGHT BEHIND.
ADMIRAL, EVEN THE BAD GUYS ARE ENTITLED TO A LUCKY BREAK NOW AND THEN.
YOU HONESTLY BELIEVE THAT?

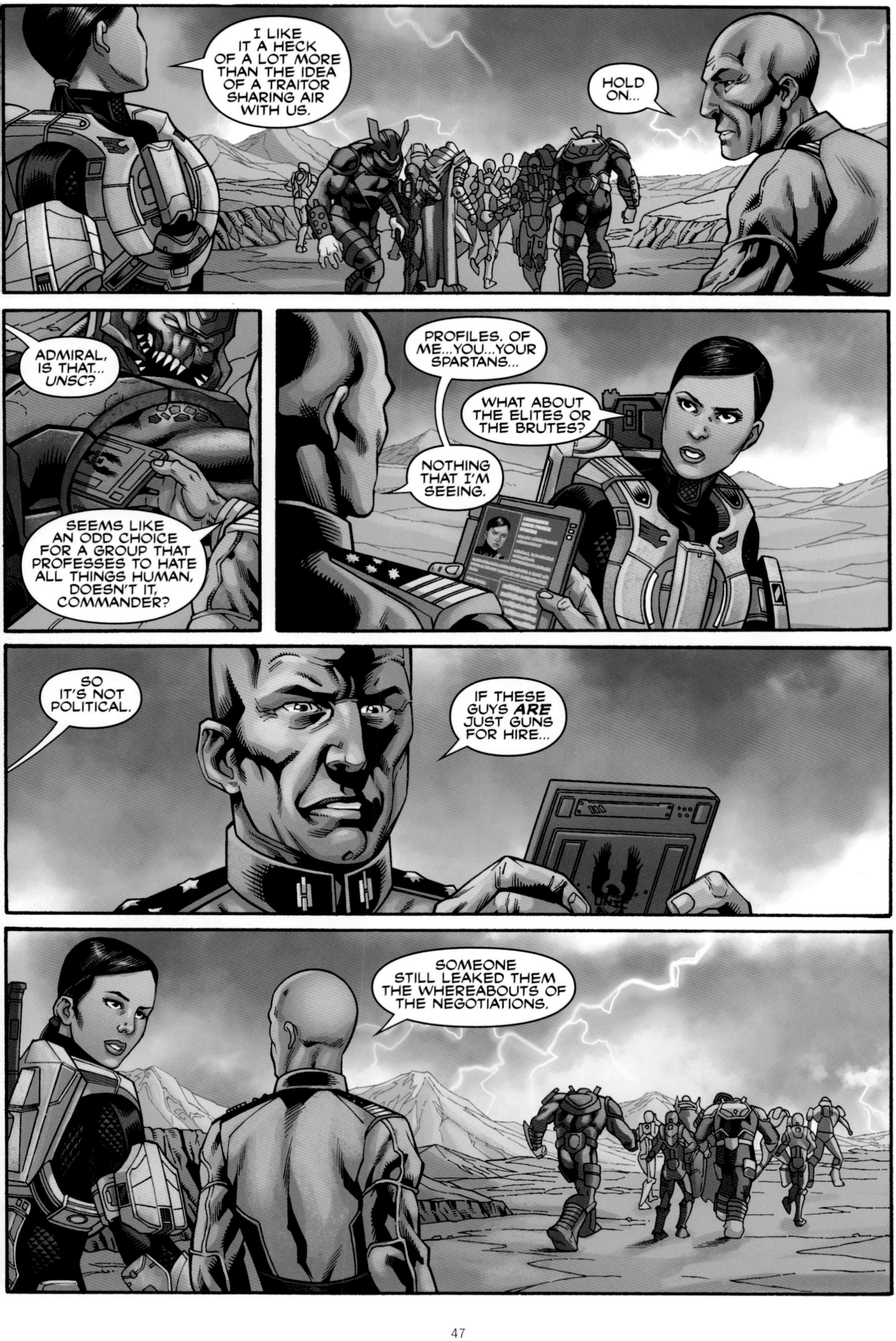
I LIKE IT A HECK OF A LOT MORE THAN THE IDEA OF A TRAITOR SHARING AIR WITH US.
HOLD ON...
ADMIRAL, IS THAT... *UNSC*?
SEEMS LIKE AN ODD CHOICE FOR A GROUP THAT PROFESSES TO HATE ALL THINGS HUMAN, DOESN'T IT, COMMANDER?
PROFILES. OF ME...YOU...YOUR SPARTANS...
WHAT ABOUT THE ELITES OR THE BRUTES?
NOTHING THAT I'M SEEING.
SO IT'S NOT POLITICAL.
IF THESE GUYS ***ARE*** JUST GUNS FOR HIRE...
SOMEONE STILL LEAKED THEM THE WHEREABOUTS OF THE NEGOTIATIONS.

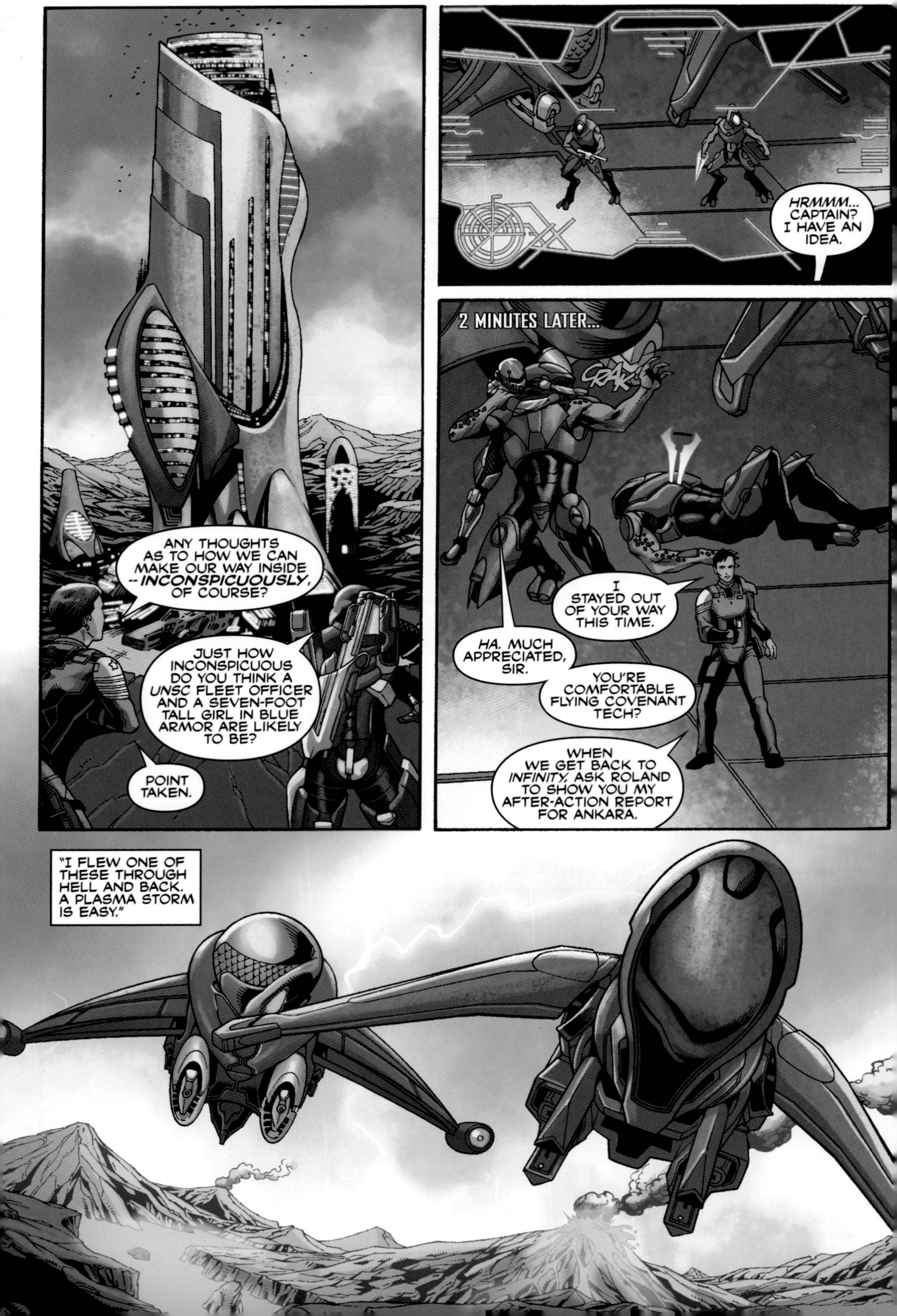
ANY THOUGHTS AS TO HOW WE CAN MAKE OUR WAY INSIDE --*INCONSPICUOUSLY*, OF COURSE?
JUST HOW INCONSPICUOUS DO YOU THINK A *UNSC* FLEET OFFICER AND A SEVEN-FOOT TALL GIRL IN BLUE ARMOR ARE LIKELY TO BE?
POINT TAKEN.
HRMMM... CAPTAIN? I HAVE AN IDEA.
2 MINUTES LATER...
CRAK
I STAYED OUT OF YOUR WAY THIS TIME.
HA. MUCH APPRECIATED, SIR.
YOU'RE COMFORTABLE FLYING COVENANT TECH?
WHEN WE GET BACK TO *INFINITY*, ASK ROLAND TO SHOW YOU MY AFTER-ACTION REPORT FOR ANKARA.
"I FLEW ONE OF THESE THROUGH HELL AND BACK. A PLASMA STORM IS EASY."

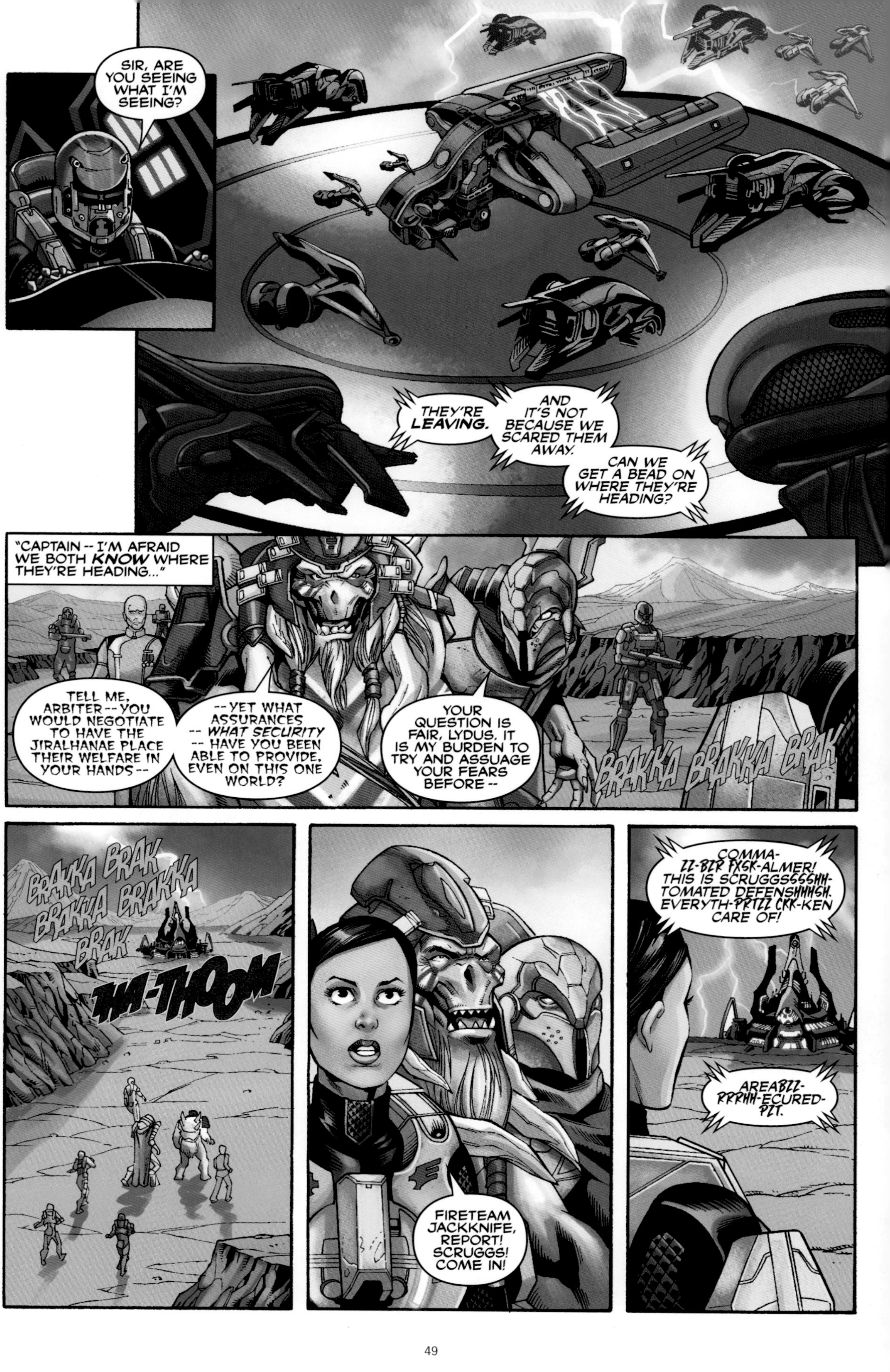
SIR, ARE YOU SEEING WHAT I'M SEEING?
THEY'RE **LEAVING.**
AND IT'S NOT BECAUSE WE SCARED THEM AWAY.
CAN WE GET A BEAD ON WHERE THEY'RE HEADING?
"CAPTAIN -- I'M AFRAID WE BOTH **KNOW** WHERE THEY'RE HEADING..."
TELL ME, ARBITER -- YOU WOULD NEGOTIATE TO HAVE THE JIRALHANAE PLACE THEIR WELFARE IN YOUR HANDS --
-- YET WHAT ASSURANCES -- *WHAT SECURITY* -- HAVE YOU BEEN ABLE TO PROVIDE, EVEN ON THIS ONE WORLD?
YOUR QUESTION IS FAIR, LYDUS. IT IS MY BURDEN TO TRY AND ASSUAGE YOUR FEARS BEFORE --
BRAKKA BRAKKA BRAK
BRAKKA BRAK BRAKKA BRAKKA BRAKKA BRAK
THA-THOOM
FIRETEAM JACKKNIFE, REPORT! SCRUGGS! COME IN!
COMMA-ZZ-BZR FXSK-ALMER! THIS IS SCRUGGSSSSHH-TOMATED DEFENSHHHSH. EVERYTH-PRTZZ CKK-KEN CARE OF!
AREABZZ-RRRHH-ECURED-PZT.

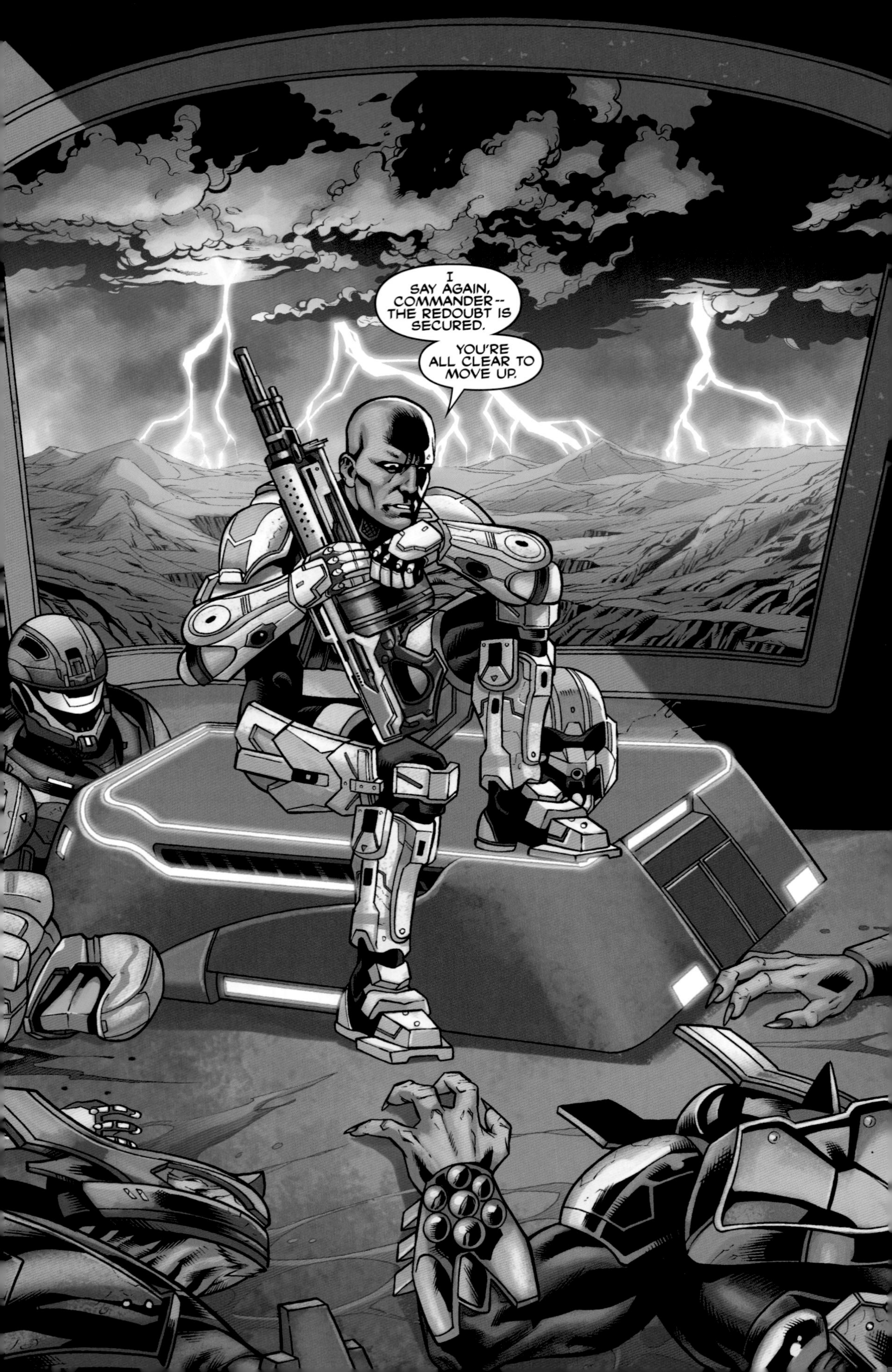
I SAY AGAIN, COMMANDER-- THE REDOUBT IS SECURED.
YOU'RE ALL CLEAR TO MOVE UP.

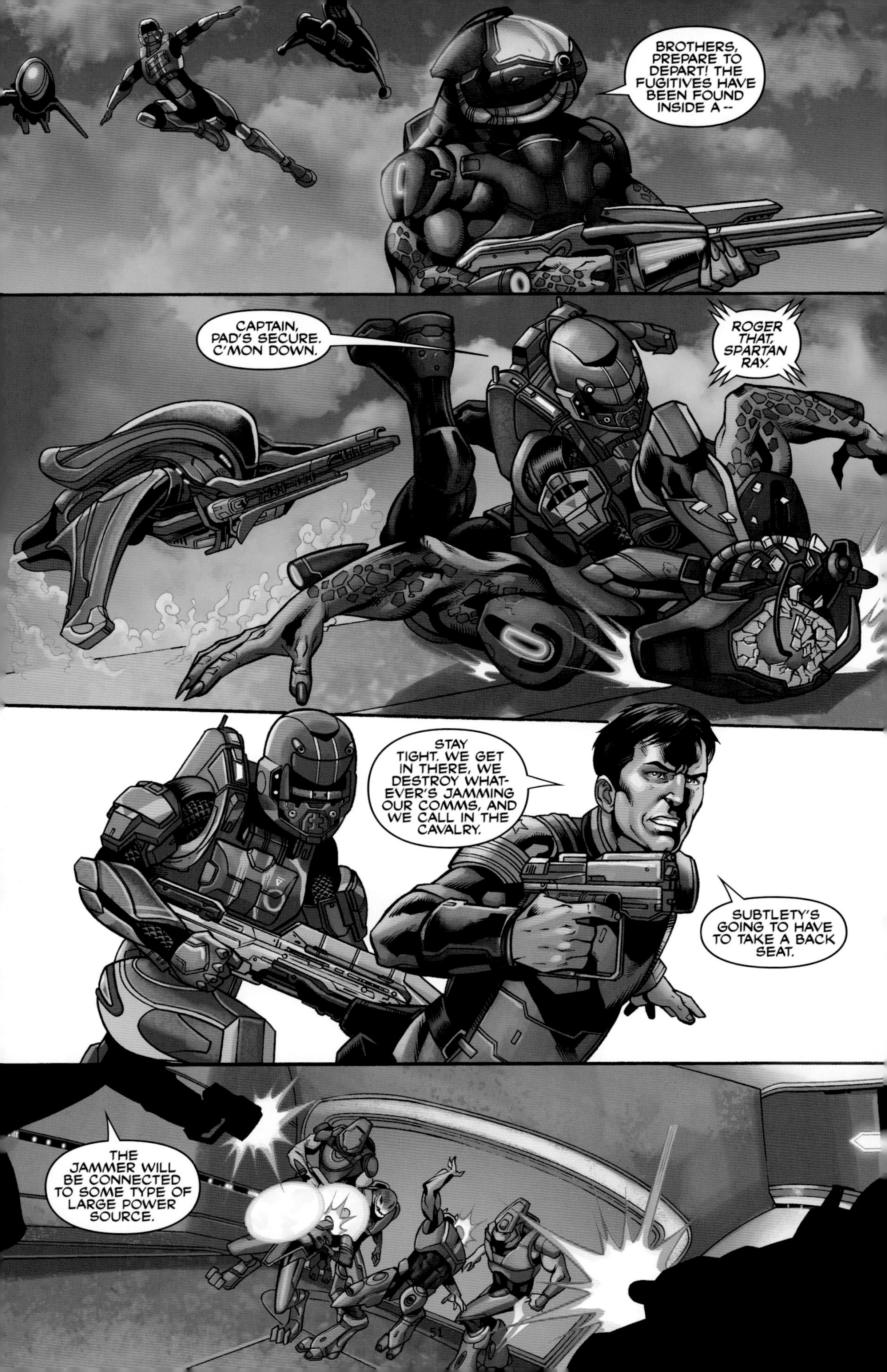
BROTHERS, PREPARE TO DEPART! THE FUGITIVES HAVE BEEN FOUND INSIDE A --
CAPTAIN, PAD'S SECURE. C'MON DOWN.
ROGER THAT, SPARTAN RAY.
STAY TIGHT. WE GET IN THERE, WE DESTROY WHAT-EVER'S JAMMING OUR COMMS, AND WE CALL IN THE CAVALRY.
SUBTLETY'S GOING TO HAVE TO TAKE A BACK SEAT.
THE JAMMER WILL BE CONNECTED TO SOME TYPE OF LARGE POWER SOURCE.

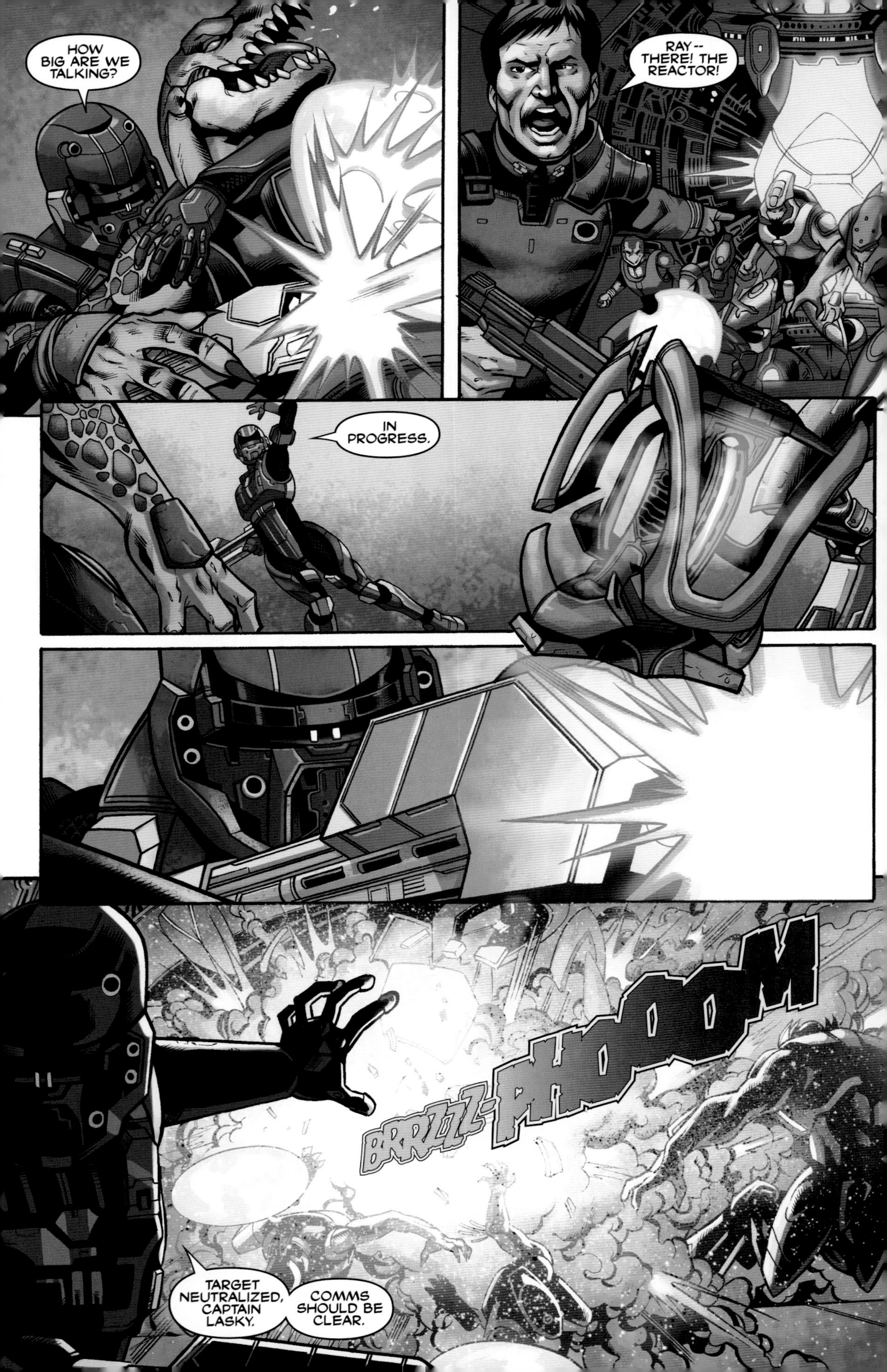
HOW BIG ARE WE TALKING?
RAY-- THERE! THE REACTOR!
IN PROGRESS.
BRRZZZ-PHOOOM
TARGET NEUTRALIZED, CAPTAIN LASKY.
COMMS SHOULD BE CLEAR.

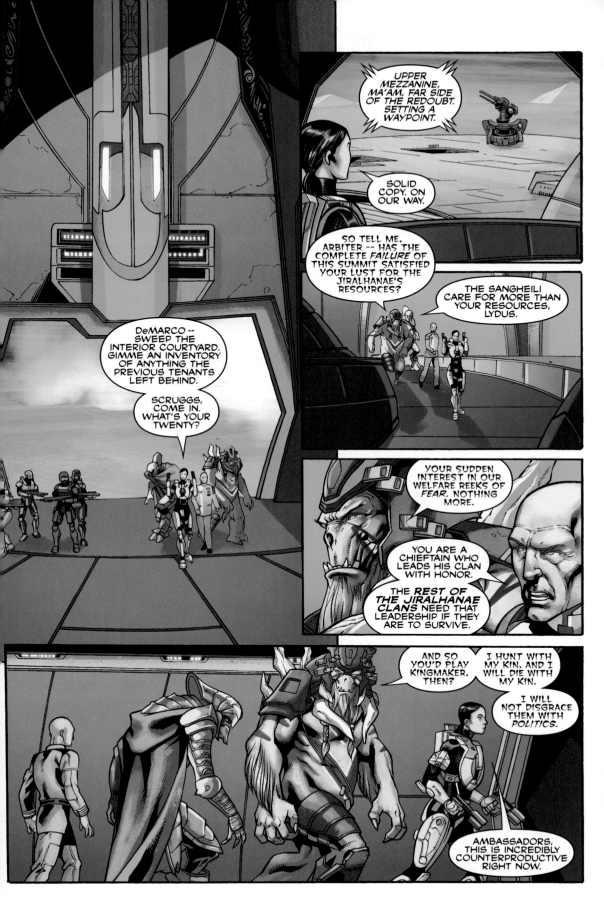

UPPER MEZZANINE, MA'AM, FAR SIDE OF THE REDOUBT. SETTING A WAYPOINT.

SOLID COPY. ON OUR WAY.

SO TELL ME, ARBITER -- HAS THE COMPLETE *FAILURE* OF THIS SUMMIT SATISFIED YOUR LUST FOR THE JIRALHANAE'S RESOURCES?

THE SANGHEILI CARE FOR MORE THAN YOUR RESOURCES, LYDUS.

DeMARCO -- SWEEP THE INTERIOR COURTYARD, GIMME AN INVENTORY OF ANYTHING THE PREVIOUS TENANTS LEFT BEHIND.

SCRUGGS, COME IN. WHAT'S YOUR TWENTY?

YOUR SUDDEN INTEREST IN OUR WELFARE REEKS OF *FEAR.* NOTHING MORE.

YOU ARE A CHIEFTAIN WHO LEADS HIS CLAN WITH HONOR.

THE *REST OF THE JIRALHANAE CLANS* NEED THAT LEADERSHIP IF THEY ARE TO SURVIVE.

AND SO YOU'D PLAY KINGMAKER, THEN?

I HUNT WITH MY KIN. AND I WILL DIE WITH MY KIN.

I WILL NOT DISGRACE THEM WITH *POLITICS.*

AMBASSADORS, THIS IS INCREDIBLY COUNTERPRODUCTIVE RIGHT NOW.

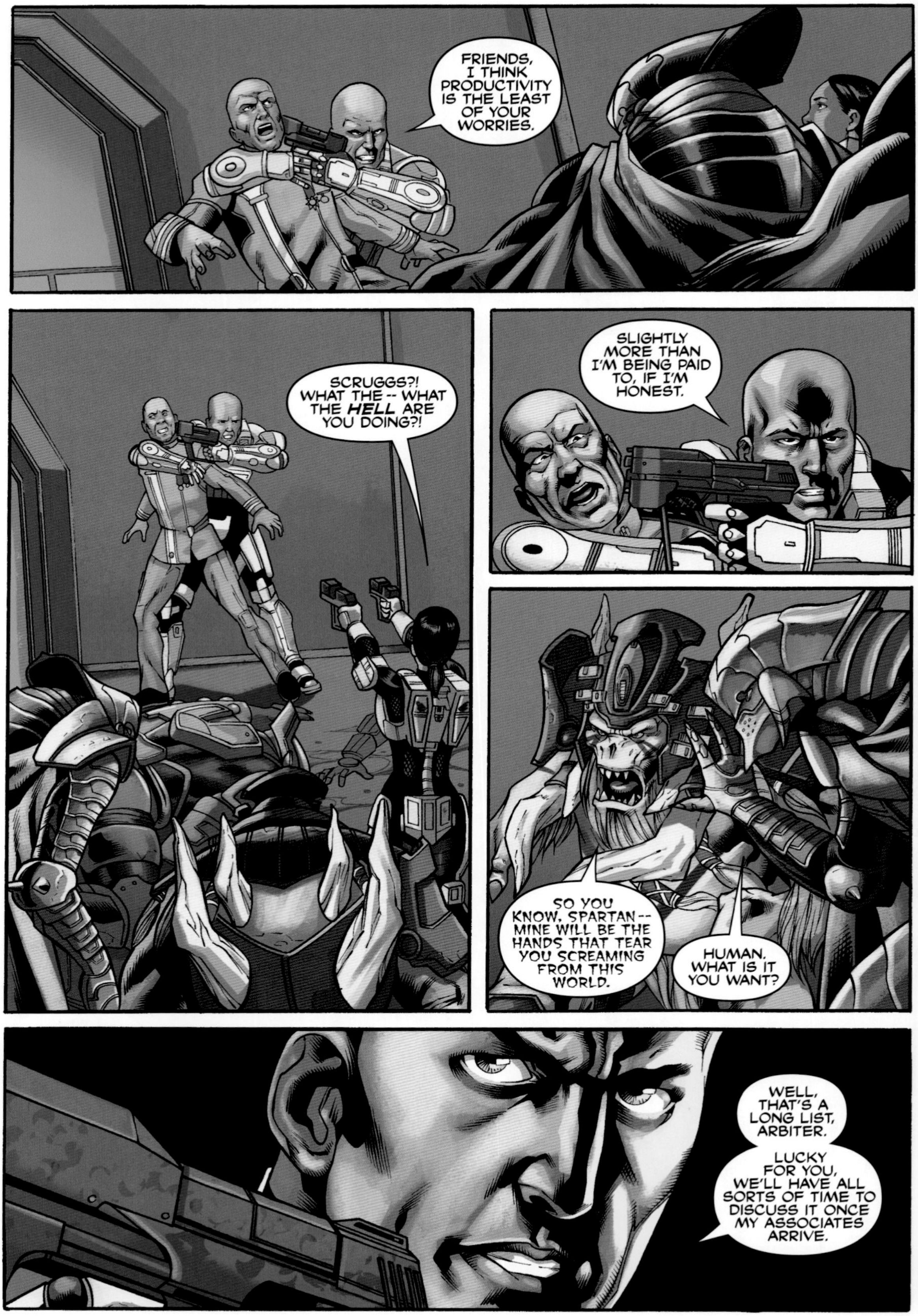
FRIENDS, I THINK PRODUCTIVITY IS THE LEAST OF YOUR WORRIES.
SCRUGGS?! WHAT THE -- WHAT THE *HELL* ARE YOU DOING?!
SLIGHTLY MORE THAN I'M BEING PAID TO, IF I'M HONEST.
SO YOU KNOW, SPARTAN -- MINE WILL BE THE HANDS THAT TEAR YOU SCREAMING FROM THIS WORLD.
HUMAN, WHAT IS IT YOU WANT?
WELL, THAT'S A LONG LIST, ARBITER.
LUCKY FOR YOU, WE'LL HAVE ALL SORTS OF TIME TO DISCUSS IT ONCE MY ASSOCIATES ARRIVE.

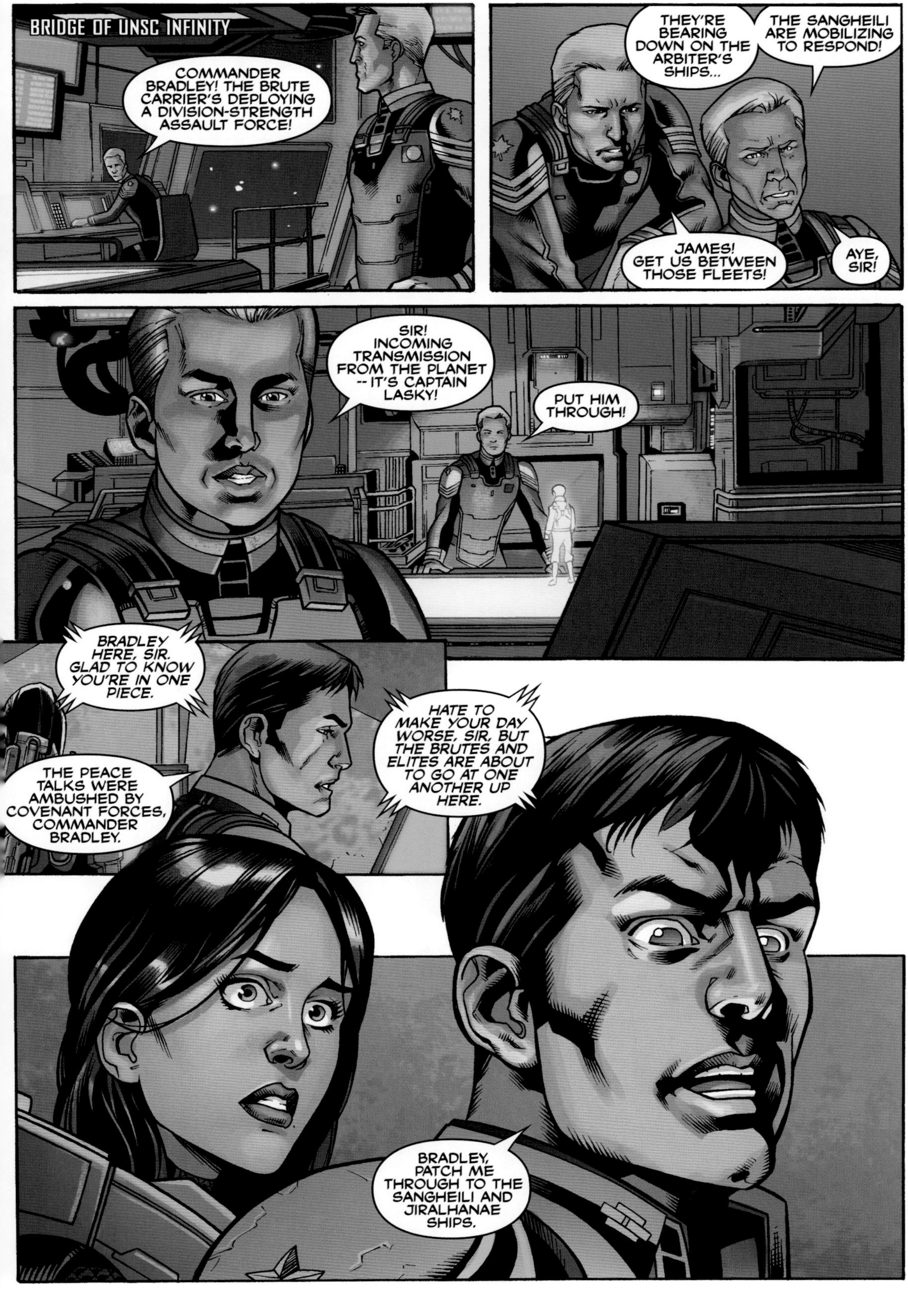
BRIDGE OF UNSC INFINITY
COMMANDER BRADLEY! THE BRUTE CARRIER'S DEPLOYING A DIVISION-STRENGTH ASSAULT FORCE!
THEY'RE BEARING DOWN ON THE ARBITER'S SHIPS...
THE SANGHEILI ARE MOBILIZING TO RESPOND!
JAMES! GET US BETWEEN THOSE FLEETS!
AYE, SIR!
SIR! INCOMING TRANSMISSION FROM THE PLANET -- IT'S CAPTAIN LASKY!
PUT HIM THROUGH!
BRADLEY HERE, SIR. GLAD TO KNOW YOU'RE IN ONE PIECE.
THE PEACE TALKS WERE AMBUSHED BY COVENANT FORCES, COMMANDER BRADLEY.
HATE TO MAKE YOUR DAY WORSE, SIR, BUT THE BRUTES AND ELITES ARE ABOUT TO GO AT ONE ANOTHER UP HERE.
BRADLEY, PATCH ME THROUGH TO THE SANGHEILI AND JIRALHANAE SHIPS.

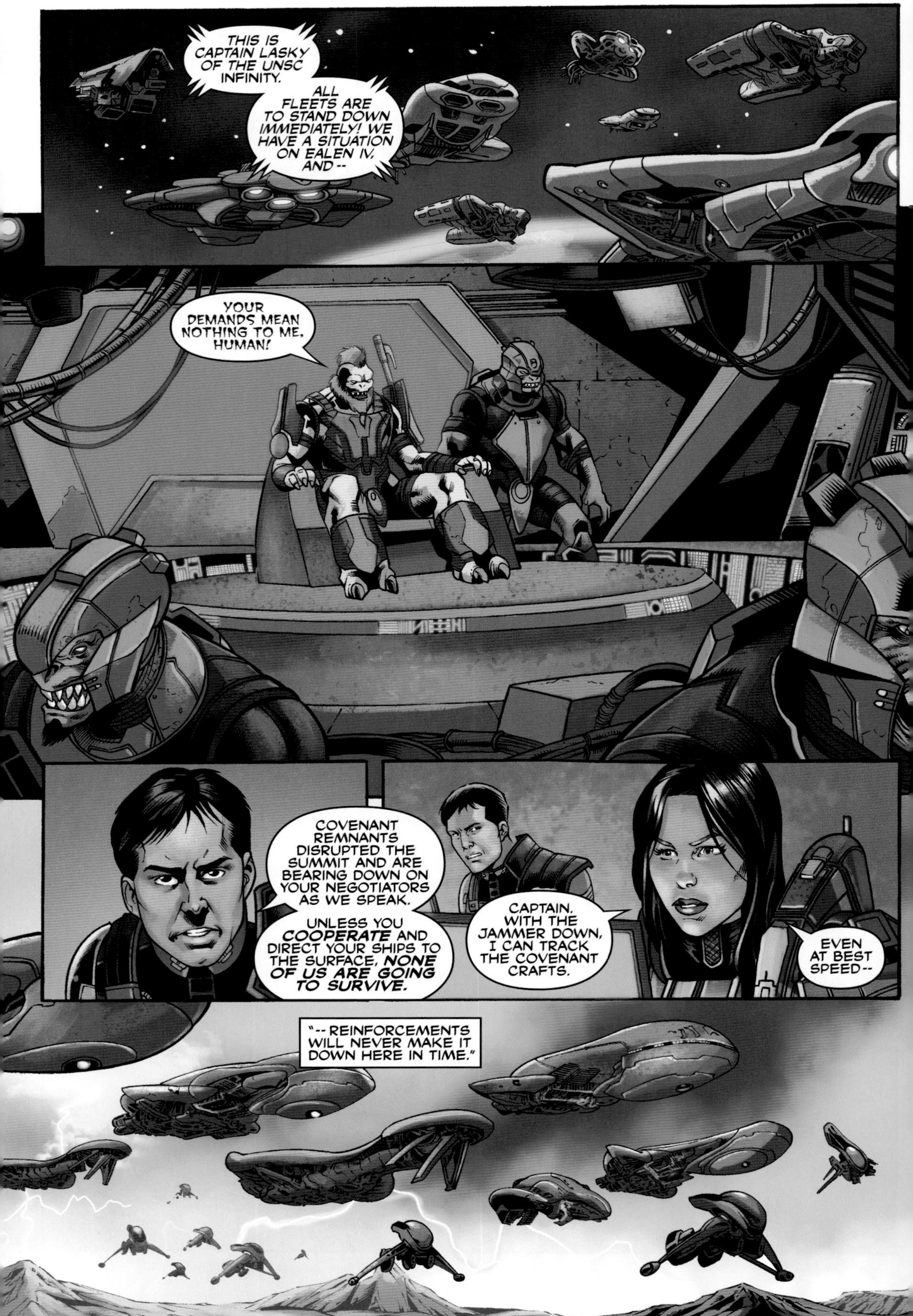
THIS IS CAPTAIN LASKY OF THE UNSC INFINITY.
ALL FLEETS ARE TO STAND DOWN IMMEDIATELY! WE HAVE A SITUATION ON EALEN IV, AND --
YOUR DEMANDS MEAN NOTHING TO ME, HUMAN!
COVENANT REMNANTS DISRUPTED THE SUMMIT AND ARE BEARING DOWN ON YOUR NEGOTIATORS AS WE SPEAK.
UNLESS YOU **COOPERATE** AND DIRECT YOUR SHIPS TO THE SURFACE, **NONE OF US ARE GOING TO SURVIVE.**
CAPTAIN. WITH THE JAMMER DOWN, I CAN TRACK THE COVENANT CRAFTS.
EVEN AT BEST SPEED--
"--REINFORCEMENTS WILL NEVER MAKE IT DOWN HERE IN TIME."

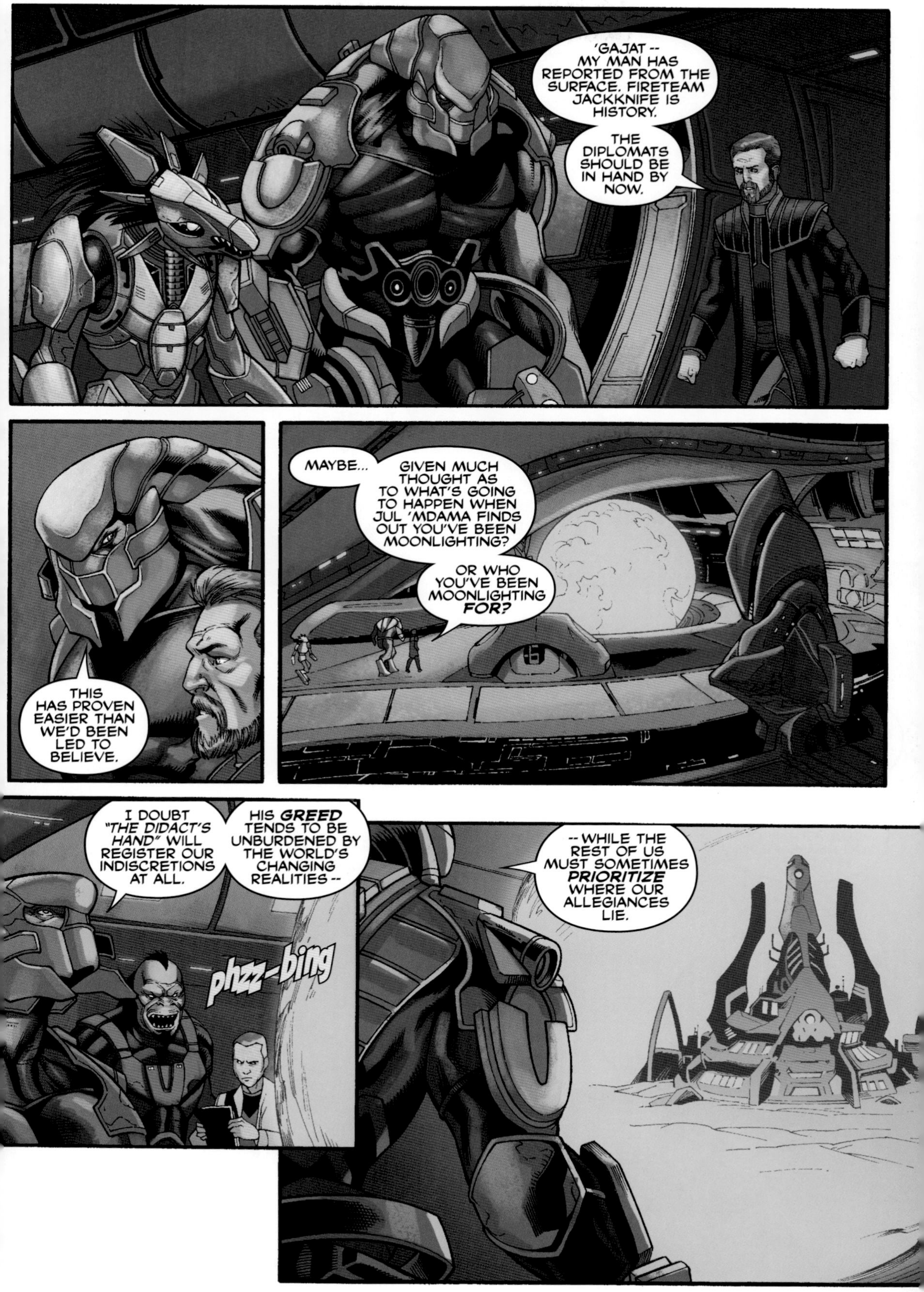
'GAJAT -- MY MAN HAS REPORTED FROM THE SURFACE. FIRETEAM JACKKNIFE IS HISTORY.
THE DIPLOMATS SHOULD BE IN HAND BY NOW.
THIS HAS PROVEN EASIER THAN WE'D BEEN LED TO BELIEVE.
MAYBE...
GIVEN MUCH THOUGHT AS TO WHAT'S GOING TO HAPPEN WHEN JUL 'MDAMA FINDS OUT YOU'VE BEEN MOONLIGHTING?
OR WHO YOU'VE BEEN MOONLIGHTING *FOR?*
I DOUBT *"THE DIDACT'S HAND"* WILL REGISTER OUR INDISCRETIONS AT ALL.
HIS *GREED* TENDS TO BE UNBURDENED BY THE WORLD'S CHANGING REALITIES --
phzz-bing
-- WHILE THE REST OF US MUST SOMETIMES *PRIORITIZE* WHERE OUR ALLEGIANCES LIE.

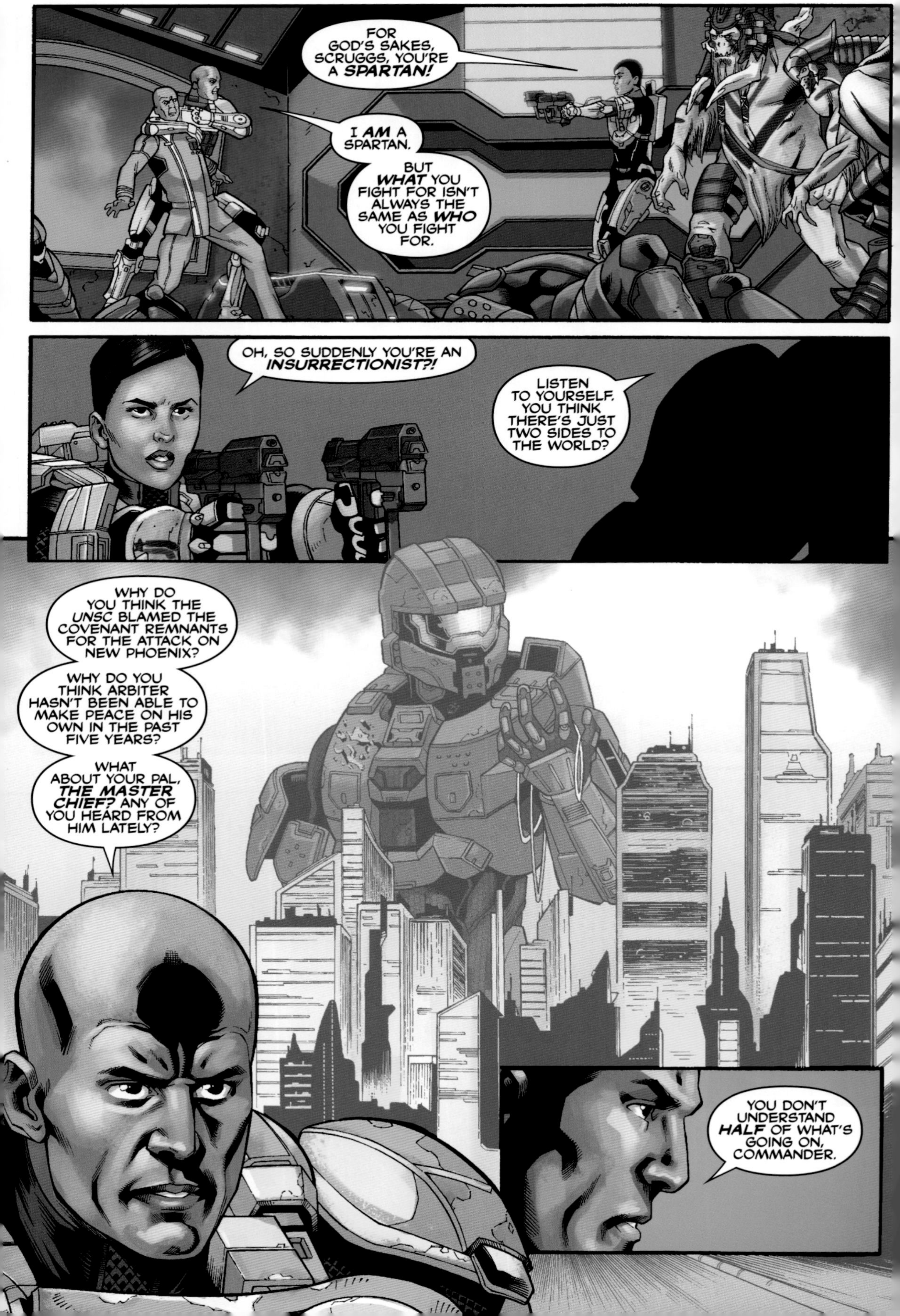
FOR GOD'S SAKES, SCRUGGS, YOU'RE A SPARTAN!
I AM A SPARTAN.
BUT WHAT YOU FIGHT FOR ISN'T ALWAYS THE SAME AS WHO YOU FIGHT FOR.
OH, SO SUDDENLY YOU'RE AN INSURRECTIONIST?!
LISTEN TO YOURSELF. YOU THINK THERE'S JUST TWO SIDES TO THE WORLD?
WHY DO YOU THINK THE UNSC BLAMED THE COVENANT REMNANTS FOR THE ATTACK ON NEW PHOENIX?
WHY DO YOU THINK ARBITER HASN'T BEEN ABLE TO MAKE PEACE ON HIS OWN IN THE PAST FIVE YEARS?
WHAT ABOUT YOUR PAL, THE MASTER CHIEF? ANY OF YOU HEARD FROM HIM LATELY?
YOU DON'T UNDERSTAND HALF OF WHAT'S GOING ON, COMMANDER.

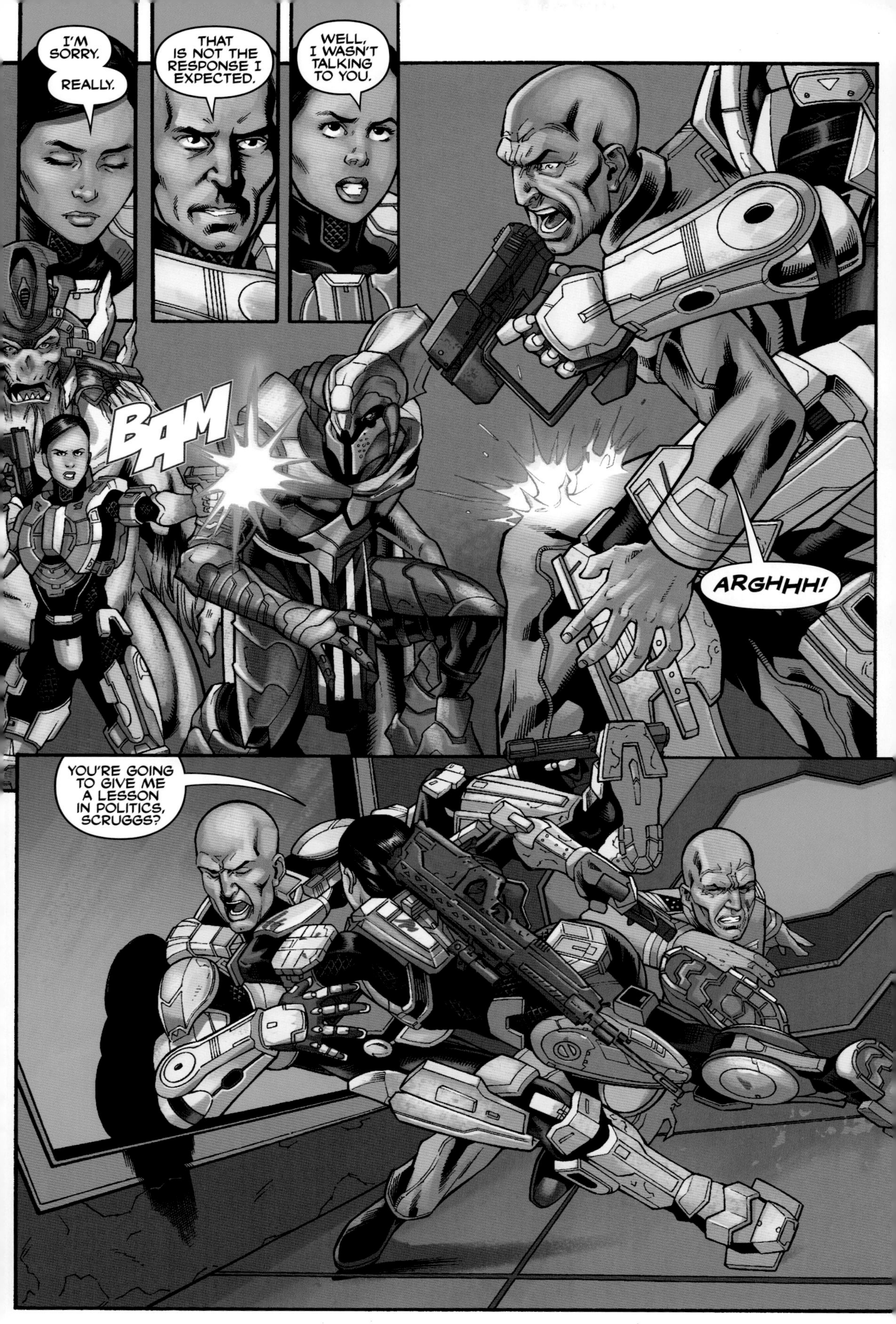
I'M SORRY.
REALLY.
THAT IS NOT THE RESPONSE I EXPECTED.
WELL, I WASN'T TALKING TO YOU.
BAM
ARGHHH!
YOU'RE GOING TO GIVE ME A LESSON IN POLITICS, SCRUGGS?

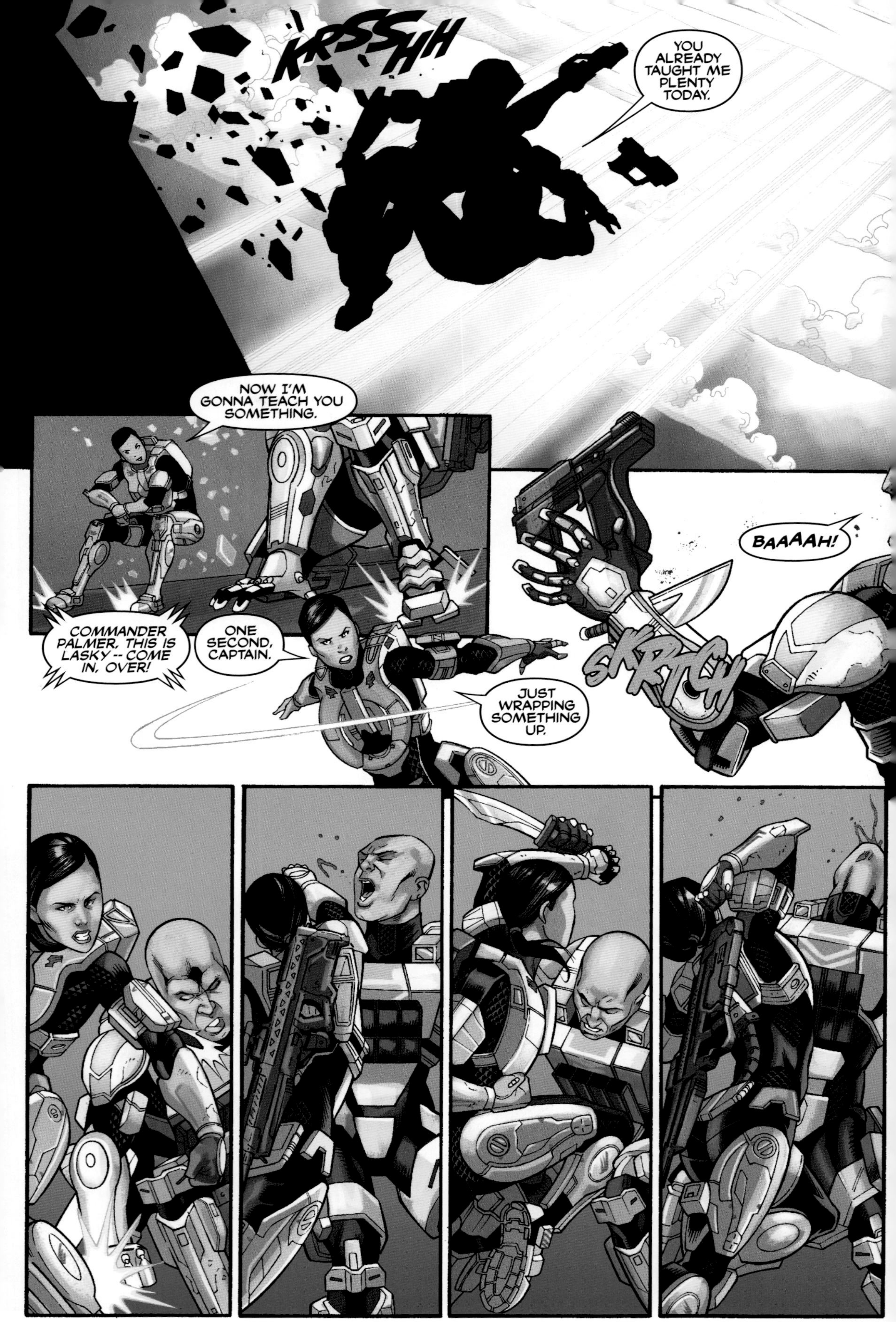
KRSSHH
YOU ALREADY TAUGHT ME PLENTY TODAY.
NOW I'M GONNA TEACH YOU SOMETHING.
BAAAAH!
SKRTCH
COMMANDER PALMER, THIS IS LASKY -- COME IN, OVER!
ONE SECOND, CAPTAIN.
JUST WRAPPING SOMETHING UP.

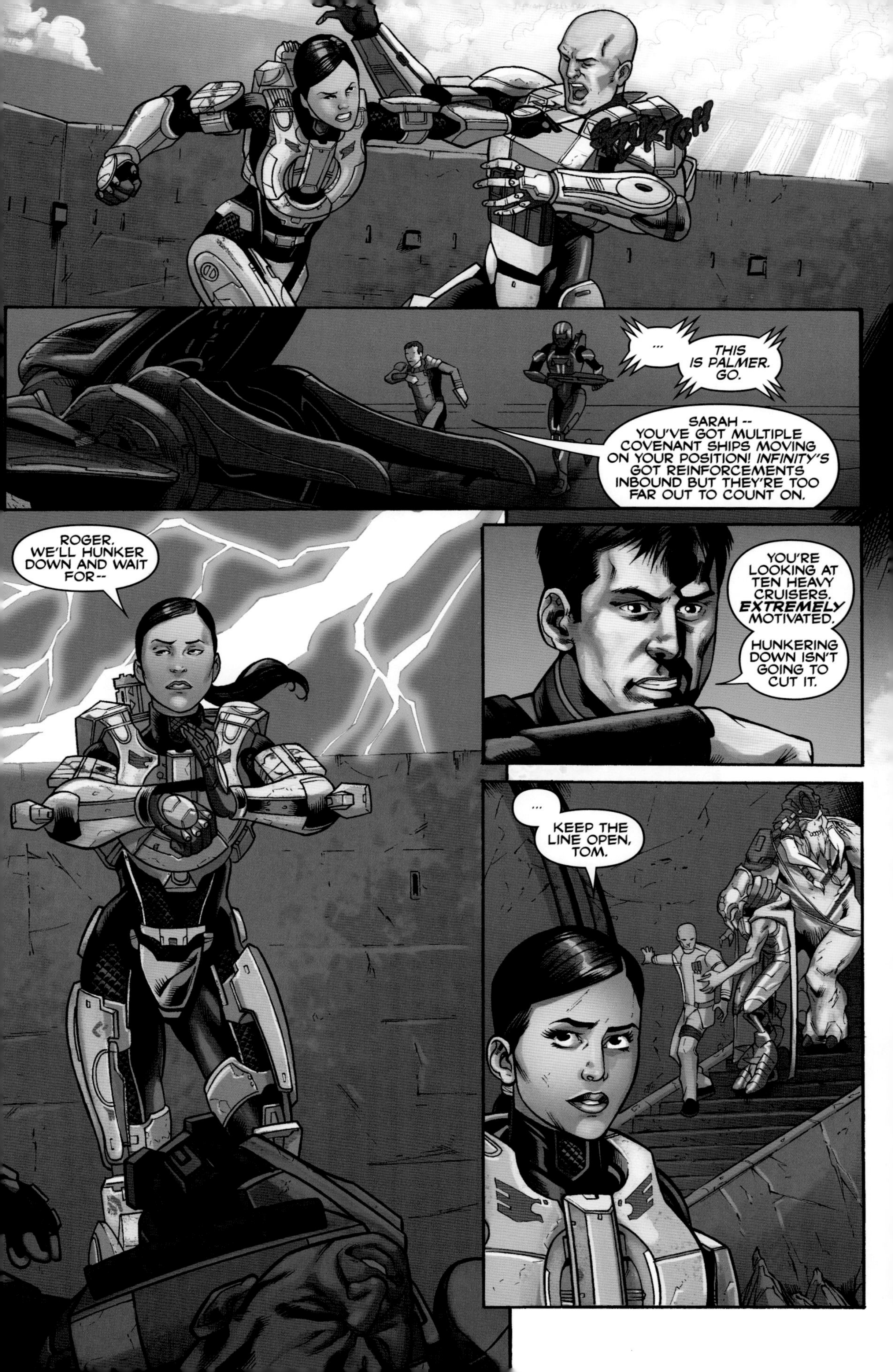
... THIS IS PALMER. GO.
SARAH -- YOU'VE GOT MULTIPLE COVENANT SHIPS MOVING ON YOUR POSITION! *INFINITY'S* GOT REINFORCEMENTS INBOUND BUT THEY'RE TOO FAR OUT TO COUNT ON.
ROGER. WE'LL HUNKER DOWN AND WAIT FOR--
YOU'RE LOOKING AT TEN HEAVY CRUISERS. ***EXTREMELY*** MOTIVATED.
HUNKERING DOWN ISN'T GOING TO CUT IT.
... KEEP THE LINE OPEN, TOM.

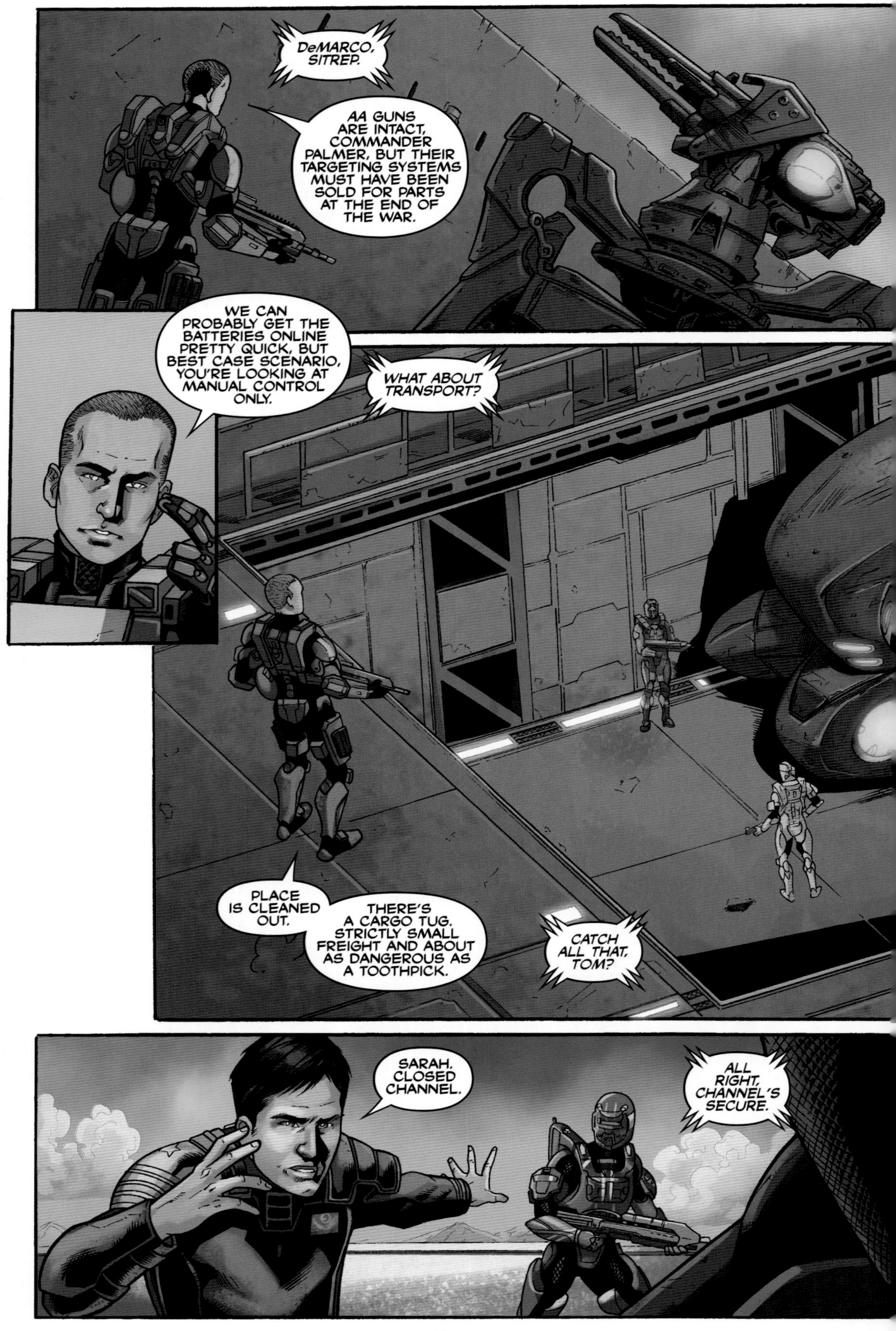
DeMARCO, SITREP.
AA GUNS ARE INTACT, COMMANDER PALMER, BUT THEIR TARGETING SYSTEMS MUST HAVE BEEN SOLD FOR PARTS AT THE END OF THE WAR.
WE CAN PROBABLY GET THE BATTERIES ONLINE PRETTY QUICK, BUT BEST CASE SCENARIO, YOU'RE LOOKING AT MANUAL CONTROL ONLY.
WHAT ABOUT TRANSPORT?
PLACE IS CLEANED OUT.
THERE'S A CARGO TUG. STRICTLY SMALL FREIGHT AND ABOUT AS DANGEROUS AS A TOOTHPICK.
CATCH ALL THAT, TOM?
SARAH. CLOSED CHANNEL.
ALL RIGHT, CHANNEL'S SECURE.

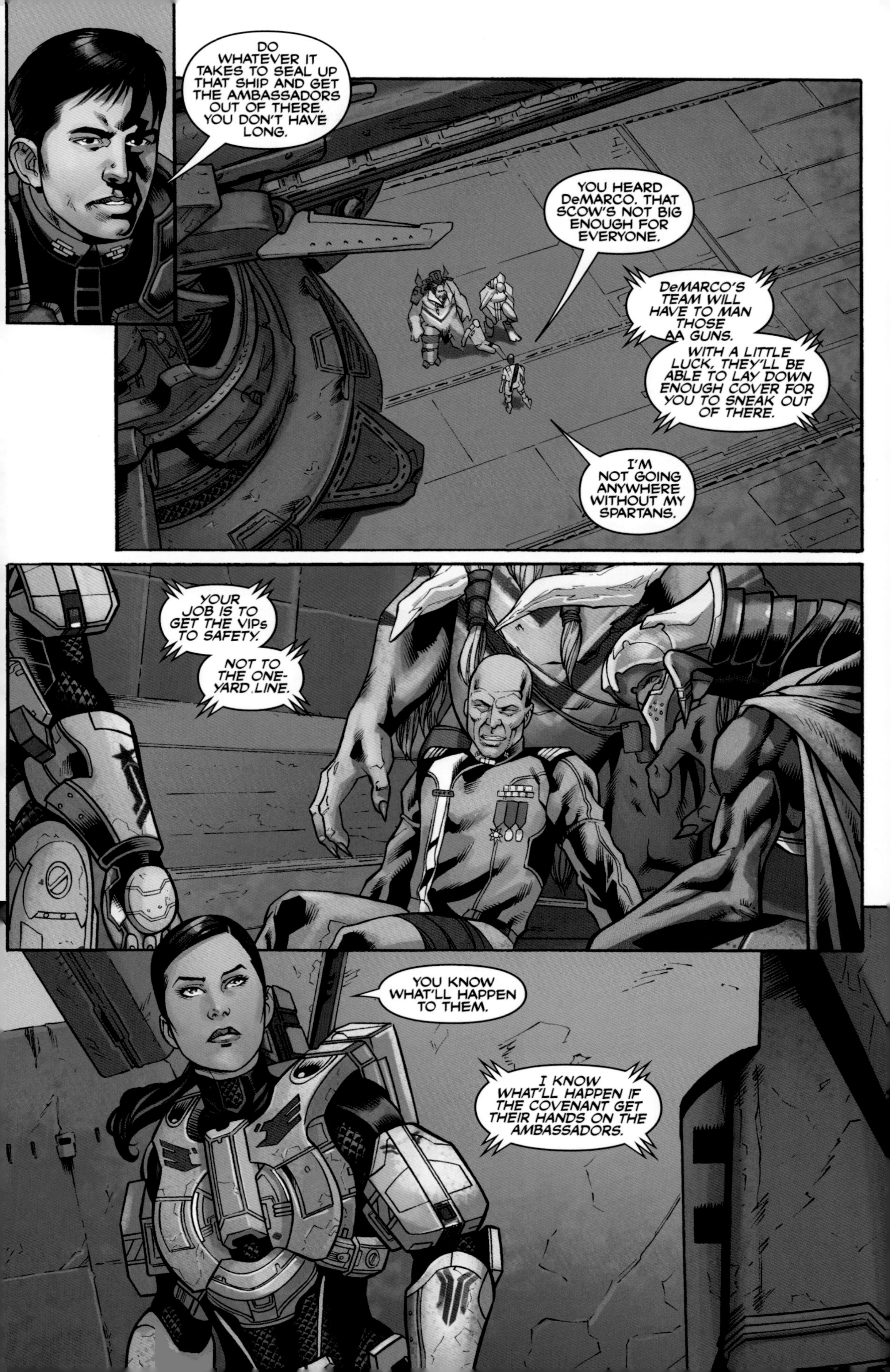
DO WHATEVER IT TAKES TO SEAL UP THAT SHIP AND GET THE AMBASSADORS OUT OF THERE. YOU DON'T HAVE LONG.
YOU HEARD DeMARCO. THAT SCOW'S NOT BIG ENOUGH FOR EVERYONE.
DeMARCO'S TEAM WILL HAVE TO MAN THOSE AA GUNS.
WITH A LITTLE LUCK, THEY'LL BE ABLE TO LAY DOWN ENOUGH COVER FOR YOU TO SNEAK OUT OF THERE.
I'M NOT GOING ANYWHERE WITHOUT MY SPARTANS.
YOUR JOB IS TO GET THE VIPs TO SAFETY.
NOT TO THE ONE-YARD LINE.
YOU KNOW WHAT'LL HAPPEN TO THEM.
I KNOW WHAT'LL HAPPEN IF THE COVENANT GET THEIR HANDS ON THE AMBASSADORS.

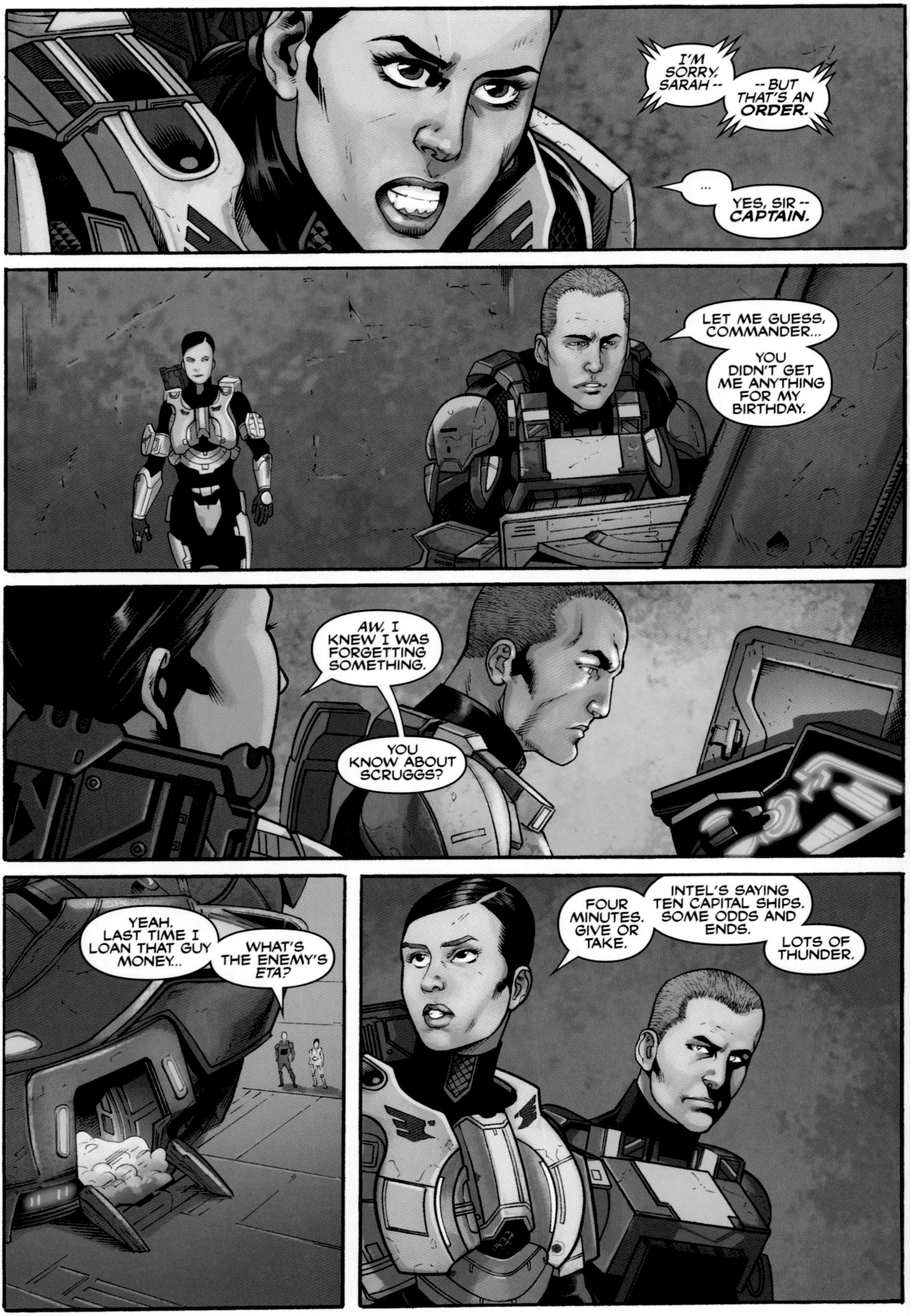
I'M SORRY, SARAH --
-- BUT THAT'S AN ORDER.
...
YES, SIR -- CAPTAIN.
LET ME GUESS, COMMANDER...
YOU DIDN'T GET ME ANYTHING FOR MY BIRTHDAY.
AW, I KNEW I WAS FORGETTING SOMETHING.
YOU KNOW ABOUT SCRUGGS?
YEAH. LAST TIME I LOAN THAT GUY MONEY...
WHAT'S THE ENEMY'S ETA?
FOUR MINUTES, GIVE OR TAKE.
INTEL'S SAYING TEN CAPITAL SHIPS. SOME ODDS AND ENDS.
LOTS OF THUNDER.

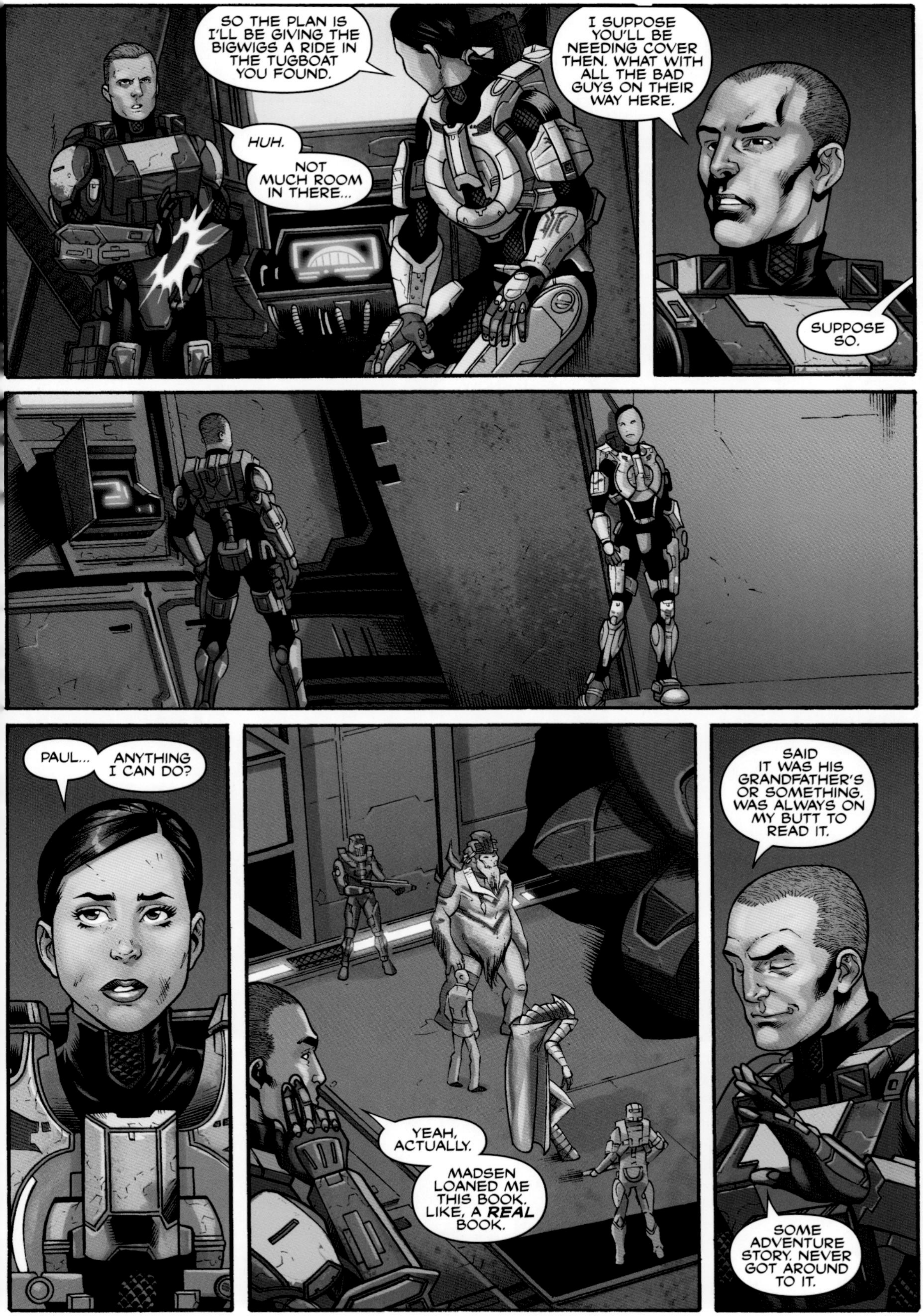
SO THE PLAN IS I'LL BE GIVING THE BIGWIGS A RIDE IN THE TUGBOAT YOU FOUND.
HUH.
NOT MUCH ROOM IN THERE...
I SUPPOSE YOU'LL BE NEEDING COVER THEN. WHAT WITH ALL THE BAD GUYS ON THEIR WAY HERE.
SUPPOSE SO.
PAUL...
ANYTHING I CAN DO?
YEAH, ACTUALLY.
MADSEN LOANED ME THIS BOOK. LIKE, A *REAL* BOOK.
SAID IT WAS HIS GRANDFATHER'S OR SOMETHING. WAS ALWAYS ON MY BUTT TO READ IT.
SOME ADVENTURE STORY. NEVER GOT AROUND TO IT.

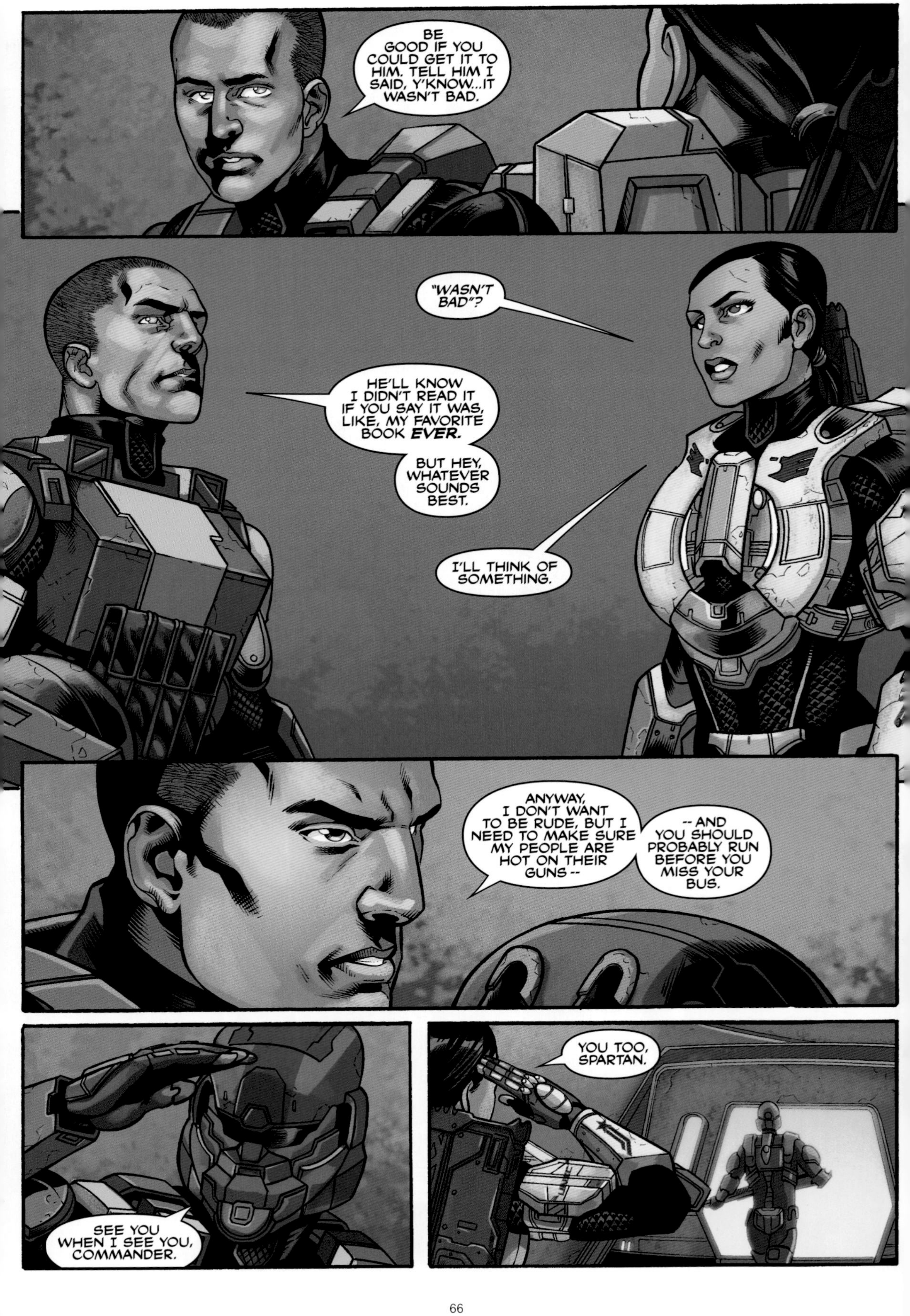
BE GOOD IF YOU COULD GET IT TO HIM. TELL HIM I SAID, Y'KNOW...IT WASN'T BAD.
"WASN'T BAD"?
HE'LL KNOW I DIDN'T READ IT IF YOU SAY IT WAS, LIKE, MY FAVORITE BOOK EVER.
BUT HEY, WHATEVER SOUNDS BEST.
I'LL THINK OF SOMETHING.
ANYWAY, I DON'T WANT TO BE RUDE, BUT I NEED TO MAKE SURE MY PEOPLE ARE HOT ON THEIR GUNS --
-- AND YOU SHOULD PROBABLY RUN BEFORE YOU MISS YOUR BUS.
SEE YOU WHEN I SEE YOU, COMMANDER.
YOU TOO, SPARTAN.

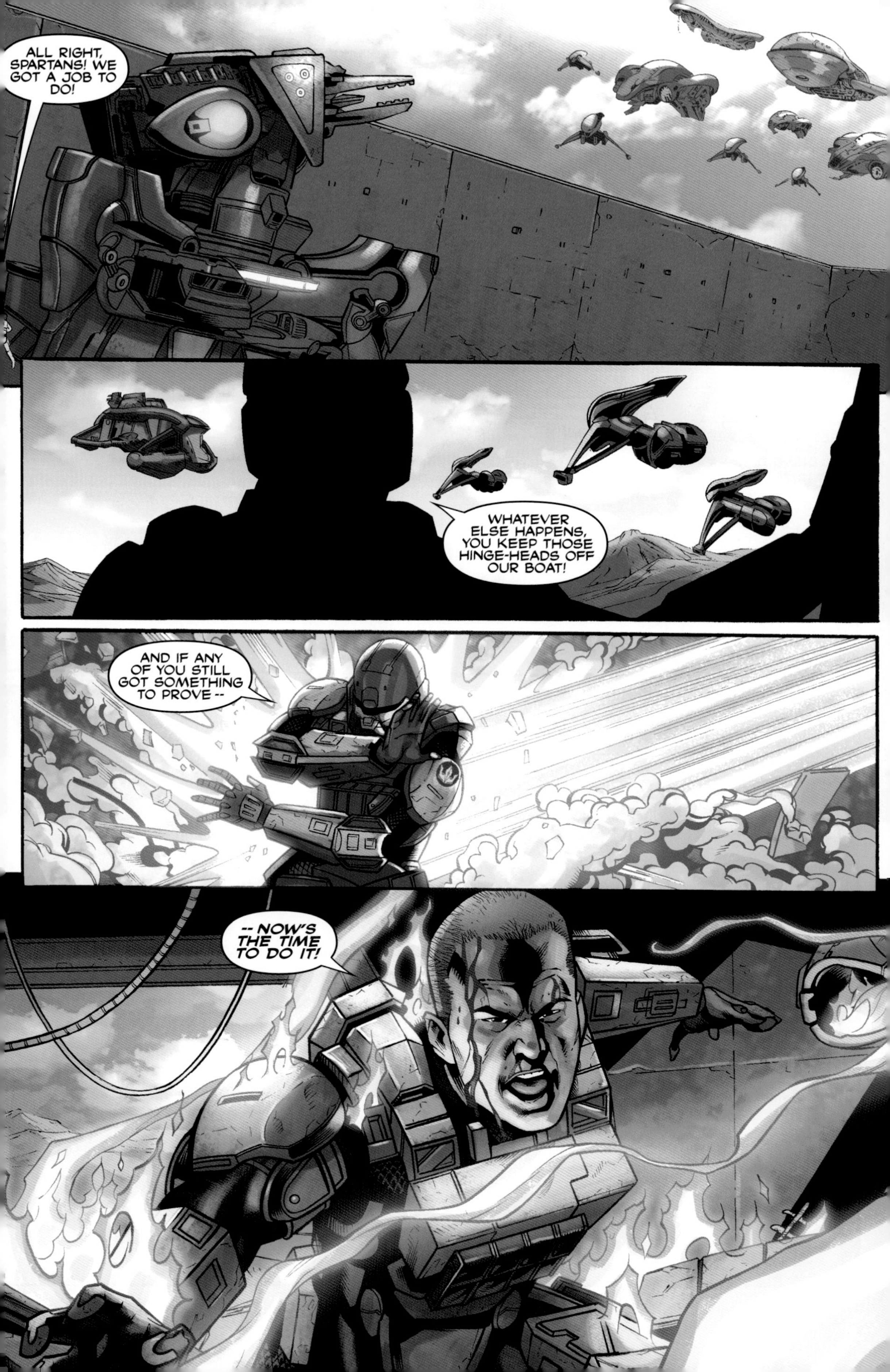
ALL RIGHT, SPARTANS! WE GOT A JOB TO DO!
WHATEVER ELSE HAPPENS, YOU KEEP THOSE HINGE-HEADS OFF OUR BOAT!
AND IF ANY OF YOU STILL GOT SOMETHING TO PROVE --
-- NOW'S THE TIME TO DO IT!

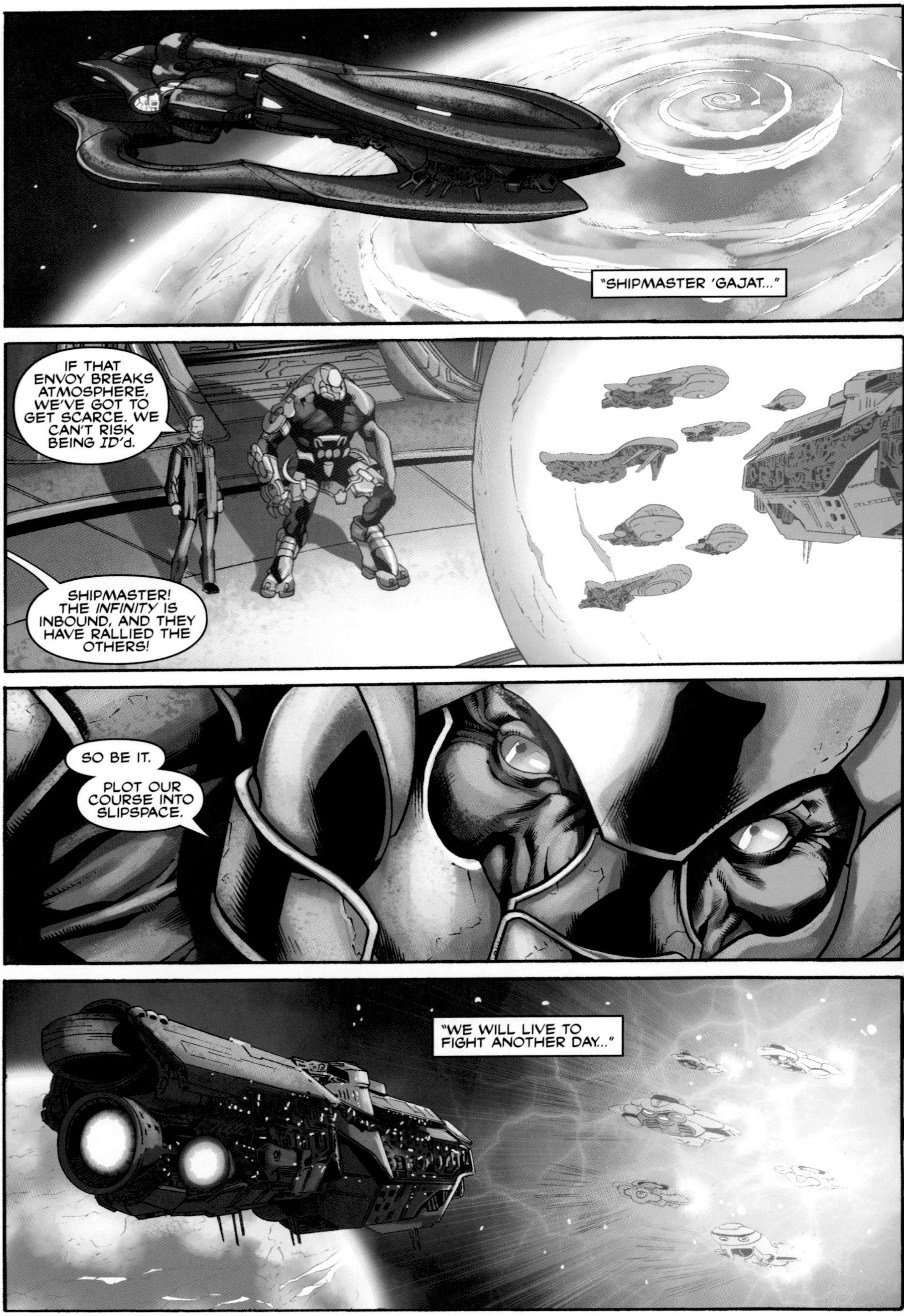
"SHIPMASTER 'GAJAT..."
IF THAT ENVOY BREAKS ATMOSPHERE, WE'VE GOT TO GET SCARCE. WE CAN'T RISK BEING *ID*'d.
SHIPMASTER! THE *INFINITY* IS INBOUND, AND THEY HAVE RALLIED THE OTHERS!
SO BE IT.
PLOT OUR COURSE INTO SLIPSPACE.
"WE WILL LIVE TO FIGHT ANOTHER DAY..."

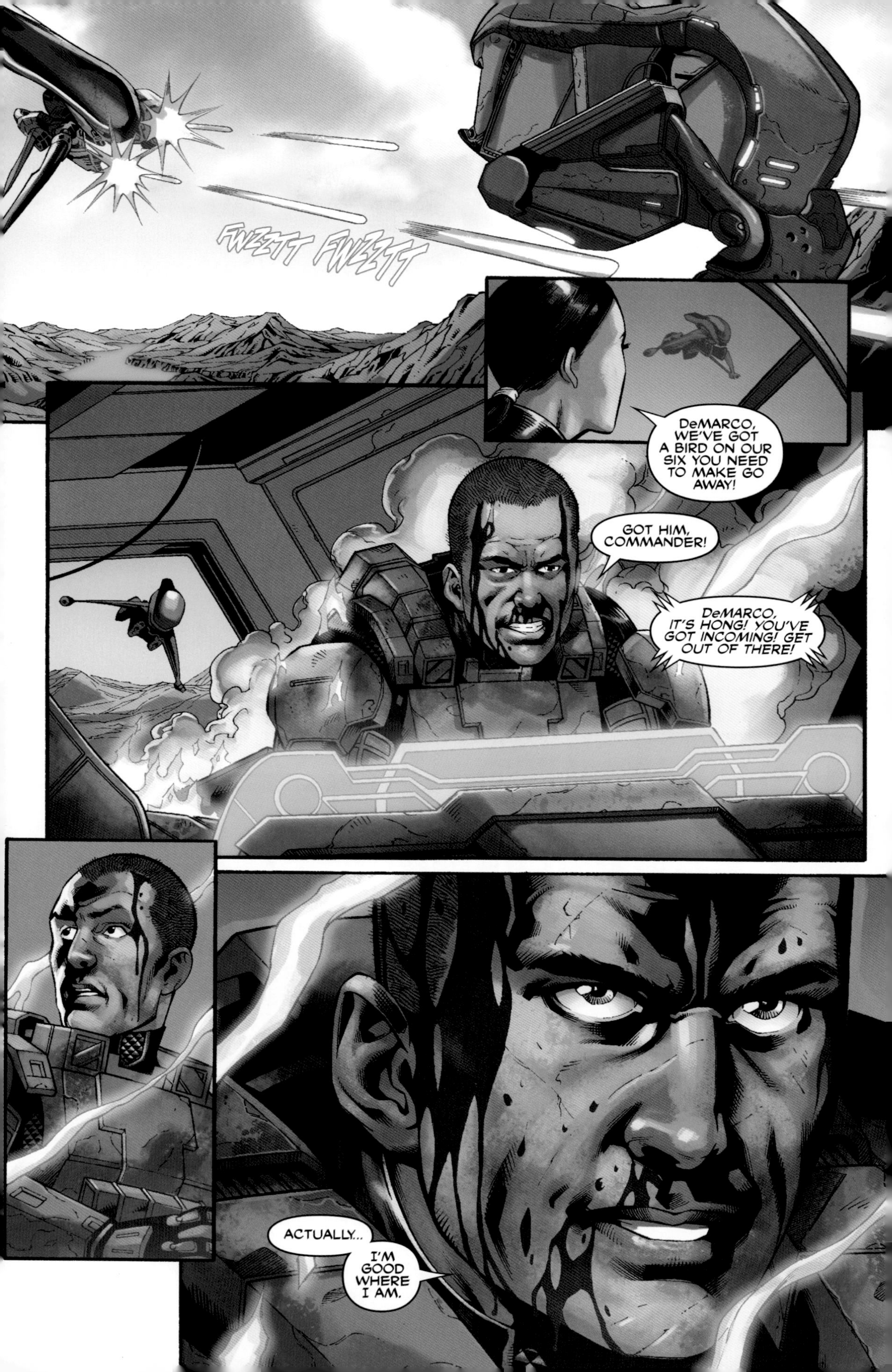
FWZZTT FWZZTT
DeMARCO, WE'VE GOT A BIRD ON OUR SIX YOU NEED TO MAKE GO AWAY!
GOT HIM, COMMANDER!
DeMARCO, IT'S HONG! YOU'VE GOT INCOMING! GET OUT OF THERE!
ACTUALLY...
I'M GOOD WHERE I AM.

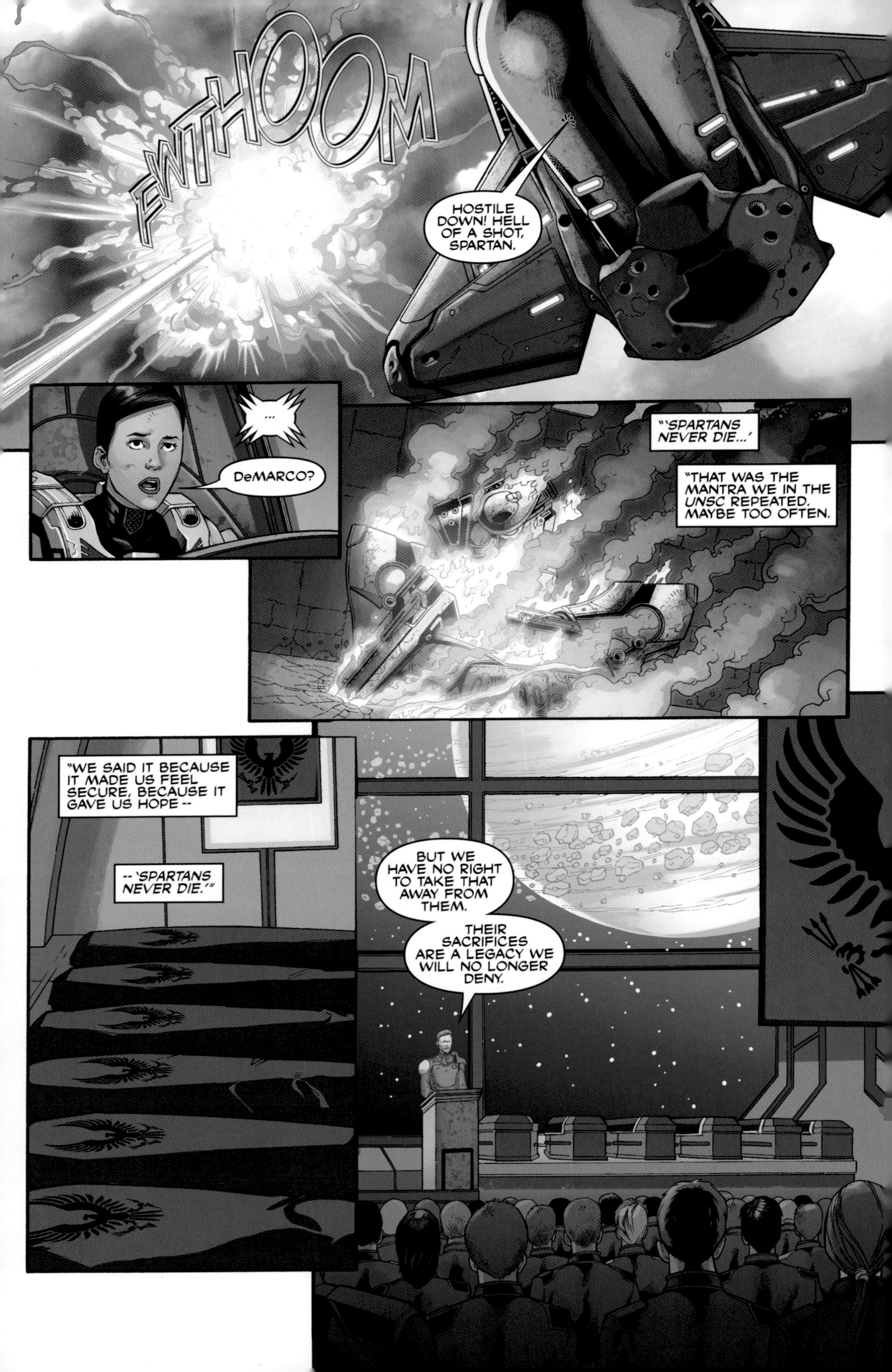
FWTHOOM
HOSTILE DOWN! HELL OF A SHOT, SPARTAN.
...
DeMARCO?
"'SPARTANS NEVER DIE...'
"THAT WAS THE MANTRA WE IN THE UNSC REPEATED. MAYBE TOO OFTEN.
"WE SAID IT BECAUSE IT MADE US FEEL SECURE, BECAUSE IT GAVE US HOPE --
-- 'SPARTANS NEVER DIE.'"
BUT WE HAVE NO RIGHT TO TAKE THAT AWAY FROM THEM.
THEIR SACRIFICES ARE A LEGACY WE WILL NO LONGER DENY.

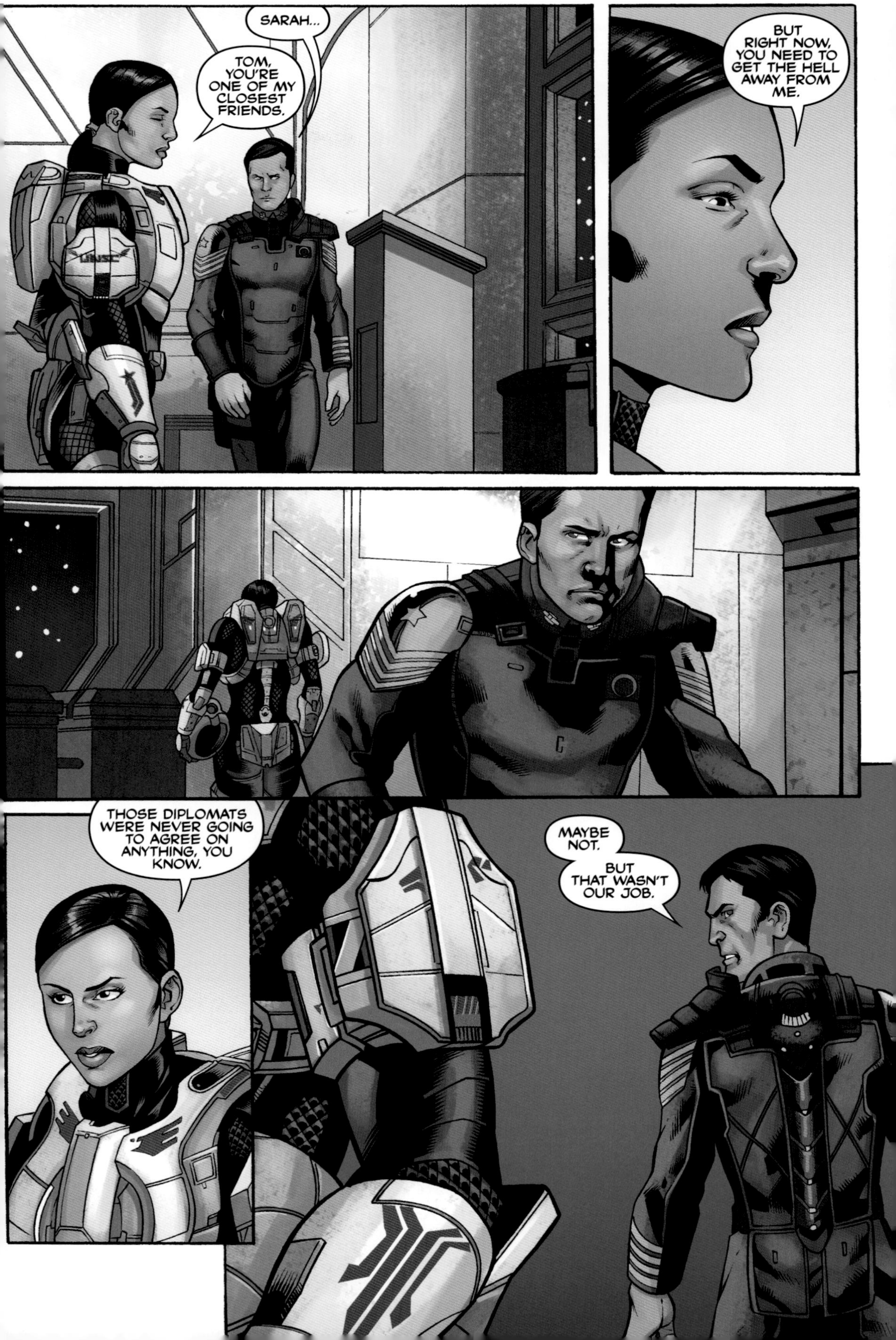
SARAH...
TOM, YOU'RE ONE OF MY CLOSEST FRIENDS.
BUT RIGHT NOW, YOU NEED TO GET THE HELL AWAY FROM ME.
THOSE DIPLOMATS WERE NEVER GOING TO AGREE ON ANYTHING, YOU KNOW.
MAYBE NOT.
BUT THAT WASN'T OUR JOB.

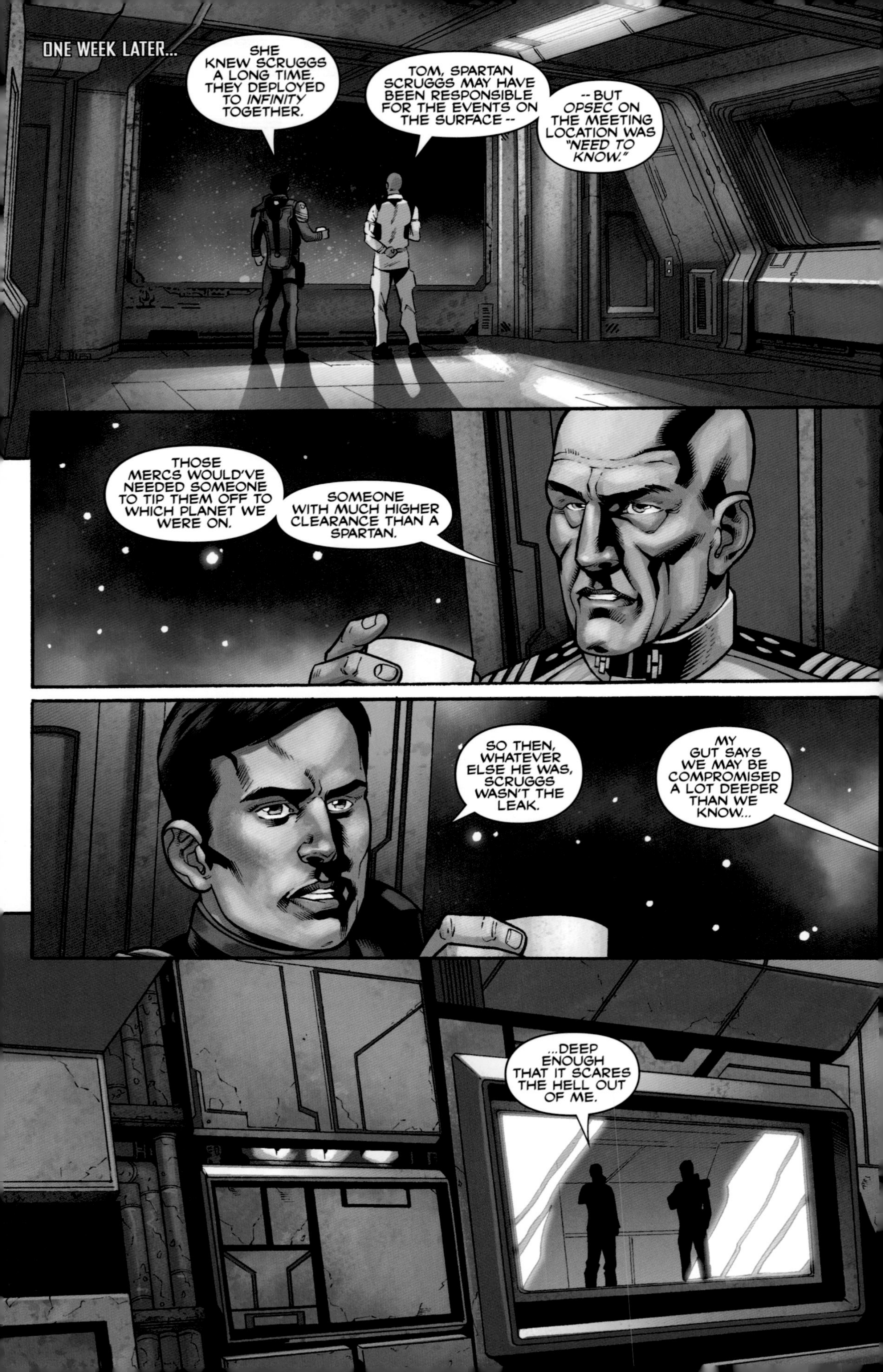
ONE WEEK LATER...
SHE KNEW SCRUGGS A LONG TIME. THEY DEPLOYED TO *INFINITY* TOGETHER.
TOM, SPARTAN SCRUGGS MAY HAVE BEEN RESPONSIBLE FOR THE EVENTS ON THE SURFACE --
-- BUT *OPSEC* ON THE MEETING LOCATION WAS *"NEED TO KNOW."*
THOSE MERCS WOULD'VE NEEDED SOMEONE TO TIP THEM OFF TO WHICH PLANET WE WERE ON.
SOMEONE WITH MUCH HIGHER CLEARANCE THAN A SPARTAN.
SO THEN, WHATEVER ELSE HE WAS, SCRUGGS WASN'T THE LEAK.
MY GUT SAYS WE MAY BE COMPROMISED A LOT DEEPER THAN WE KNOW...
...DEEP ENOUGH THAT IT SCARES THE HELL OUT OF ME.

Illustration by Anthony Palumbo

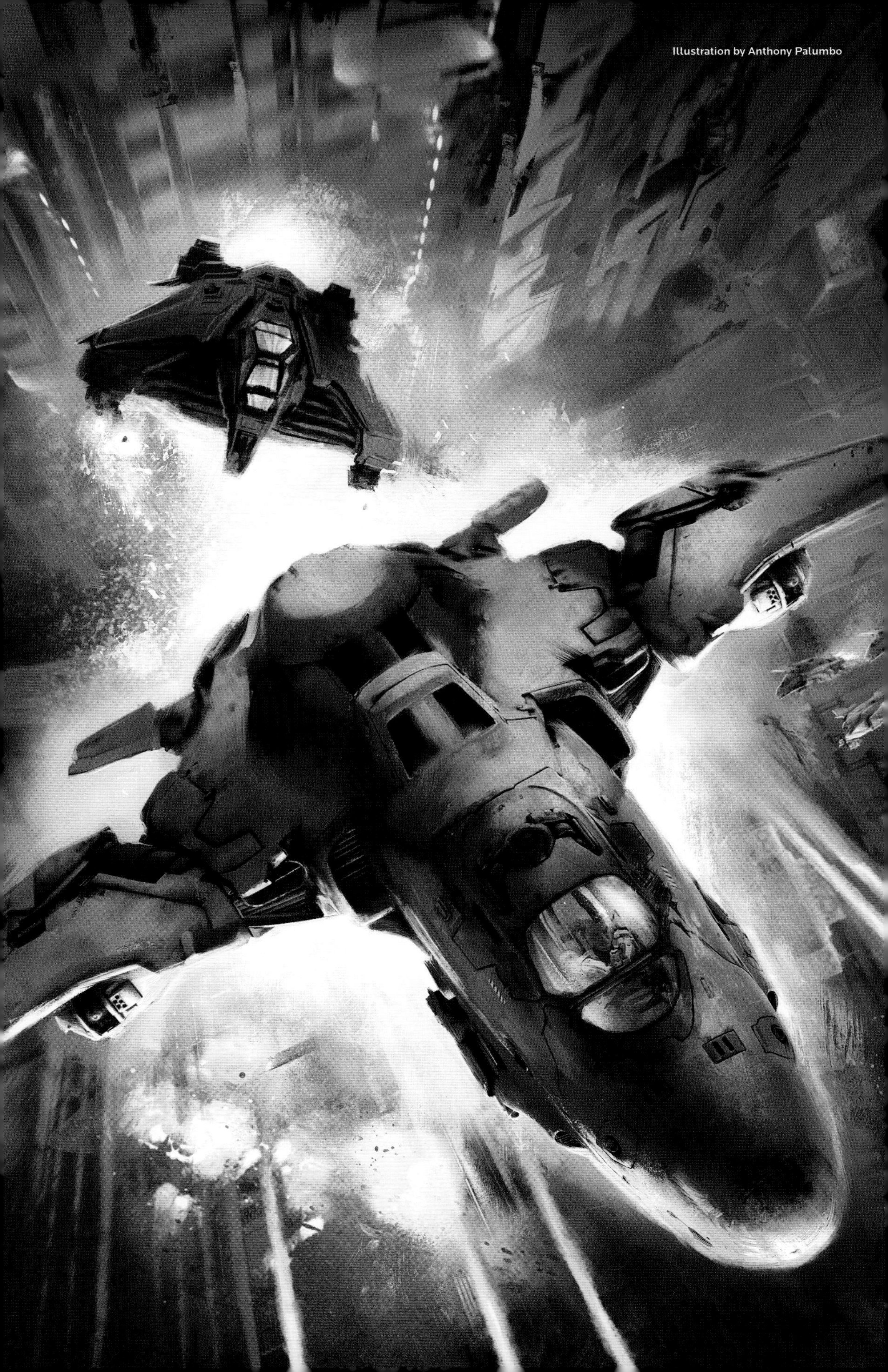

Facing an inescapable onslaught by the mercenary fleet, Spartan DeMarco and the other members of Fireteam Bailey sacrifice themselves to provide cover for the Arbiter and Lydus's retreat. Onboard UNSC *Infinity*, Captain Lasky and Admiral Hood determine someone must have leaked the details of the peace talks as they ponder their next move.

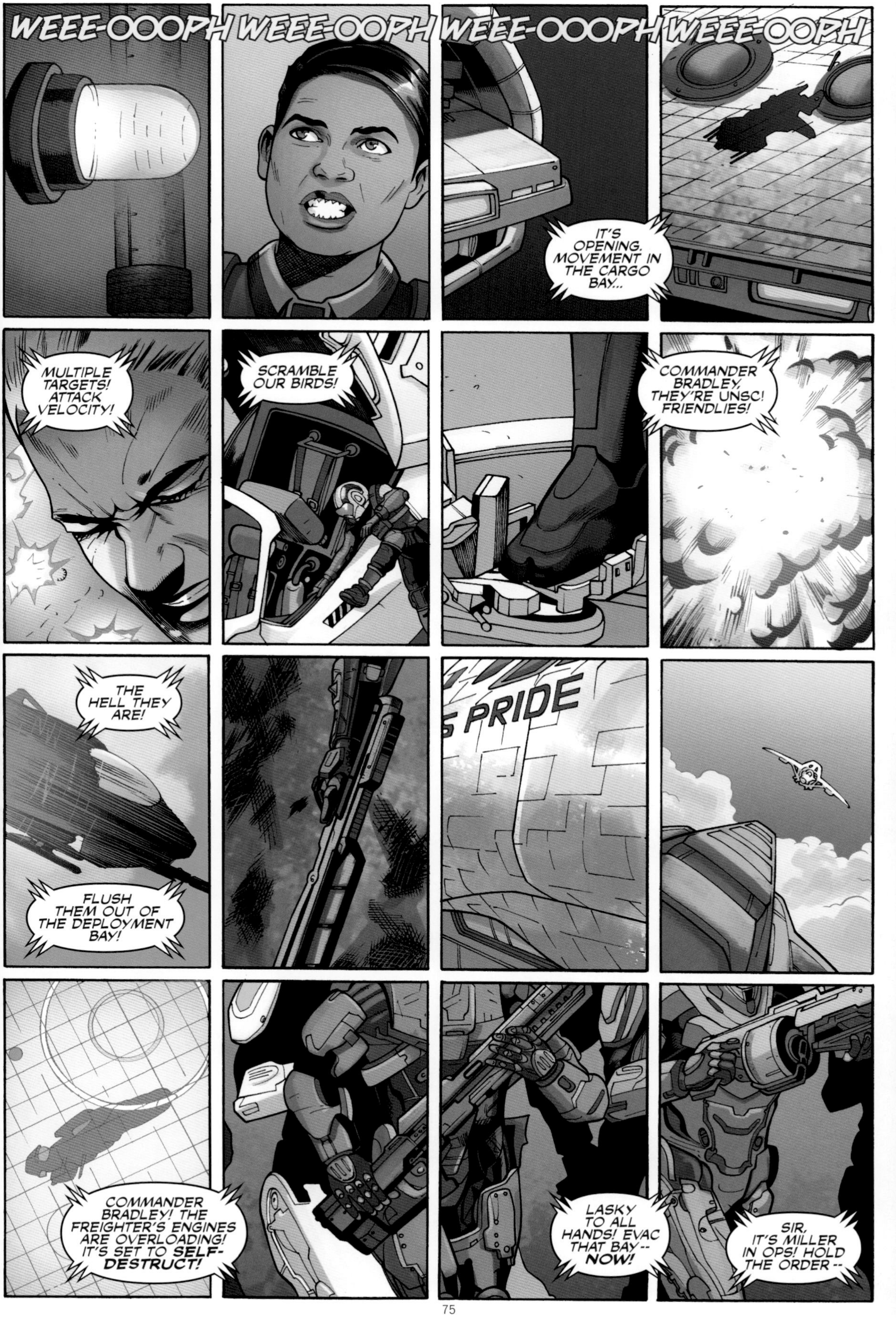
WEEE-OOOPH WEEE-OOPH WEEE-OOOPH WEEE-OOPH
IT'S OPENING. MOVEMENT IN THE CARGO BAY...
MULTIPLE TARGETS! ATTACK VELOCITY!
SCRAMBLE OUR BIRDS!
COMMANDER BRADLEY, THEY'RE UNSC! FRIENDLIES!
THE HELL THEY ARE!
FLUSH THEM OUT OF THE DEPLOYMENT BAY!
S PRIDE
COMMANDER BRADLEY! THE FREIGHTER'S ENGINES ARE OVERLOADING! IT'S SET TO SELF-DESTRUCT!
LASKY TO ALL HANDS! EVAC THAT BAY -- NOW!
SIR, IT'S MILLER IN OPS! HOLD THE ORDER --

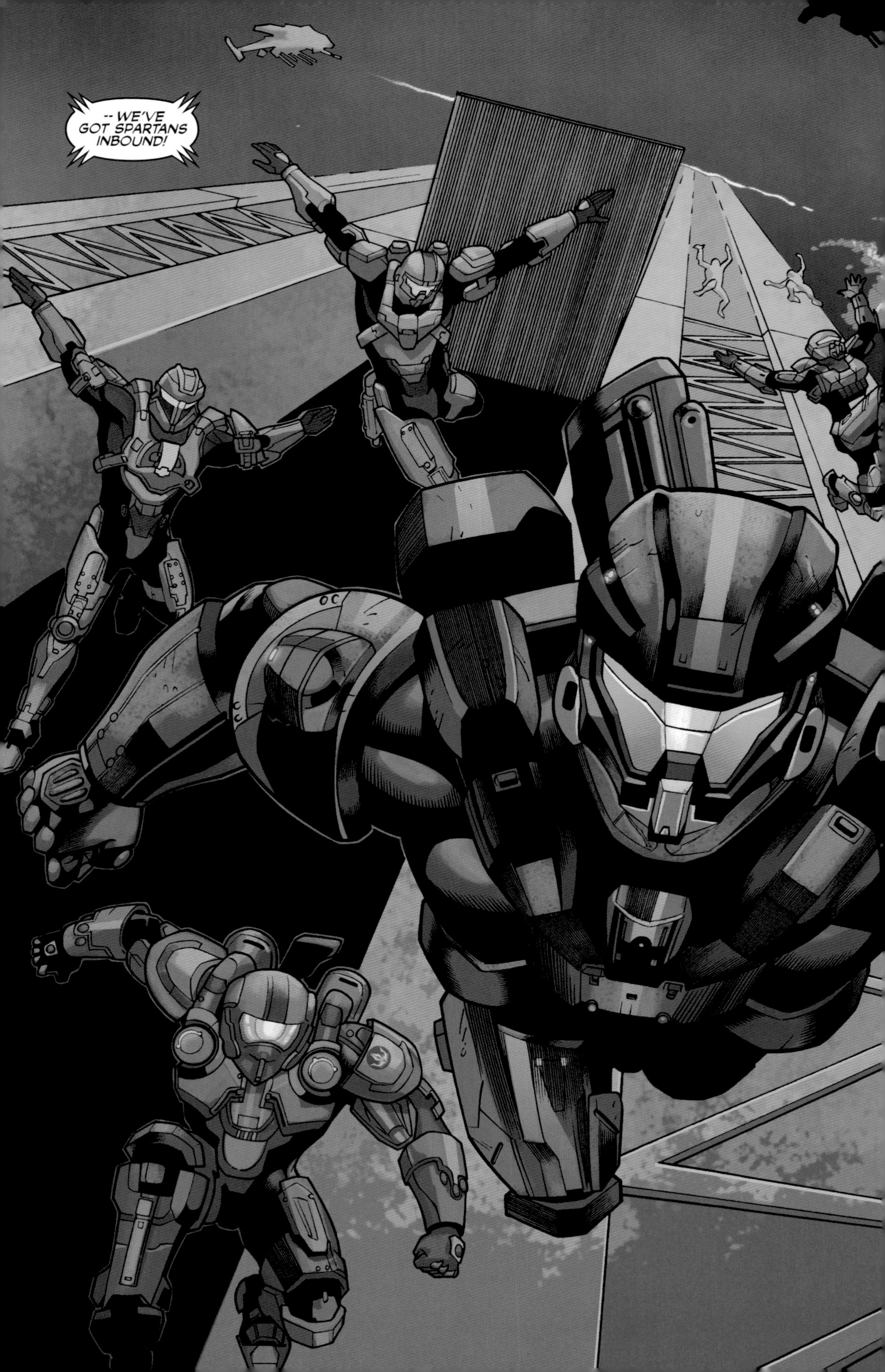
-- WE'VE GOT SPARTANS INBOUND!

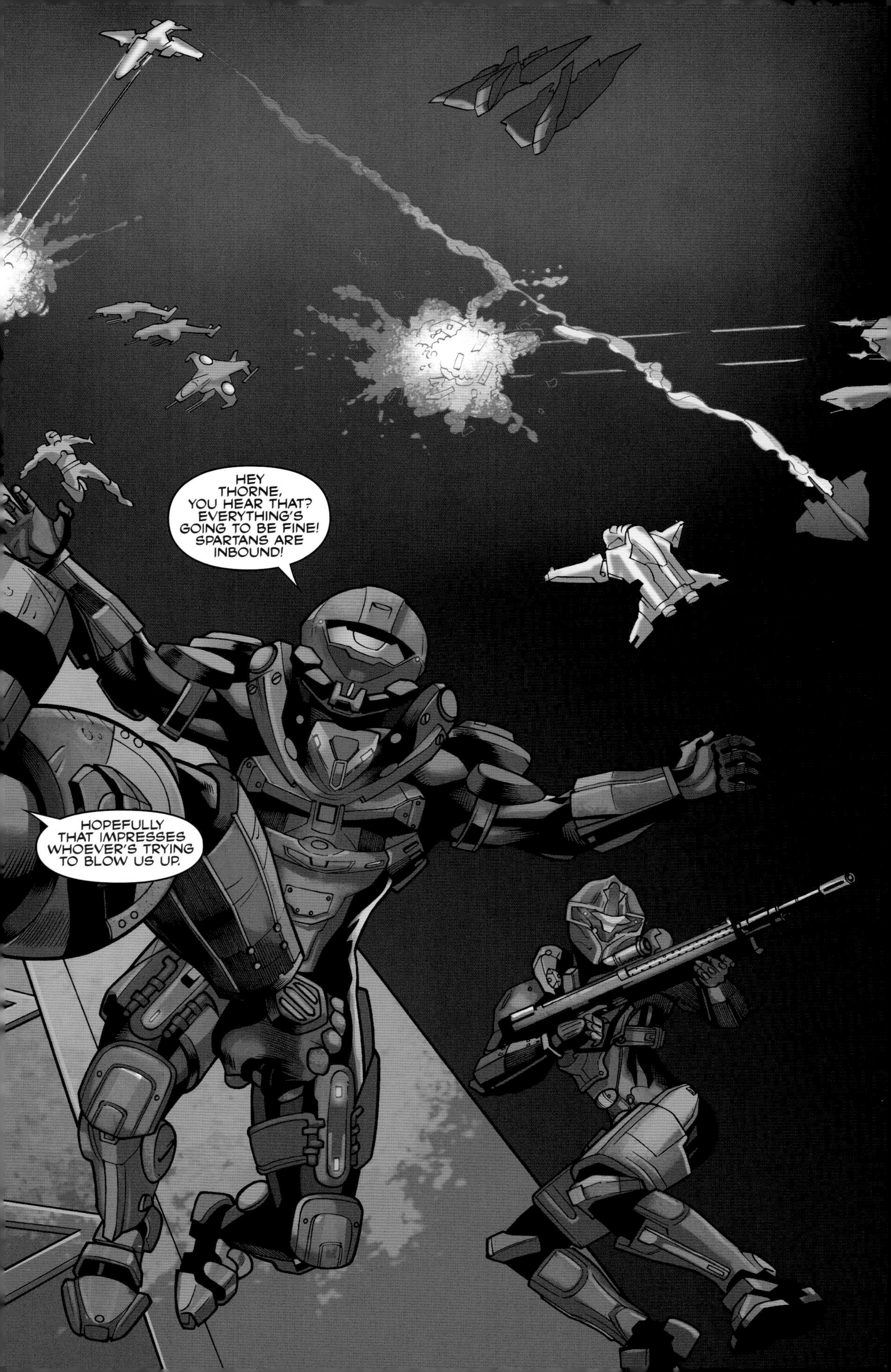
HEY THORNE, YOU HEAR THAT? EVERYTHING'S GOING TO BE FINE! SPARTANS ARE INBOUND!
HOPEFULLY THAT IMPRESSES WHOEVER'S TRYING TO BLOW US UP.

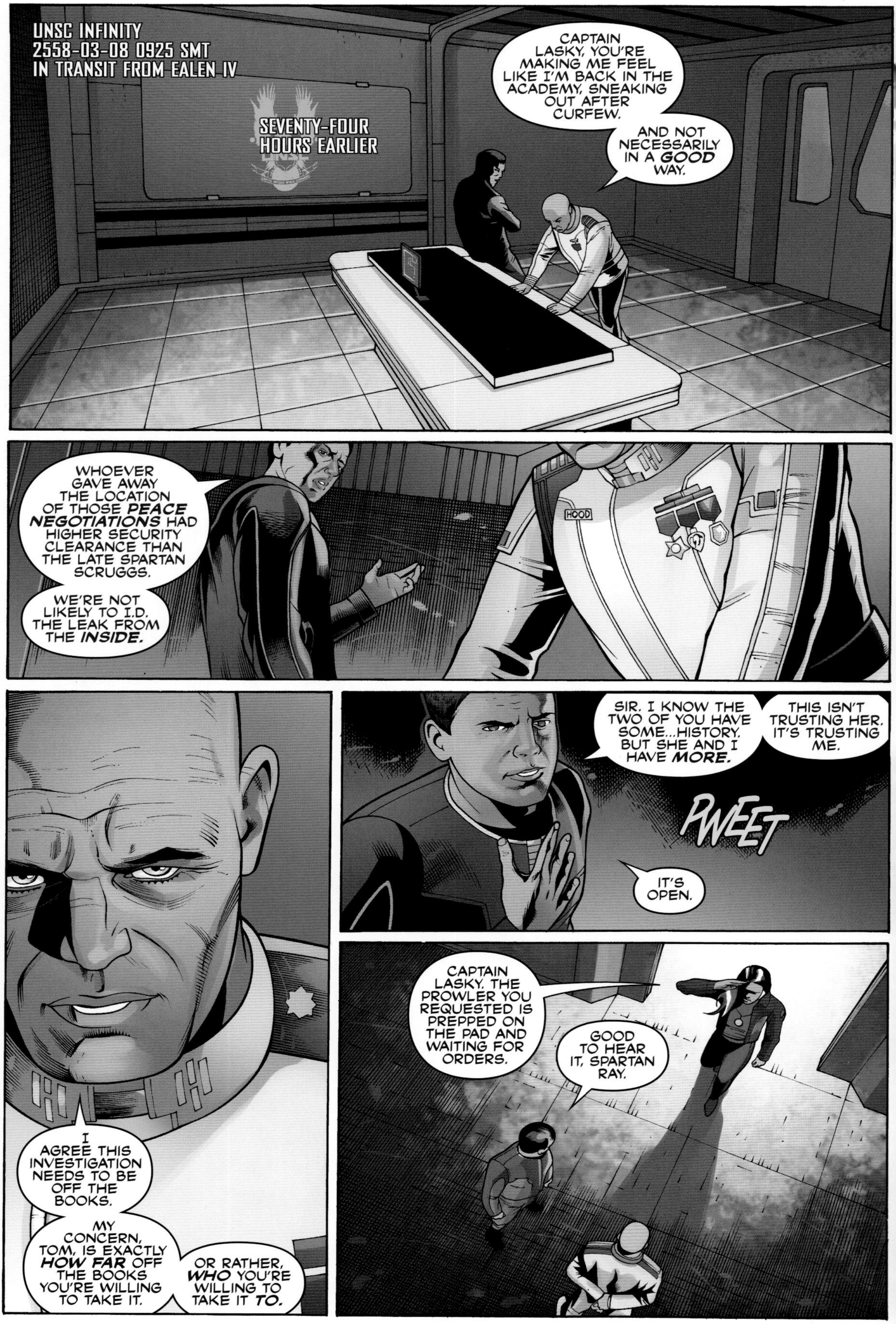
UNSC INFINITY
2558-03-08 0925 SMT
IN TRANSIT FROM EALEN IV
SEVENTY-FOUR HOURS EARLIER
CAPTAIN LASKY, YOU'RE MAKING ME FEEL LIKE I'M BACK IN THE ACADEMY, SNEAKING OUT AFTER CURFEW.
AND NOT NECESSARILY IN A GOOD WAY.
WHOEVER GAVE AWAY THE LOCATION OF THOSE PEACE NEGOTIATIONS HAD HIGHER SECURITY CLEARANCE THAN THE LATE SPARTAN SCRUGGS.
WE'RE NOT LIKELY TO I.D. THE LEAK FROM THE INSIDE.
HOOD
I AGREE THIS INVESTIGATION NEEDS TO BE OFF THE BOOKS.
MY CONCERN, TOM, IS EXACTLY HOW FAR OFF THE BOOKS YOU'RE WILLING TO TAKE IT.
OR RATHER, WHO YOU'RE WILLING TO TAKE IT TO.
SIR. I KNOW THE TWO OF YOU HAVE SOME...HISTORY. BUT SHE AND I HAVE MORE.
THIS ISN'T TRUSTING HER. IT'S TRUSTING ME.
PWEET
IT'S OPEN.
CAPTAIN LASKY. THE PROWLER YOU REQUESTED IS PREPPED ON THE PAD AND WAITING FOR ORDERS.
GOOD TO HEAR IT, SPARTAN RAY.

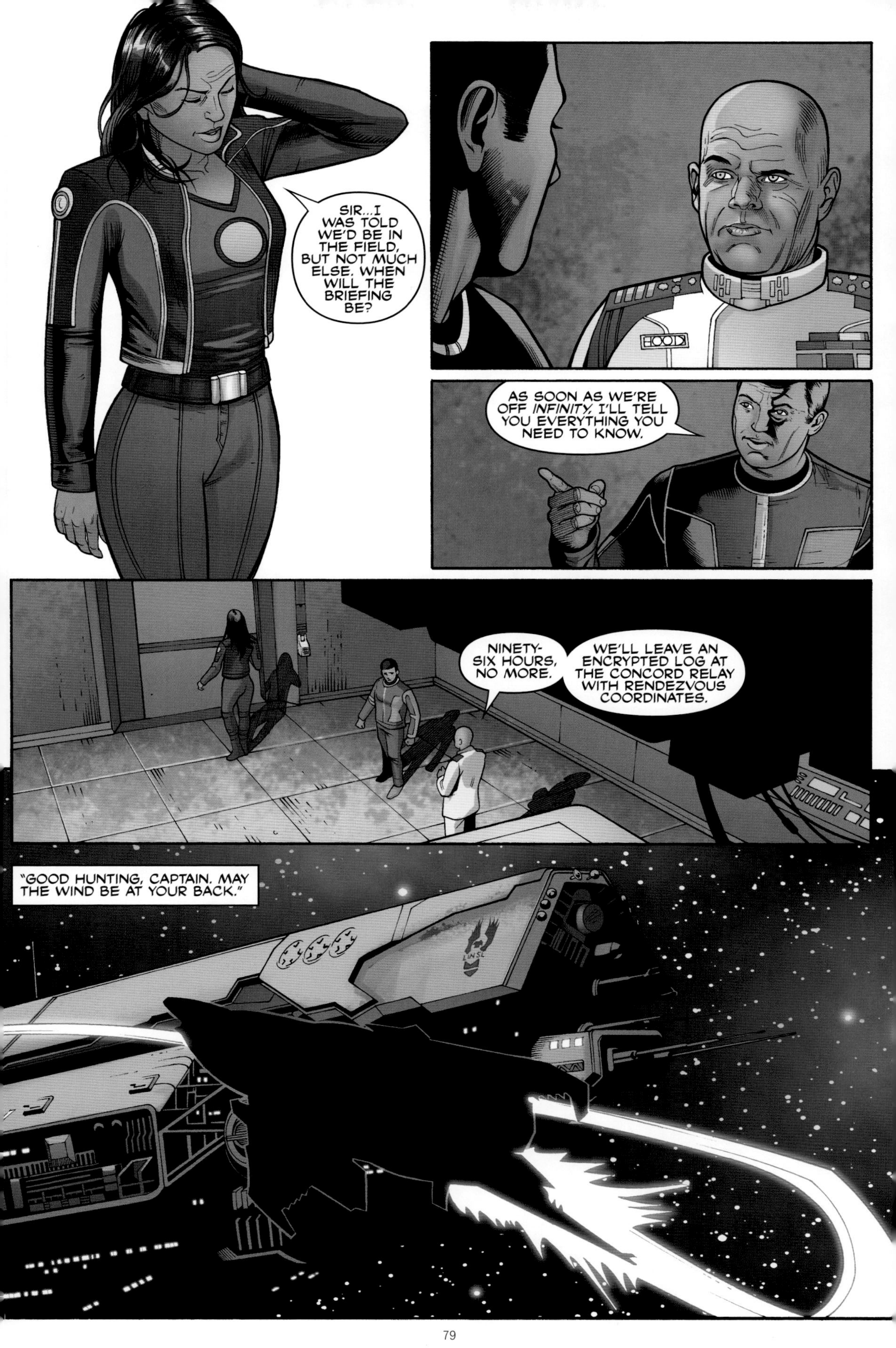
SIR...I WAS TOLD WE'D BE IN THE FIELD, BUT NOT MUCH ELSE. WHEN WILL THE BRIEFING BE?
AS SOON AS WE'RE OFF *INFINITY*, I'LL TELL YOU EVERYTHING YOU NEED TO KNOW.
NINETY-SIX HOURS, NO MORE.
WE'LL LEAVE AN ENCRYPTED LOG AT THE CONCORD RELAY WITH RENDEZVOUS COORDINATES.
"GOOD HUNTING, CAPTAIN. MAY THE WIND BE AT YOUR BACK."

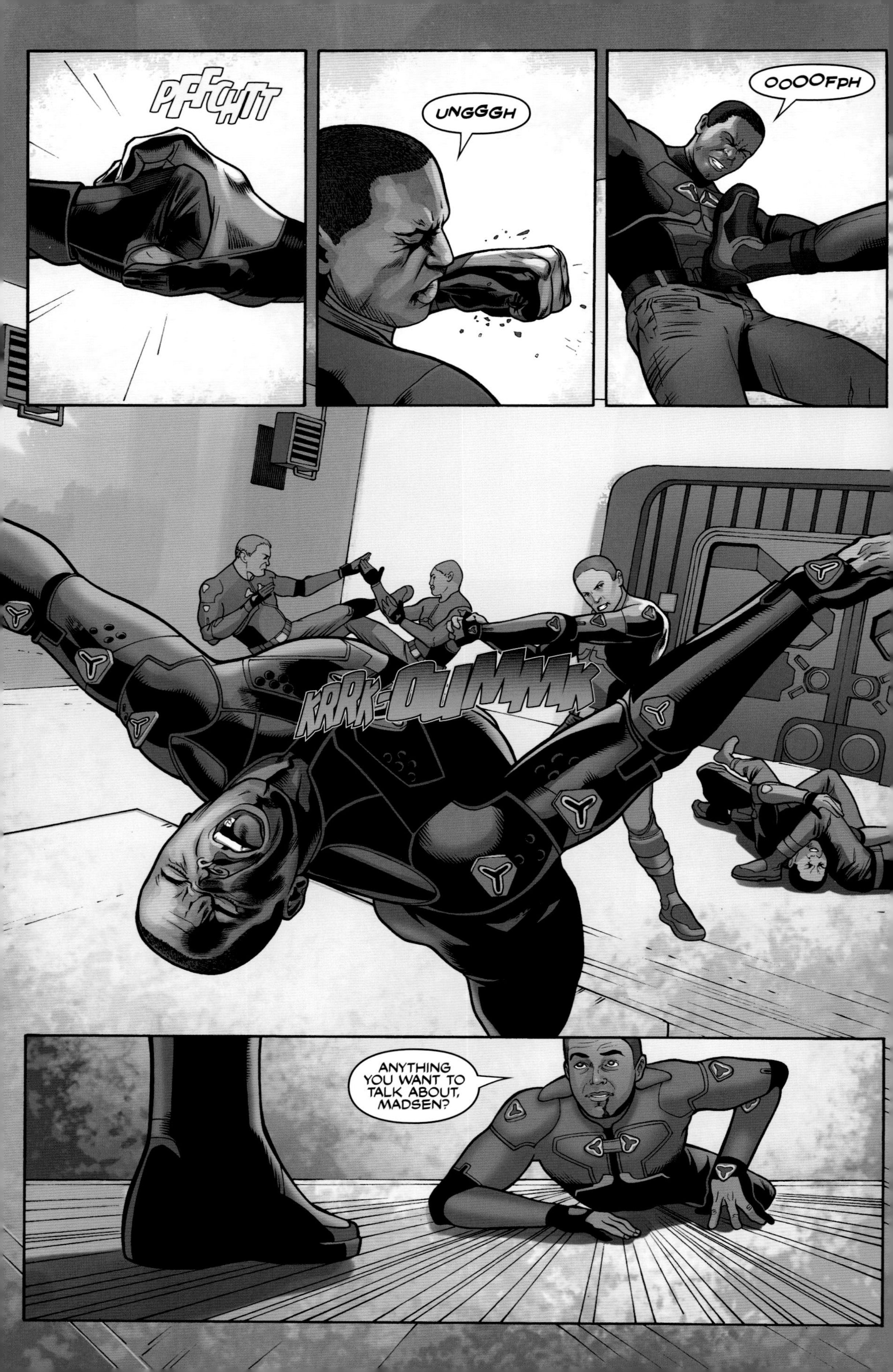
PFFCHTT
UNGGGH
OOOOFPH
KRRK-OOMMMK
ANYTHING YOU WANT TO TALK ABOUT, MADSEN?

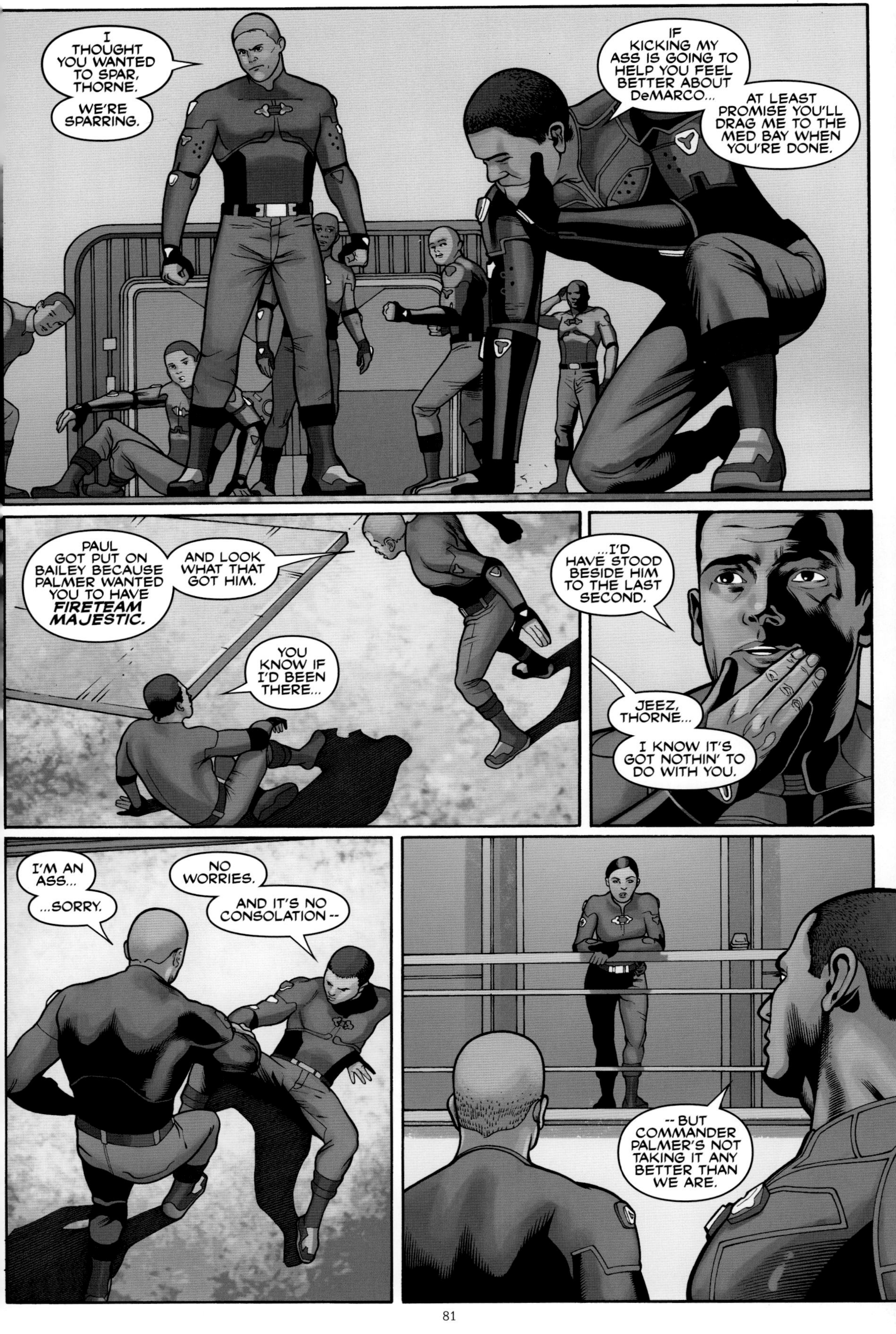
I THOUGHT YOU WANTED TO SPAR, THORNE.
WE'RE SPARRING.
IF KICKING MY ASS IS GOING TO HELP YOU FEEL BETTER ABOUT DeMARCO...
AT LEAST PROMISE YOU'LL DRAG ME TO THE MED BAY WHEN YOU'RE DONE.
PAUL GOT PUT ON BAILEY BECAUSE PALMER WANTED YOU TO HAVE FIRETEAM MAJESTIC.
AND LOOK WHAT THAT GOT HIM.
YOU KNOW IF I'D BEEN THERE...
...I'D HAVE STOOD BESIDE HIM TO THE LAST SECOND.
JEEZ, THORNE...
I KNOW IT'S GOT NOTHIN' TO DO WITH YOU.
I'M AN ASS...
...SORRY.
NO WORRIES.
AND IT'S NO CONSOLATION --
-- BUT COMMANDER PALMER'S NOT TAKING IT ANY BETTER THAN WE ARE.

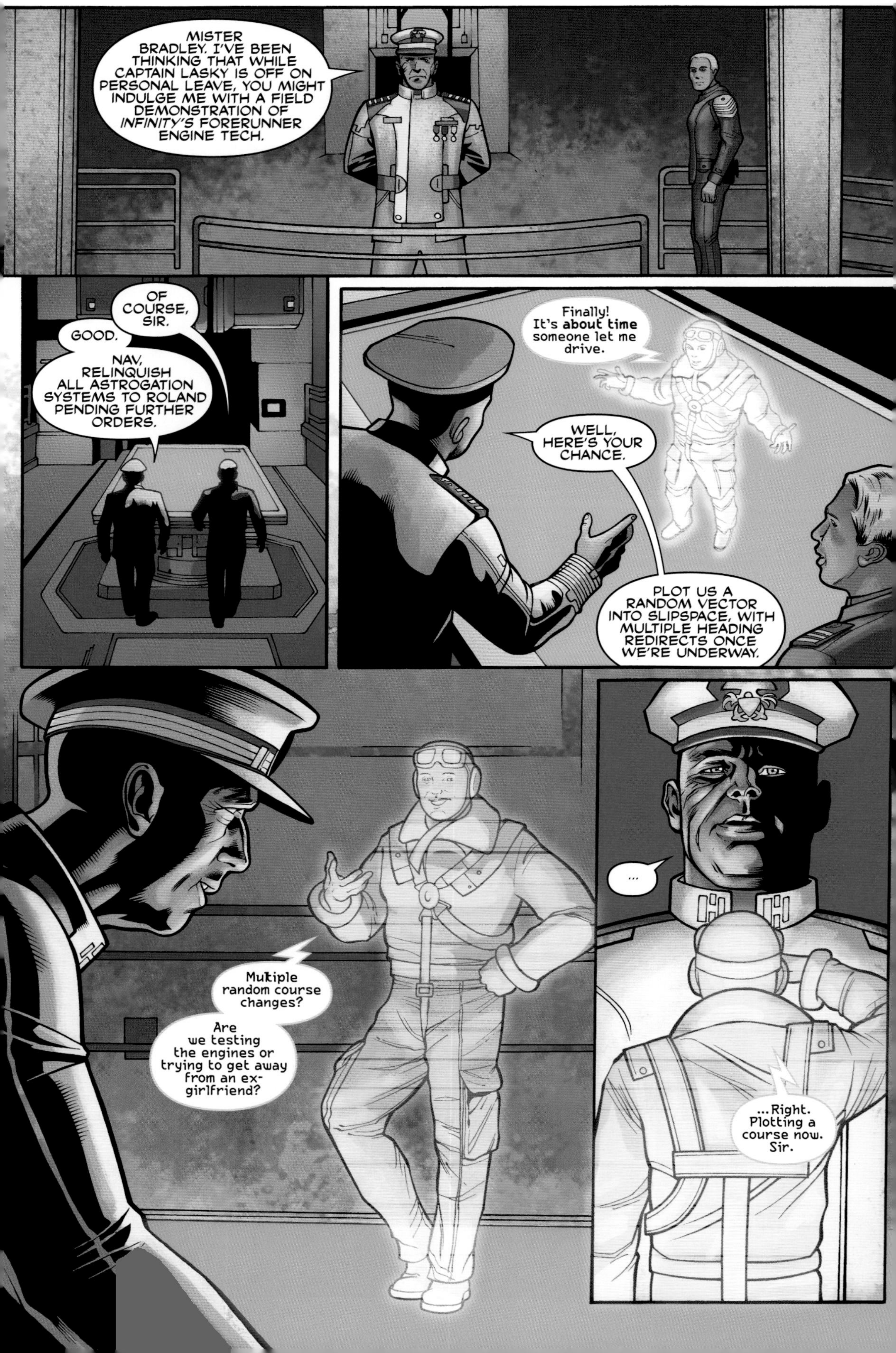
MISTER BRADLEY. I'VE BEEN THINKING THAT WHILE CAPTAIN LASKY IS OFF ON PERSONAL LEAVE, YOU MIGHT INDULGE ME WITH A FIELD DEMONSTRATION OF *INFINITY'S* FORERUNNER ENGINE TECH.
OF COURSE, SIR.
GOOD.
NAV, RELINQUISH ALL ASTROGATION SYSTEMS TO ROLAND PENDING FURTHER ORDERS.
Finally! It's **about time** someone let me drive.
WELL, HERE'S YOUR CHANCE.
PLOT US A RANDOM VECTOR INTO SLIPSPACE, WITH MULTIPLE HEADING REDIRECTS ONCE WE'RE UNDERWAY.
Multiple random course changes?
Are we testing the engines or trying to get away from an ex-girlfriend?
...
...Right. Plotting a course now. Sir.

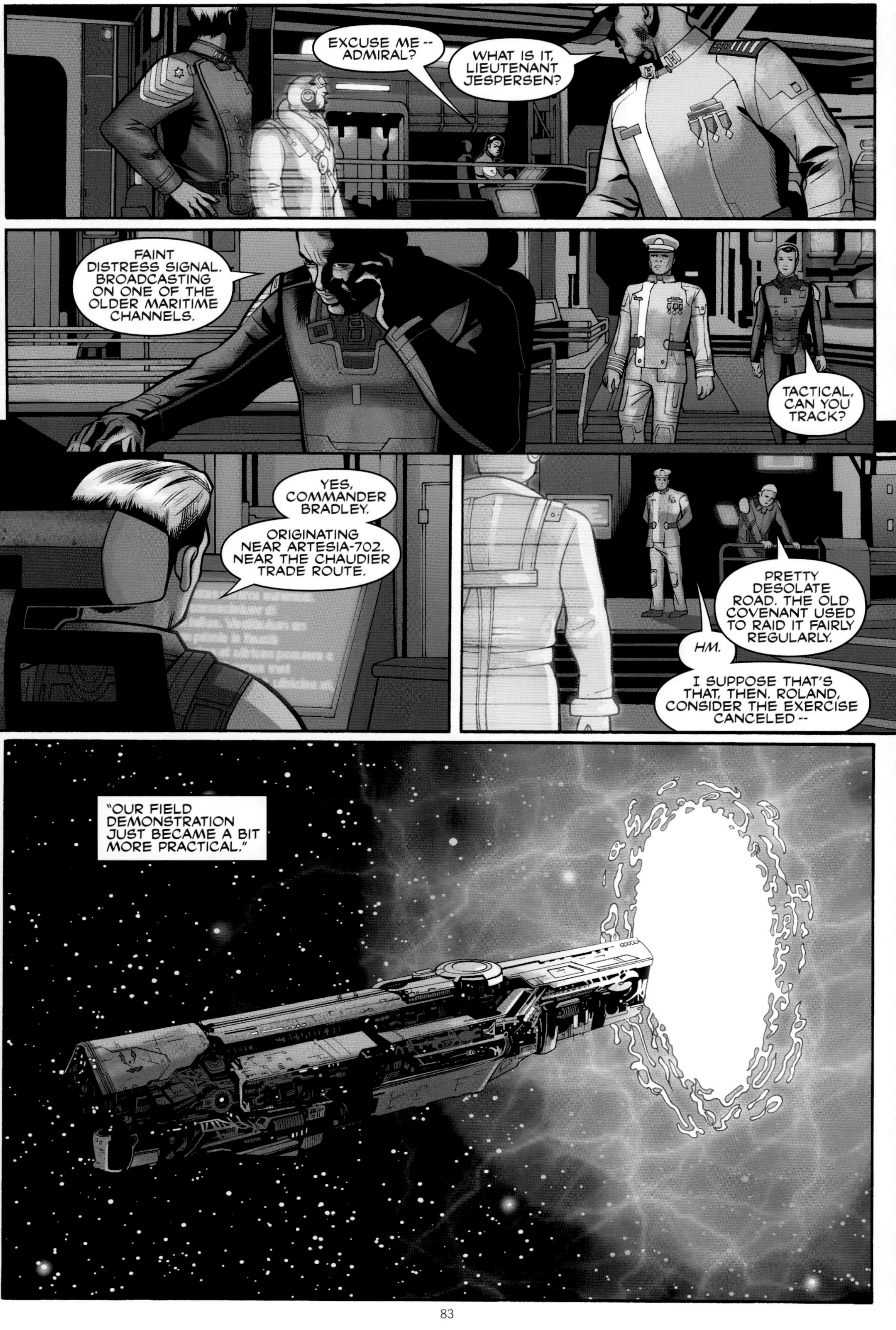
EXCUSE ME -- ADMIRAL?
WHAT IS IT, LIEUTENANT JESPERSEN?
FAINT DISTRESS SIGNAL. BROADCASTING ON ONE OF THE OLDER MARITIME CHANNELS.
TACTICAL, CAN YOU TRACK?
YES, COMMANDER BRADLEY.
ORIGINATING NEAR ARTESIA-702. NEAR THE CHAUDIER TRADE ROUTE.
PRETTY DESOLATE ROAD. THE OLD COVENANT USED TO RAID IT FAIRLY REGULARLY.
HM.
I SUPPOSE THAT'S THAT, THEN. ROLAND, CONSIDER THE EXERCISE CANCELED --
"OUR FIELD DEMONSTRATION JUST BECAME A BIT MORE PRACTICAL."

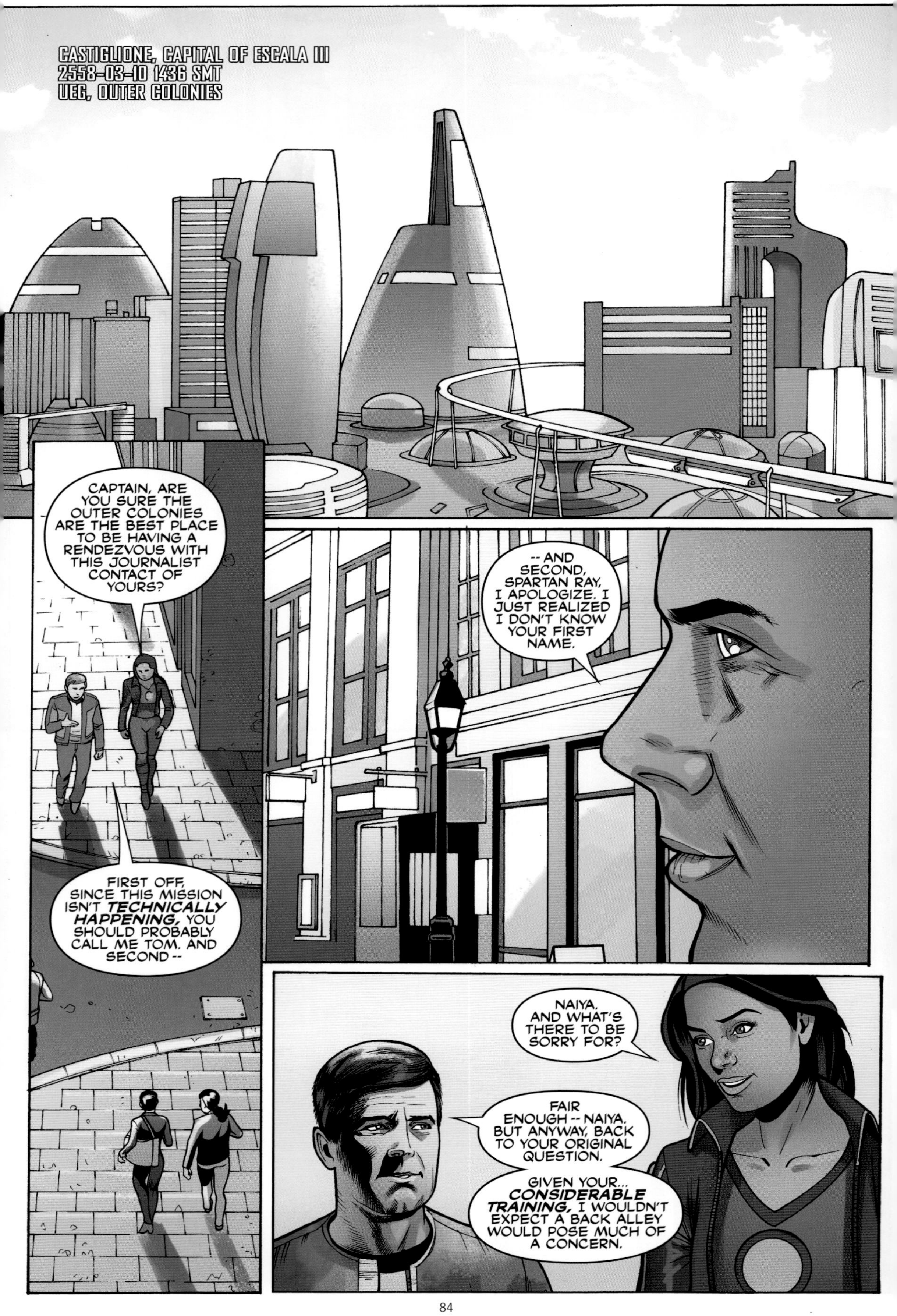
CASTIGLIONE, CAPITAL OF ESCALA III
2558-03-10 1436 SMT
UEG, OUTER COLONIES
CAPTAIN, ARE YOU SURE THE OUTER COLONIES ARE THE BEST PLACE TO BE HAVING A RENDEZVOUS WITH THIS JOURNALIST CONTACT OF YOURS?
FIRST OFF, SINCE THIS MISSION ISN'T ***TECHNICALLY HAPPENING,*** YOU SHOULD PROBABLY CALL ME TOM. AND SECOND --
-- AND SECOND, SPARTAN RAY, I APOLOGIZE. I JUST REALIZED I DON'T KNOW YOUR FIRST NAME.
NAIYA. AND WHAT'S THERE TO BE SORRY FOR?
FAIR ENOUGH -- NAIYA. BUT ANYWAY, BACK TO YOUR ORIGINAL QUESTION.
GIVEN YOUR... ***CONSIDERABLE TRAINING,*** I WOULDN'T EXPECT A BACK ALLEY WOULD POSE MUCH OF A CONCERN.

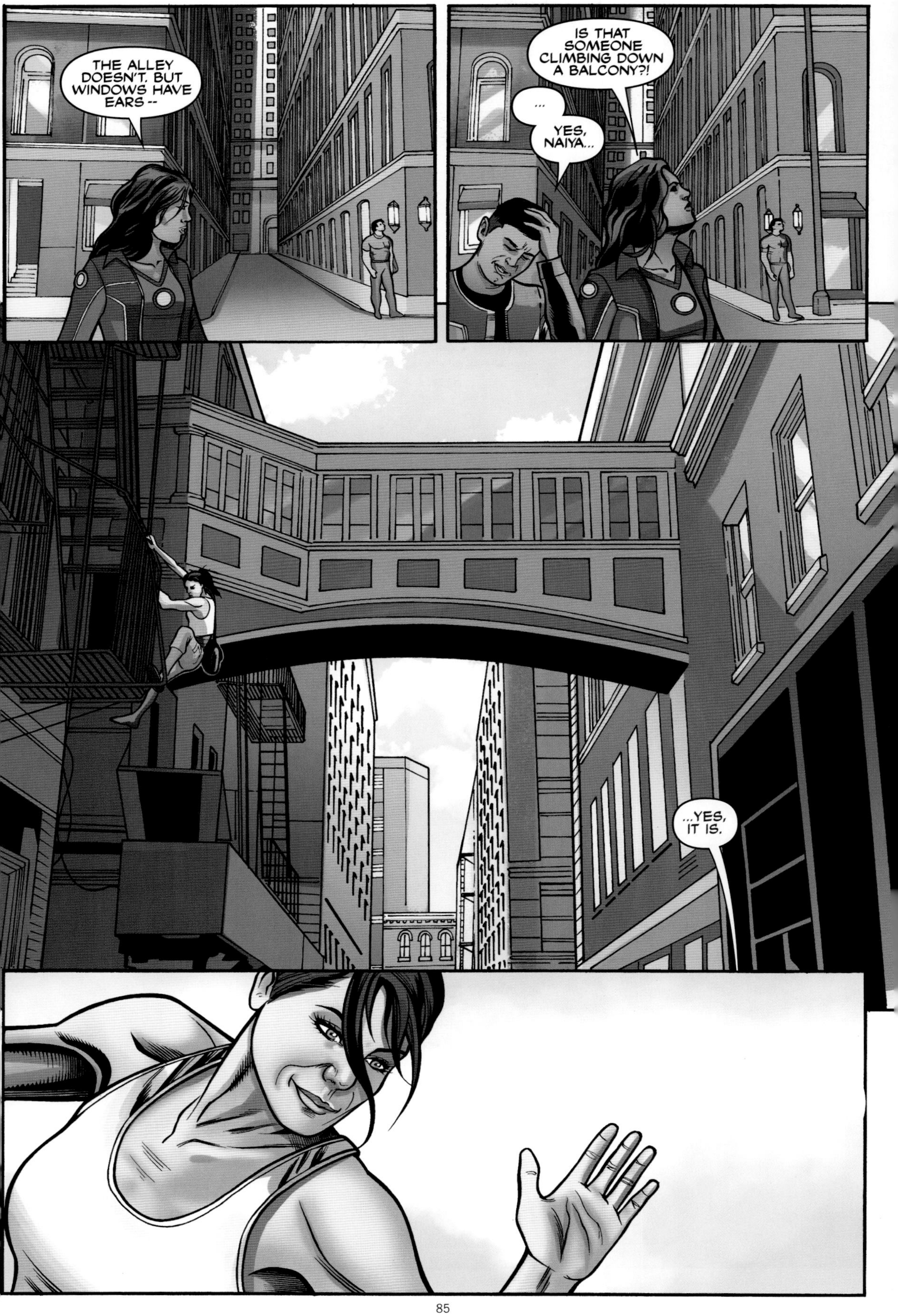
THE ALLEY DOESN'T. BUT WINDOWS HAVE EARS --
IS THAT SOMEONE CLIMBING DOWN A BALCONY?!
...
YES, NAIYA...
...YES, IT IS.

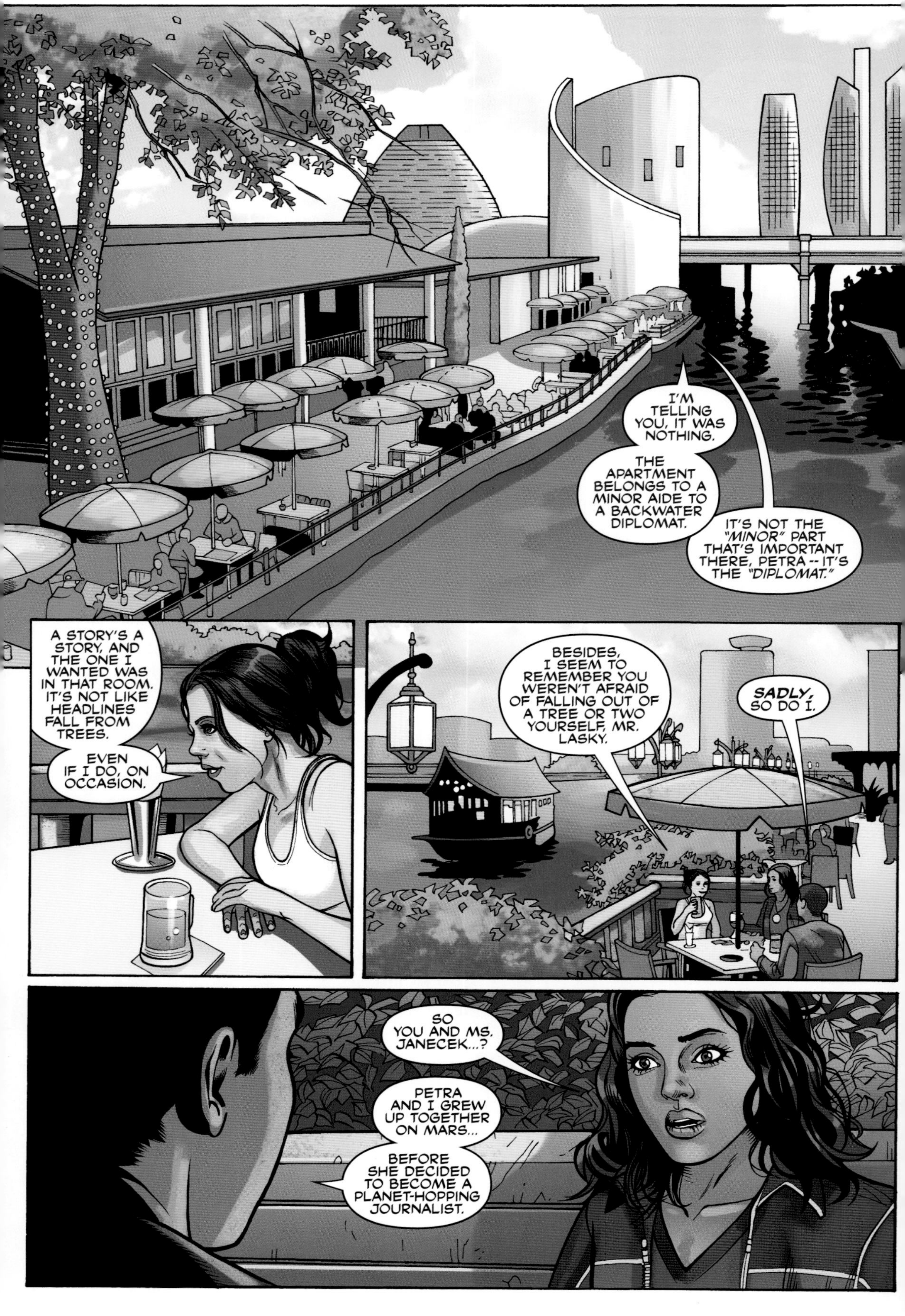
I'M TELLING YOU, IT WAS NOTHING.
THE APARTMENT BELONGS TO A MINOR AIDE TO A BACKWATER DIPLOMAT.
IT'S NOT THE *"MINOR"* PART THAT'S IMPORTANT THERE, PETRA -- IT'S THE *"DIPLOMAT."*
A STORY'S A STORY, AND THE ONE I WANTED WAS IN THAT ROOM. IT'S NOT LIKE HEADLINES FALL FROM TREES.
EVEN IF I DO, ON OCCASION.
BESIDES, I SEEM TO REMEMBER YOU WEREN'T AFRAID OF FALLING OUT OF A TREE OR TWO YOURSELF, MR. LASKY.
SADLY, SO DO I.
SO YOU AND MS. JANECEK...?
PETRA AND I GREW UP TOGETHER ON MARS...
BEFORE SHE DECIDED TO BECOME A PLANET-HOPPING JOURNALIST.

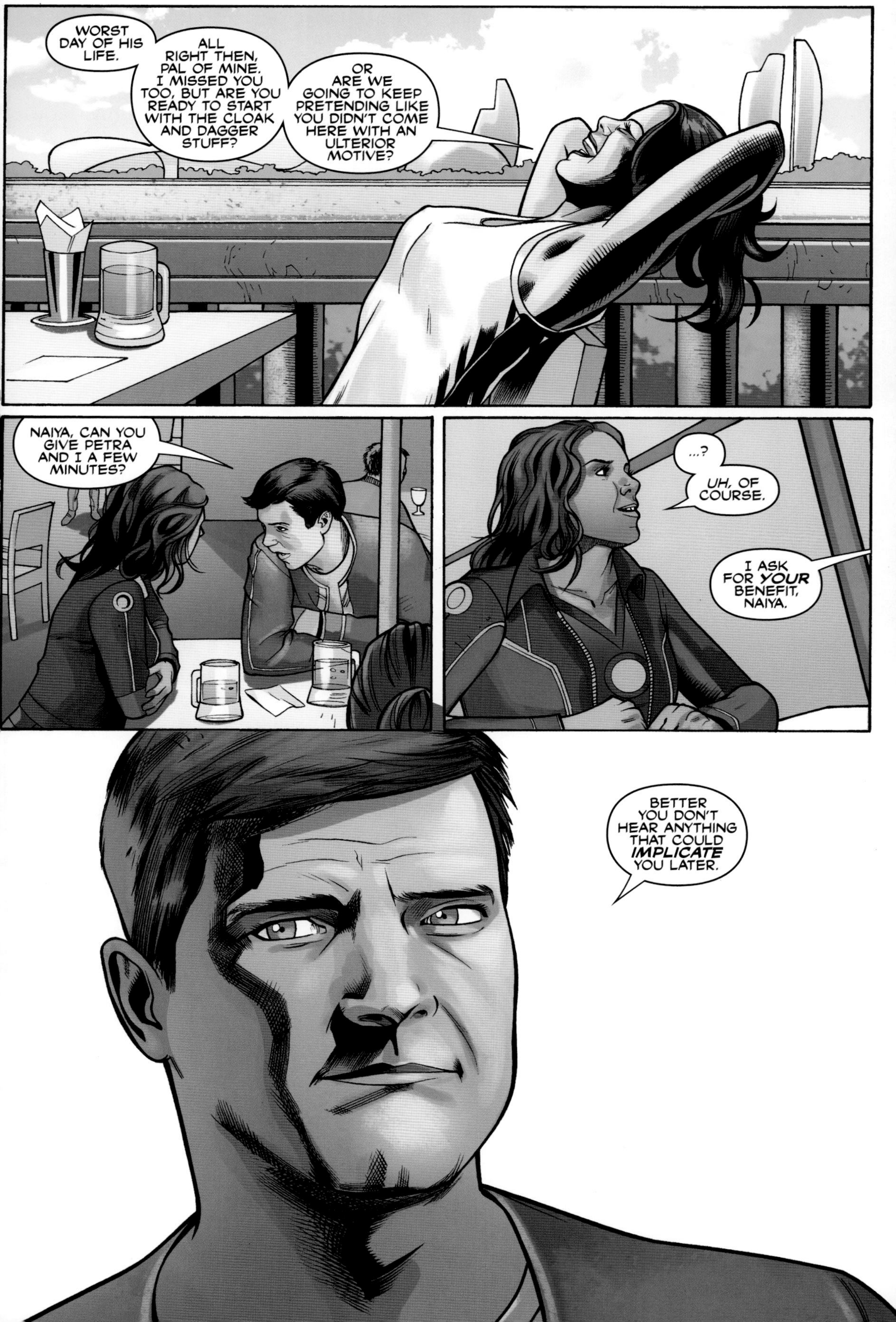
WORST DAY OF HIS LIFE.
ALL RIGHT THEN, PAL OF MINE. I MISSED YOU TOO, BUT ARE YOU READY TO START WITH THE CLOAK AND DAGGER STUFF?
OR ARE WE GOING TO KEEP PRETENDING LIKE YOU DIDN'T COME HERE WITH AN ULTERIOR MOTIVE?
NAIYA, CAN YOU GIVE PETRA AND I A FEW MINUTES?
...?
UH, OF COURSE.
I ASK FOR ***YOUR*** BENEFIT, NAIYA.
BETTER YOU DON'T HEAR ANYTHING THAT COULD ***IMPLICATE*** YOU LATER.

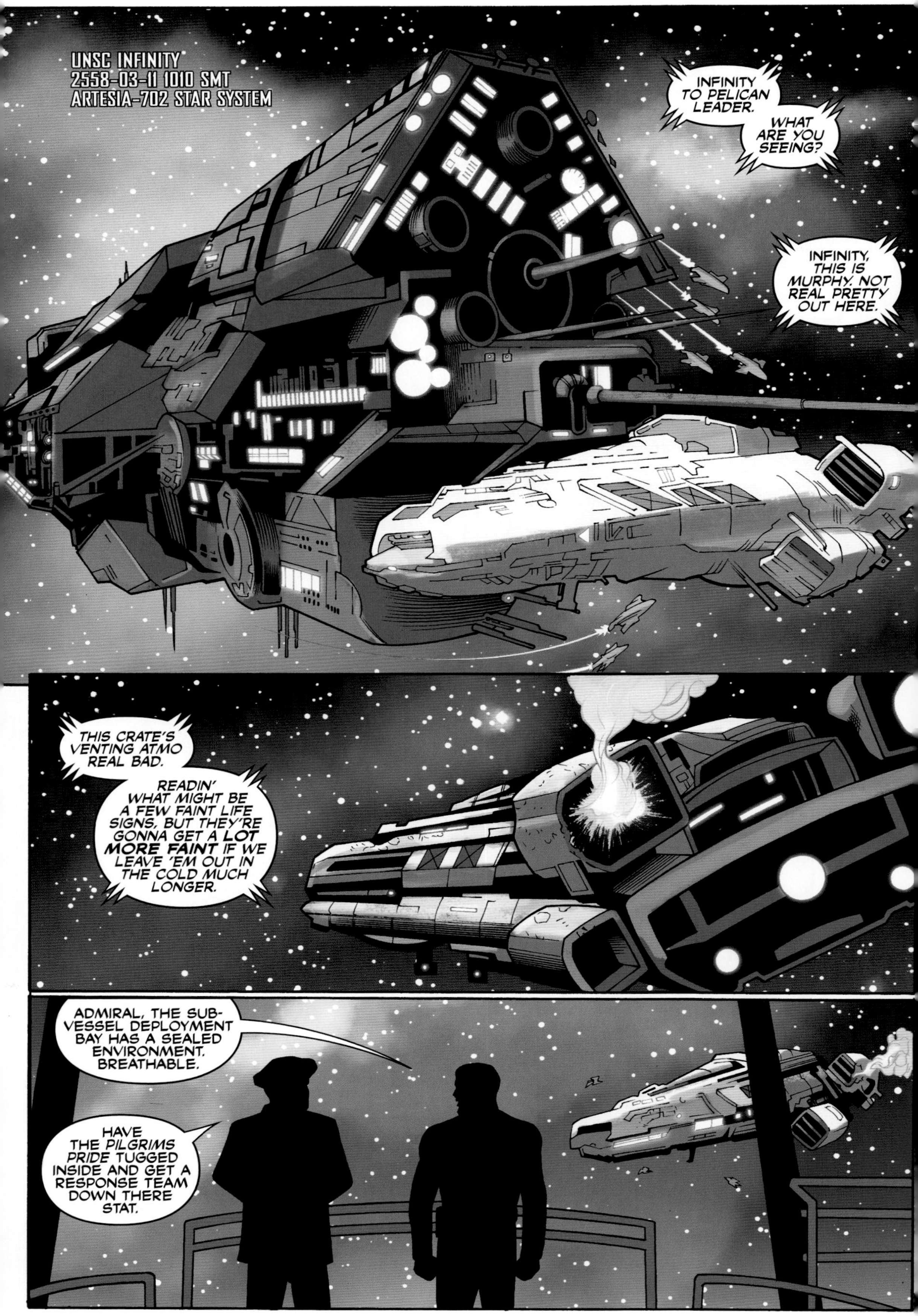
UNSC INFINITY
2558-03-11 1010 SMT
ARTESIA-702 STAR SYSTEM
INFINITY TO PELICAN LEADER.
WHAT ARE YOU SEEING?
INFINITY, THIS IS MURPHY. NOT REAL PRETTY OUT HERE.
THIS CRATE'S VENTING ATMO REAL BAD.
READIN' WHAT MIGHT BE A FEW FAINT LIFE SIGNS, BUT THEY'RE GONNA GET A **LOT MORE FAINT** IF WE LEAVE 'EM OUT IN THE COLD MUCH LONGER.
ADMIRAL, THE SUB-VESSEL DEPLOYMENT BAY HAS A SEALED ENVIRONMENT. BREATHABLE.
HAVE THE *PILGRIMS PRIDE* TUGGED INSIDE AND GET A RESPONSE TEAM DOWN THERE STAT.

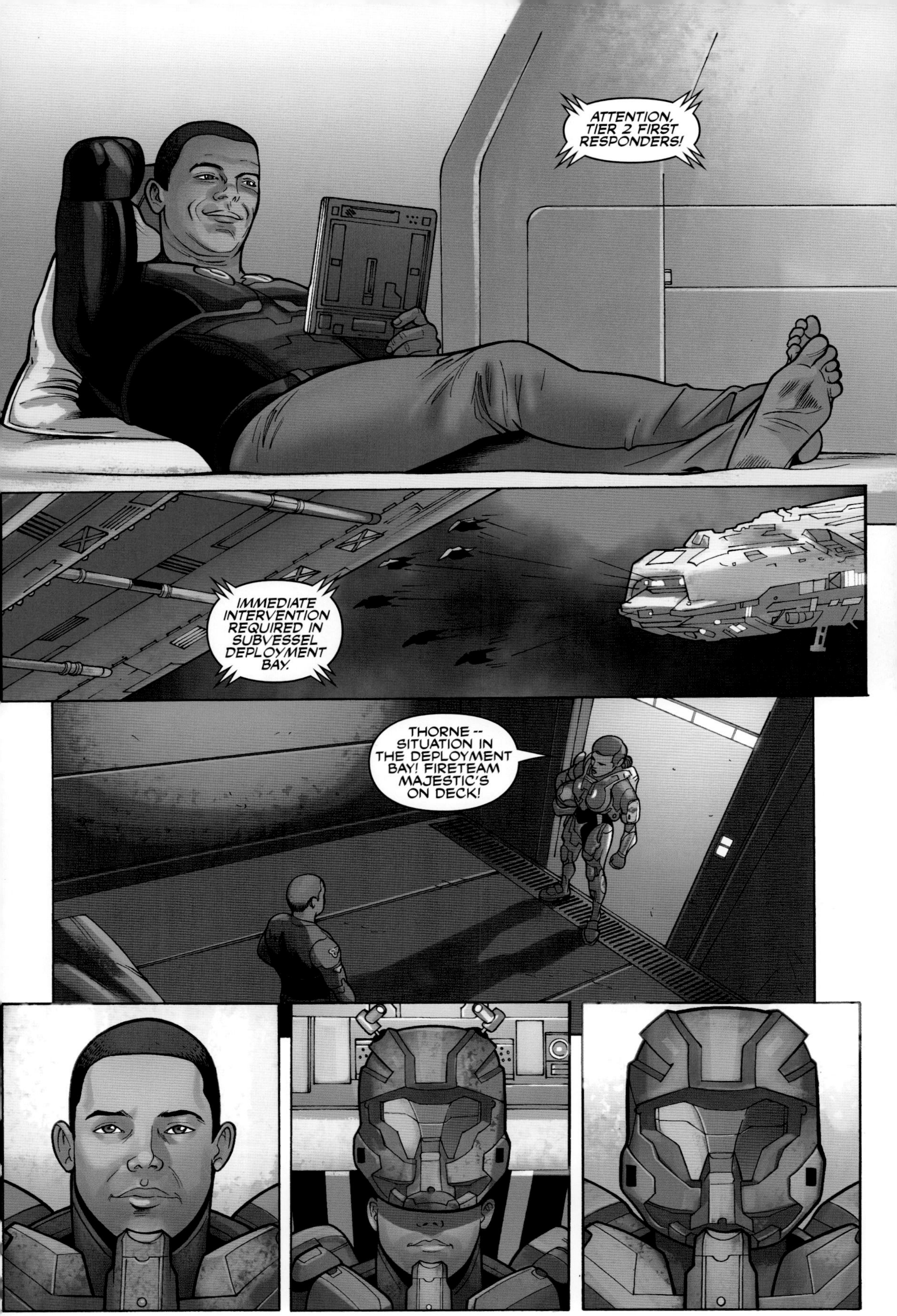
ATTENTION, TIER 2 FIRST RESPONDERS!
IMMEDIATE INTERVENTION REQUIRED IN SUBVESSEL DEPLOYMENT BAY.
THORNE -- SITUATION IN THE DEPLOYMENT BAY! FIRETEAM MAJESTIC'S ON DECK!

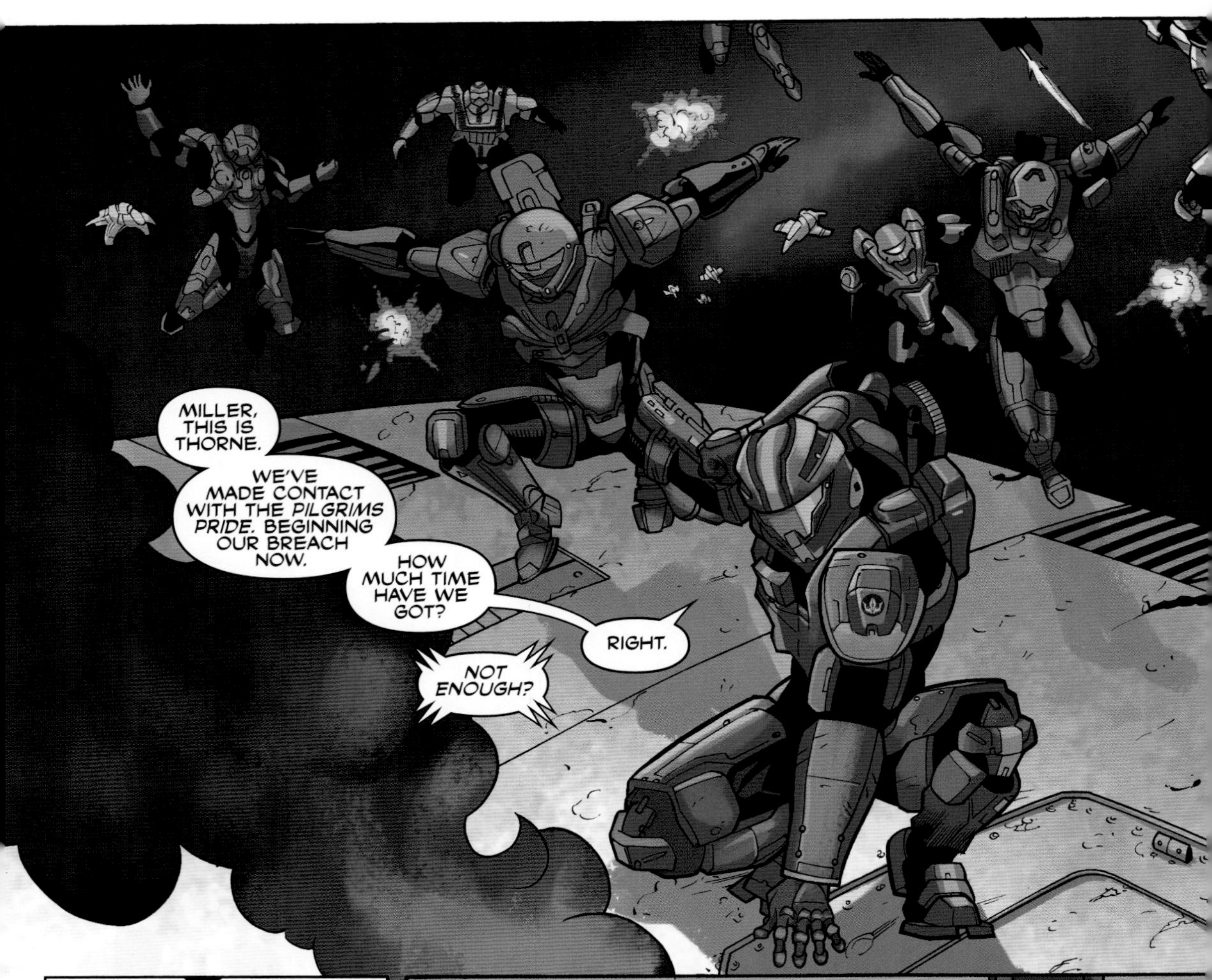
MILLER, THIS IS THORNE.
WE'VE MADE CONTACT WITH THE *PILGRIMS PRIDE*. BEGINNING OUR BREACH NOW.
HOW MUCH TIME HAVE WE GOT?
NOT ENOUGH?
RIGHT.

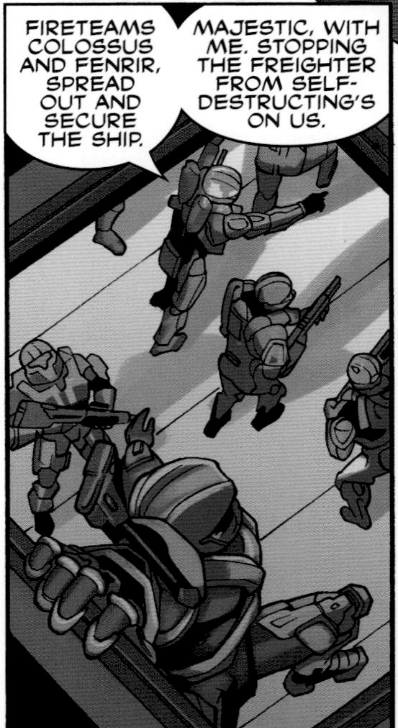
FIRETEAMS COLOSSUS AND FENRIR, SPREAD OUT AND SECURE THE SHIP.
MAJESTIC, WITH ME. STOPPING THE FREIGHTER FROM SELF-DESTRUCTING'S ON US.

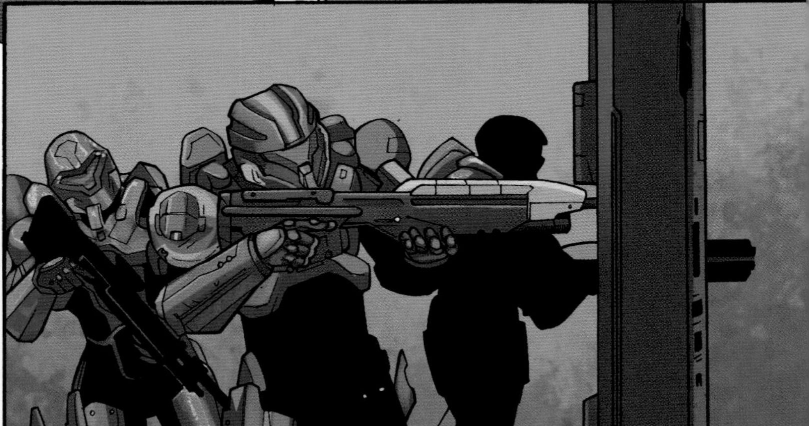

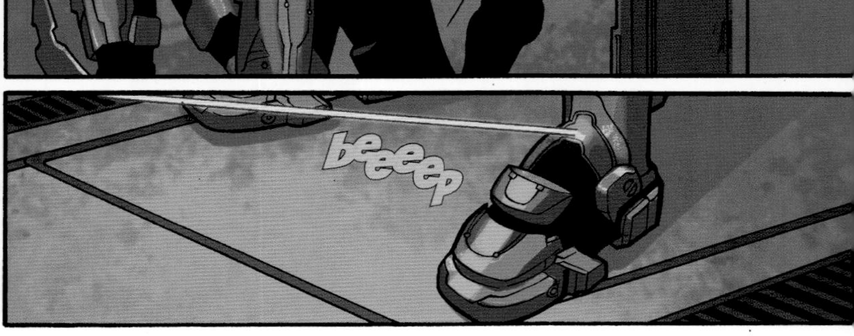
beeeep

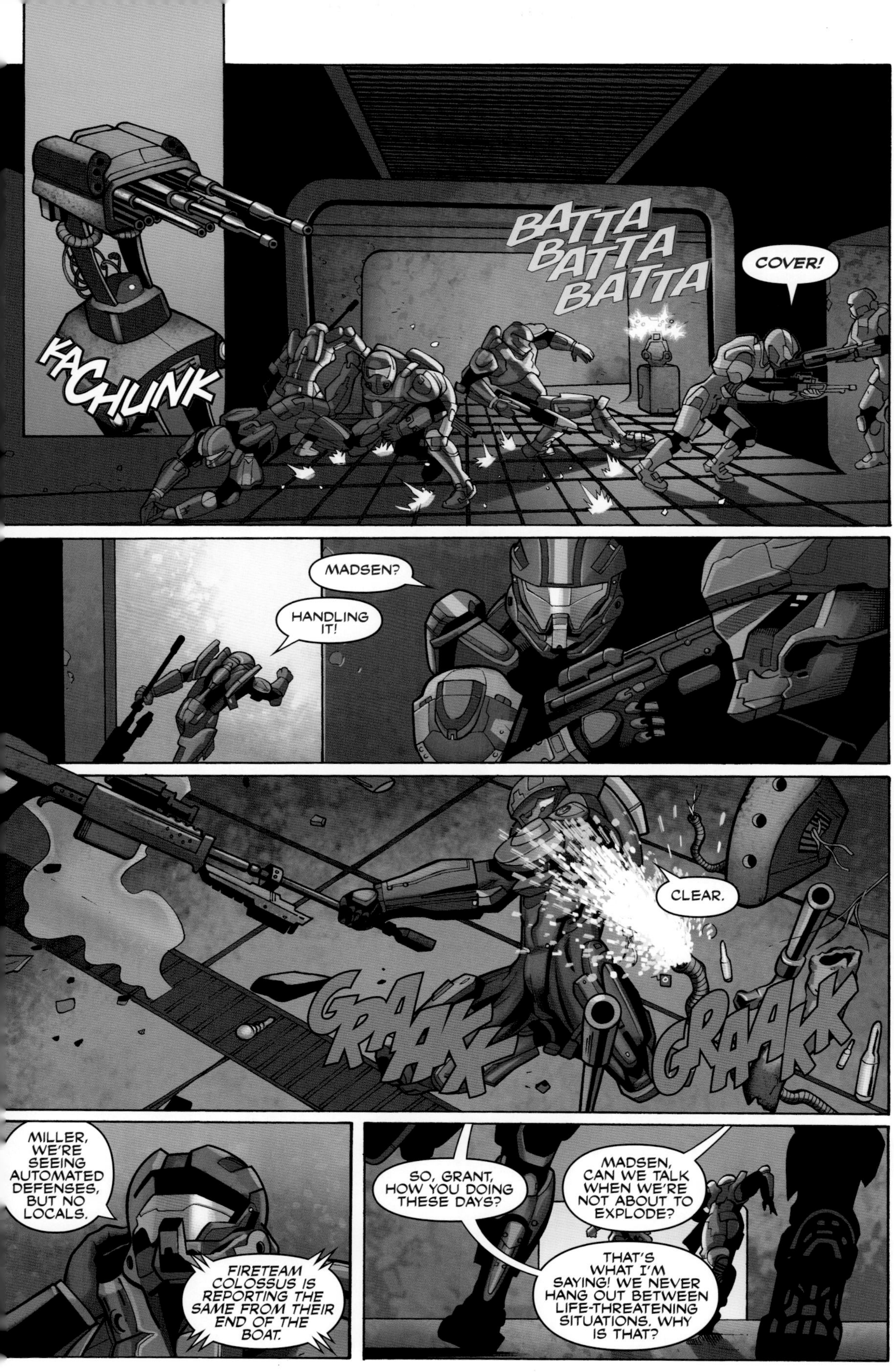
KA-CHUNK
BATTA BATTA BATTA
COVER!
MADSEN?
HANDLING IT!
CLEAR.
GRAAK GRAAK
MILLER, WE'RE SEEING AUTOMATED DEFENSES, BUT NO LOCALS.
FIRETEAM COLOSSUS IS REPORTING THE SAME FROM THEIR END OF THE BOAT.
SO, GRANT, HOW YOU DOING THESE DAYS?
MADSEN, CAN WE TALK WHEN WE'RE NOT ABOUT TO EXPLODE?
THAT'S WHAT I'M SAYING! WE NEVER HANG OUT BETWEEN LIFE-THREATENING SITUATIONS, WHY IS THAT?

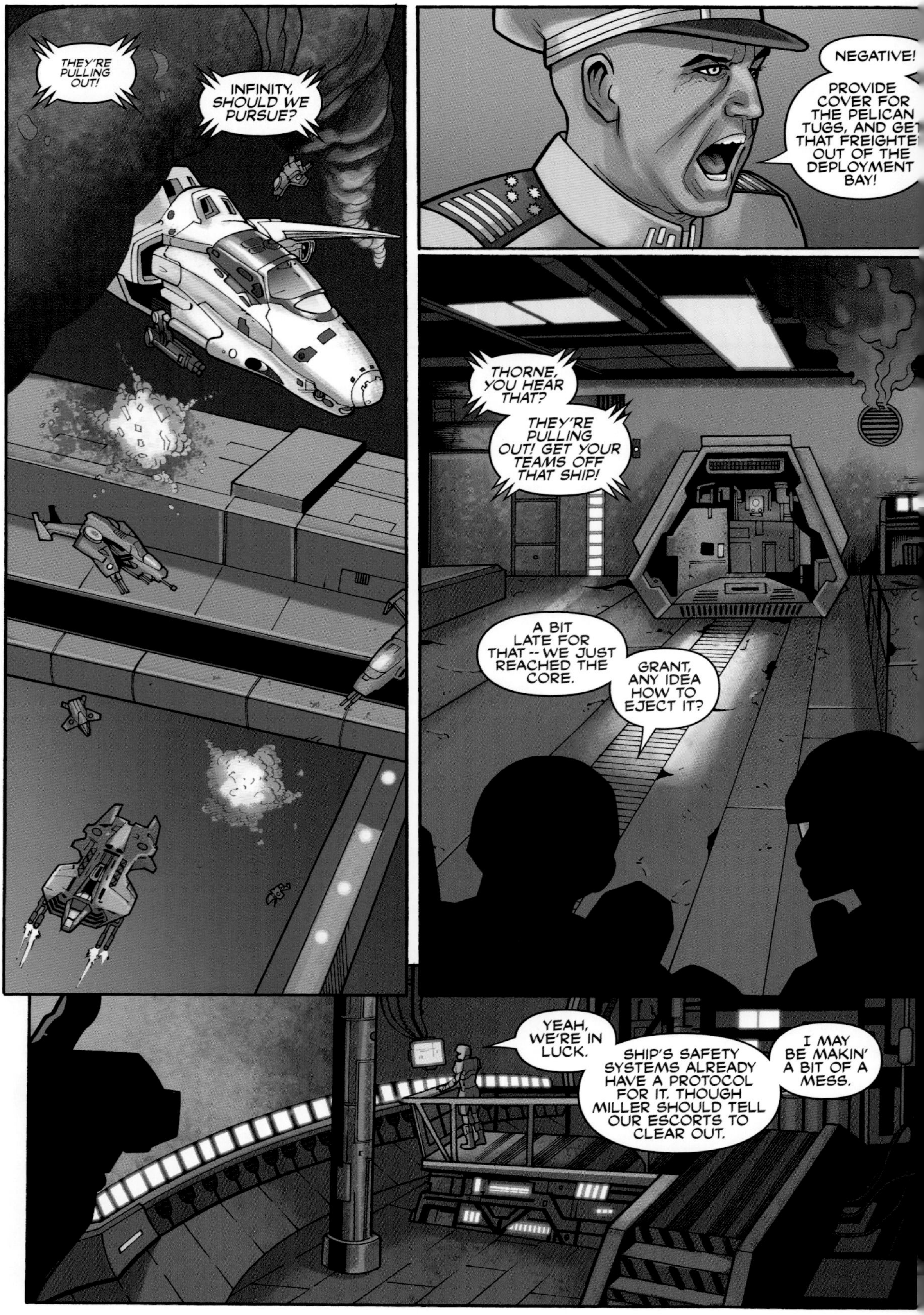

THEY'RE PULLING OUT!
INFINITY, SHOULD WE PURSUE?
NEGATIVE!
PROVIDE COVER FOR THE PELICAN TUGS, AND GET THAT FREIGHTER OUT OF THE DEPLOYMENT BAY!
THORNE, YOU HEAR THAT?
THEY'RE PULLING OUT! GET YOUR TEAMS OFF THAT SHIP!
A BIT LATE FOR THAT -- WE JUST REACHED THE CORE.
GRANT, ANY IDEA HOW TO EJECT IT?
YEAH, WE'RE IN LUCK.
SHIP'S SAFETY SYSTEMS ALREADY HAVE A PROTOCOL FOR IT. THOUGH MILLER SHOULD TELL OUR ESCORTS TO CLEAR OUT.
I MAY BE MAKIN' A BIT OF A MESS.

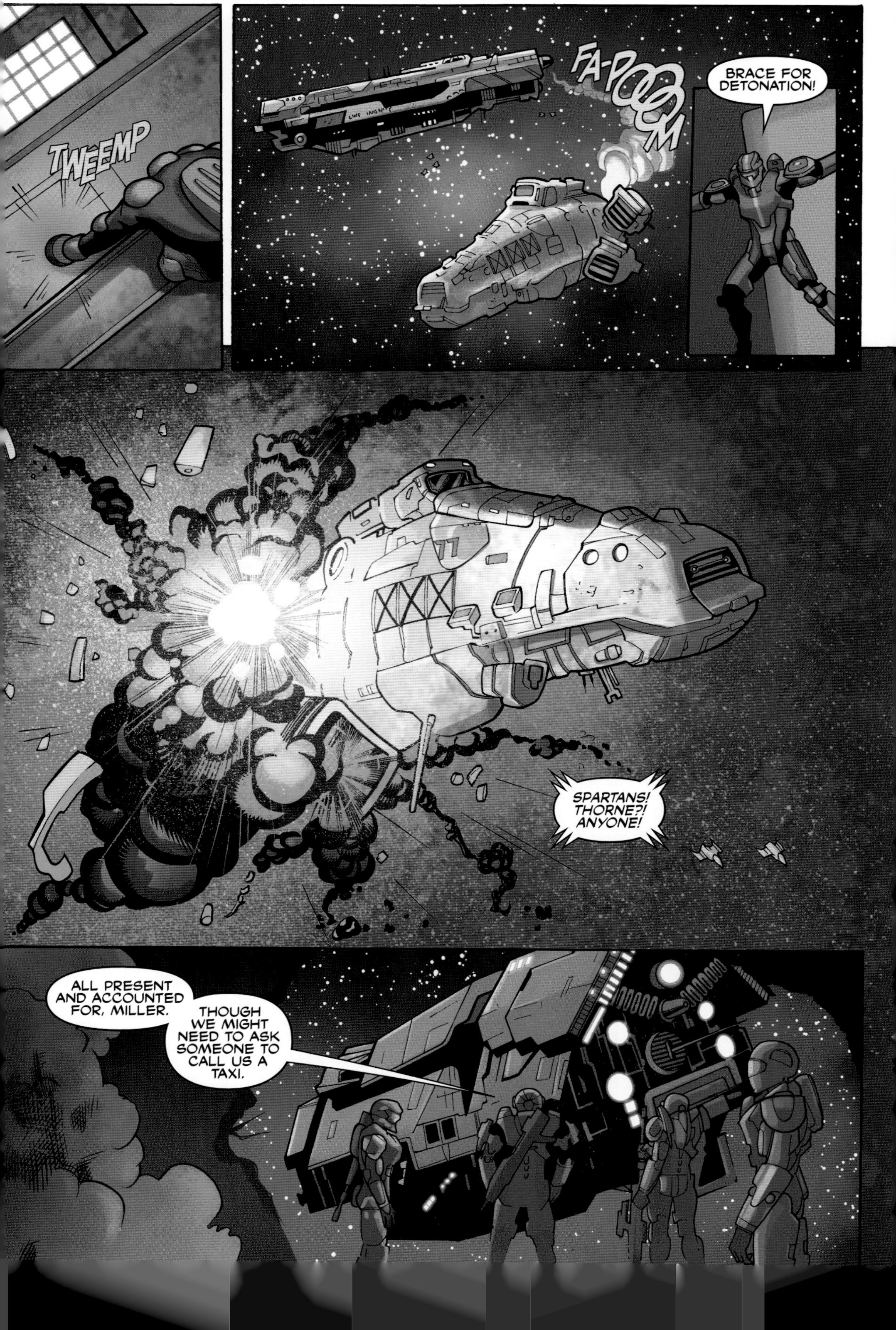
TWEEMP
FA-POOOM
BRACE FOR DETONATION!
SPARTANS! THORNE?! ANYONE!
ALL PRESENT AND ACCOUNTED FOR, MILLER.
THOUGH WE MIGHT NEED TO ASK SOMEONE TO CALL US A TAXI.

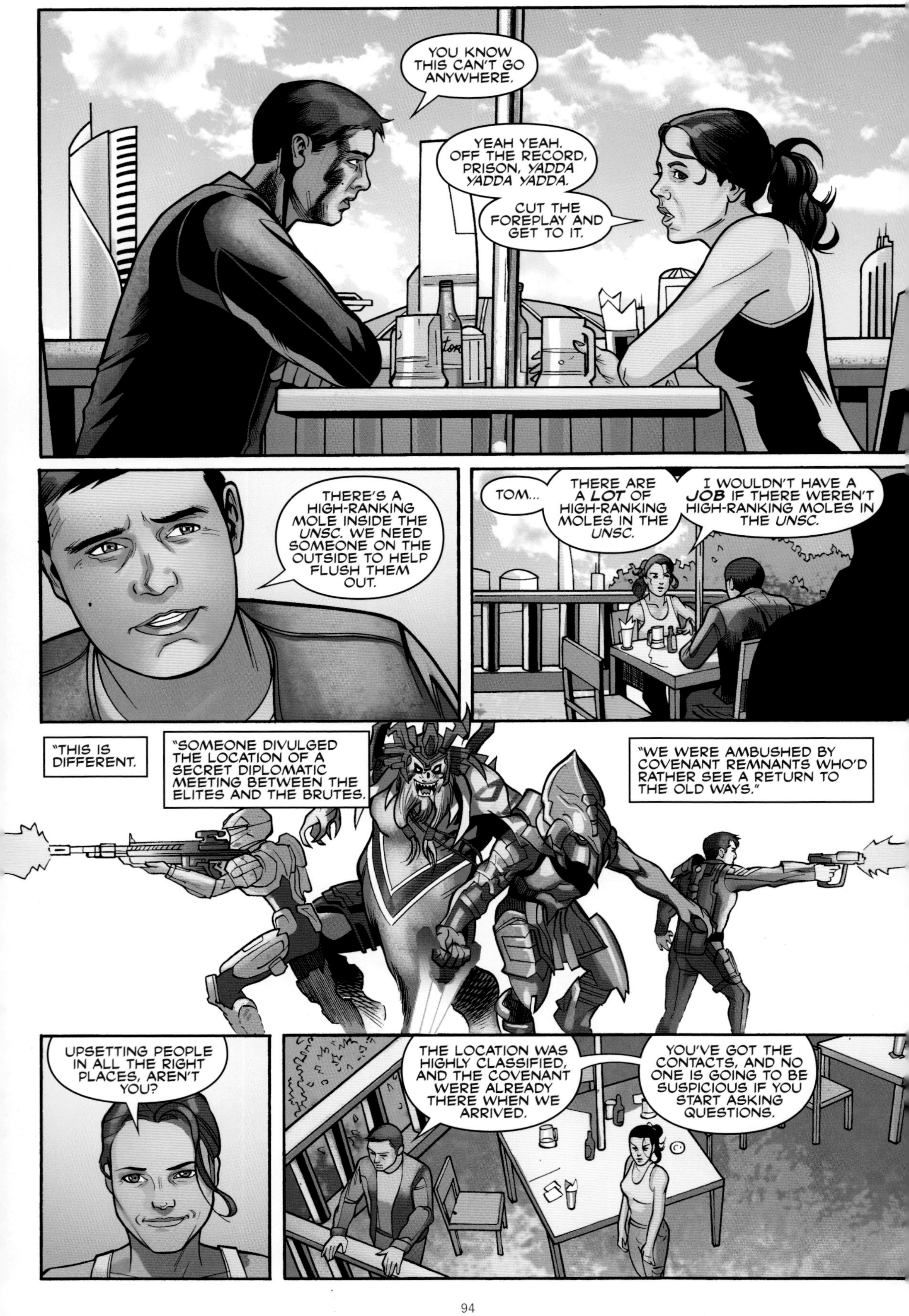

YOU KNOW THIS CAN'T GO ANYWHERE.
YEAH YEAH. OFF THE RECORD, PRISON, *YADDA YADDA YADDA.*
CUT THE FOREPLAY AND GET TO IT.
THERE'S A HIGH-RANKING MOLE INSIDE THE *UNSC.* WE NEED SOMEONE ON THE OUTSIDE TO HELP FLUSH THEM OUT.
TOM...
THERE ARE A ***LOT*** OF HIGH-RANKING MOLES IN THE *UNSC.*
I WOULDN'T HAVE A ***JOB*** IF THERE WEREN'T HIGH-RANKING MOLES IN THE *UNSC.*
"THIS IS DIFFERENT.
"SOMEONE DIVULGED THE LOCATION OF A SECRET DIPLOMATIC MEETING BETWEEN THE ELITES AND THE BRUTES.
"WE WERE AMBUSHED BY COVENANT REMNANTS WHO'D RATHER SEE A RETURN TO THE OLD WAYS."
UPSETTING PEOPLE IN ALL THE RIGHT PLACES, AREN'T YOU?
THE LOCATION WAS HIGHLY CLASSIFIED, AND THE COVENANT WERE ALREADY THERE WHEN WE ARRIVED.
YOU'VE GOT THE CONTACTS, AND NO ONE IS GOING TO BE SUSPICIOUS IF YOU START ASKING QUESTIONS.

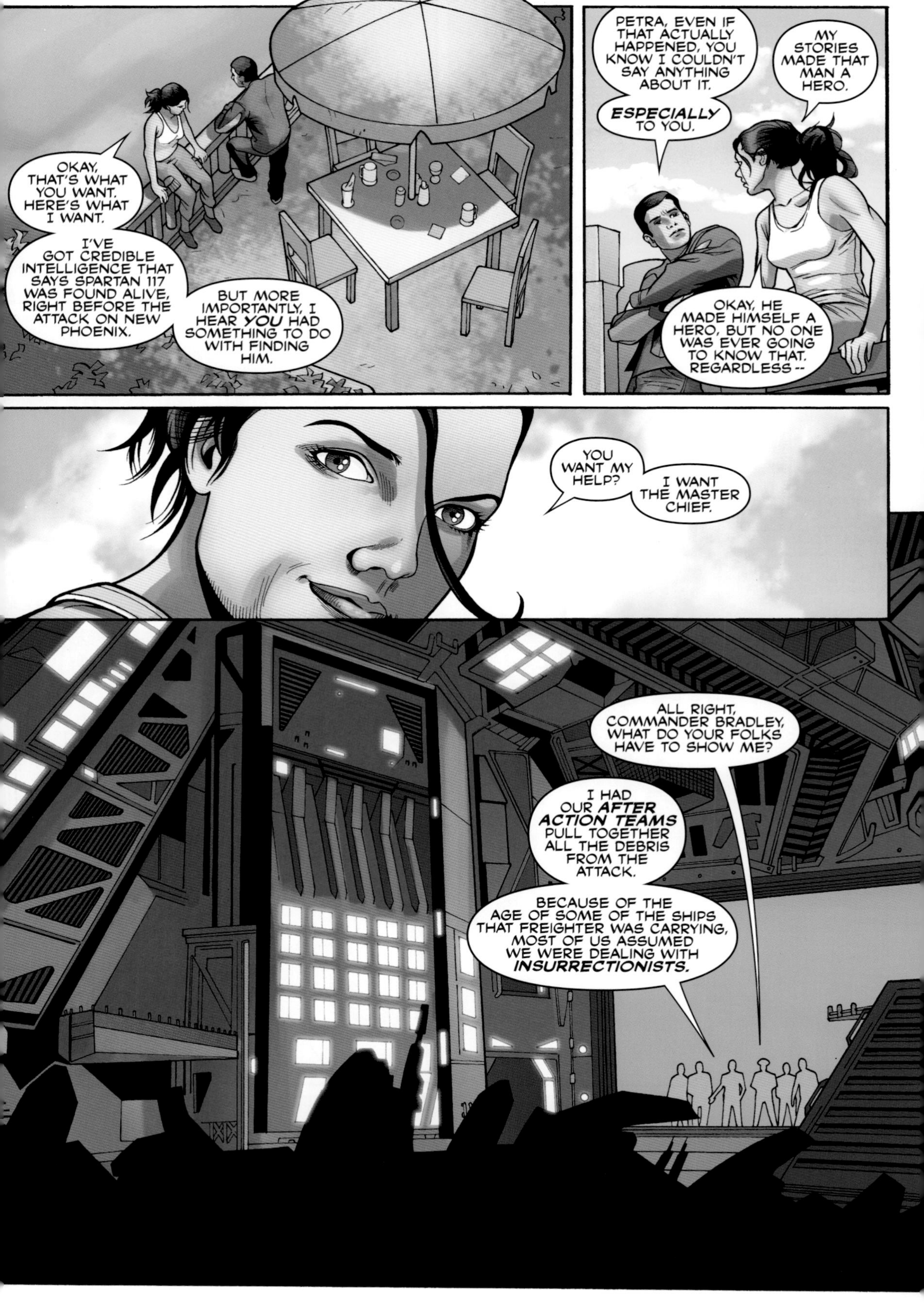
OKAY, THAT'S WHAT YOU WANT. HERE'S WHAT I WANT.
I'VE GOT CREDIBLE INTELLIGENCE THAT SAYS SPARTAN 117 WAS FOUND ALIVE, RIGHT BEFORE THE ATTACK ON NEW PHOENIX.
BUT MORE IMPORTANTLY, I HEAR YOU HAD SOMETHING TO DO WITH FINDING HIM.
PETRA, EVEN IF THAT ACTUALLY HAPPENED, YOU KNOW I COULDN'T SAY ANYTHING ABOUT IT.
ESPECIALLY TO YOU.
MY STORIES MADE THAT MAN A HERO.
OKAY, HE MADE HIMSELF A HERO, BUT NO ONE WAS EVER GOING TO KNOW THAT. REGARDLESS --
YOU WANT MY HELP?
I WANT THE MASTER CHIEF.
ALL RIGHT, COMMANDER BRADLEY. WHAT DO YOUR FOLKS HAVE TO SHOW ME?
I HAD OUR AFTER ACTION TEAMS PULL TOGETHER ALL THE DEBRIS FROM THE ATTACK.
BECAUSE OF THE AGE OF SOME OF THE SHIPS THAT FREIGHTER WAS CARRYING, MOST OF US ASSUMED WE WERE DEALING WITH INSURRECTIONISTS.

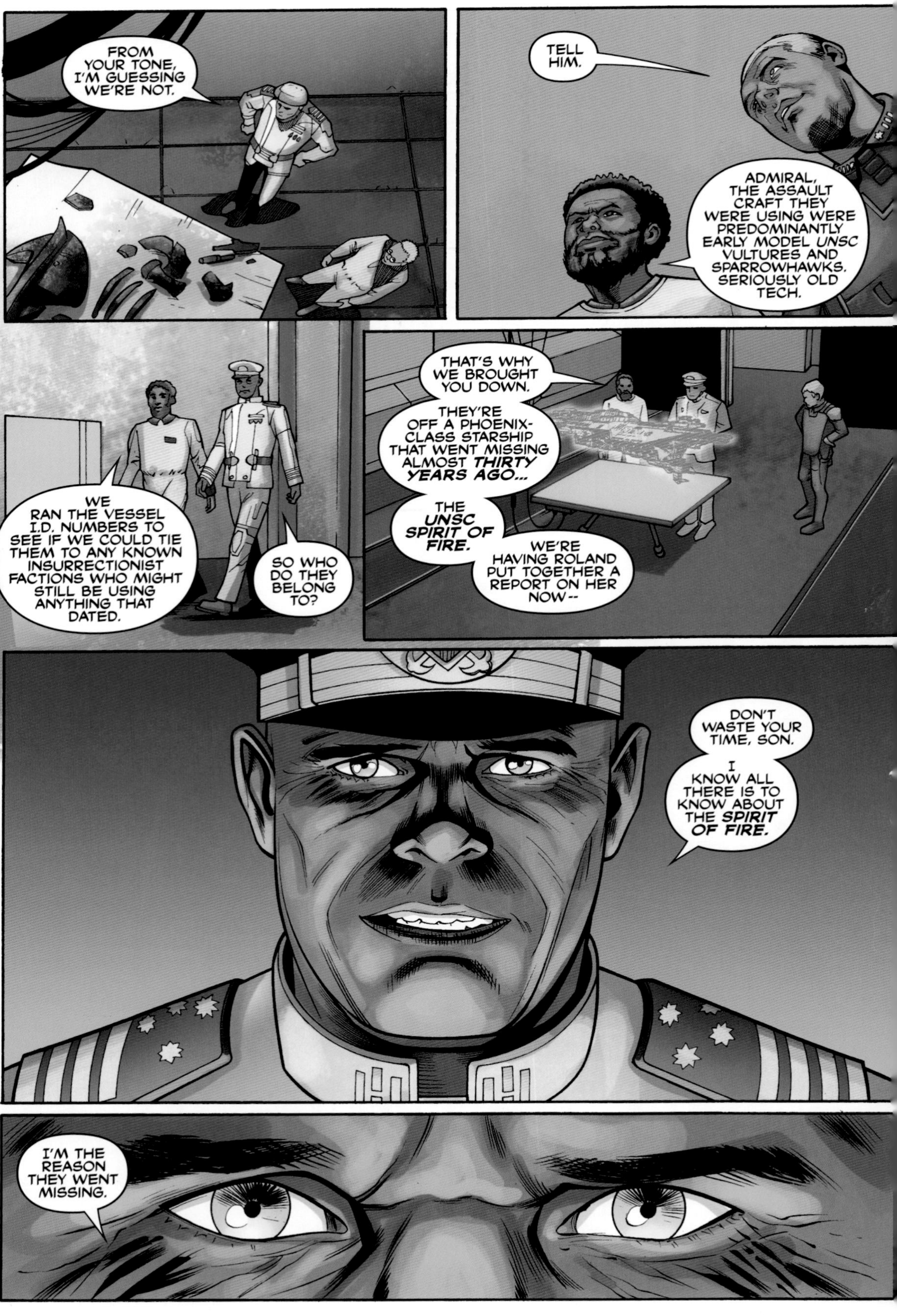

FROM YOUR TONE, I'M GUESSING WE'RE NOT.
TELL HIM.
ADMIRAL, THE ASSAULT CRAFT THEY WERE USING WERE PREDOMINANTLY EARLY MODEL *UNSC* VULTURES AND SPARROWHAWKS. SERIOUSLY OLD TECH.
WE RAN THE VESSEL I.D. NUMBERS TO SEE IF WE COULD TIE THEM TO ANY KNOWN INSURRECTIONIST FACTIONS WHO MIGHT STILL BE USING ANYTHING THAT DATED.
SO WHO DO THEY BELONG TO?
THAT'S WHY WE BROUGHT YOU DOWN.
THEY'RE OFF A PHOENIX-CLASS STARSHIP THAT WENT MISSING ALMOST ***THIRTY YEARS AGO...***
THE ***UNSC SPIRIT OF FIRE.***
WE'RE HAVING ROLAND PUT TOGETHER A REPORT ON HER NOW--
DON'T WASTE YOUR TIME, SON.
I KNOW ALL THERE IS TO KNOW ABOUT THE ***SPIRIT OF FIRE.***
I'M THE REASON THEY WENT MISSING.

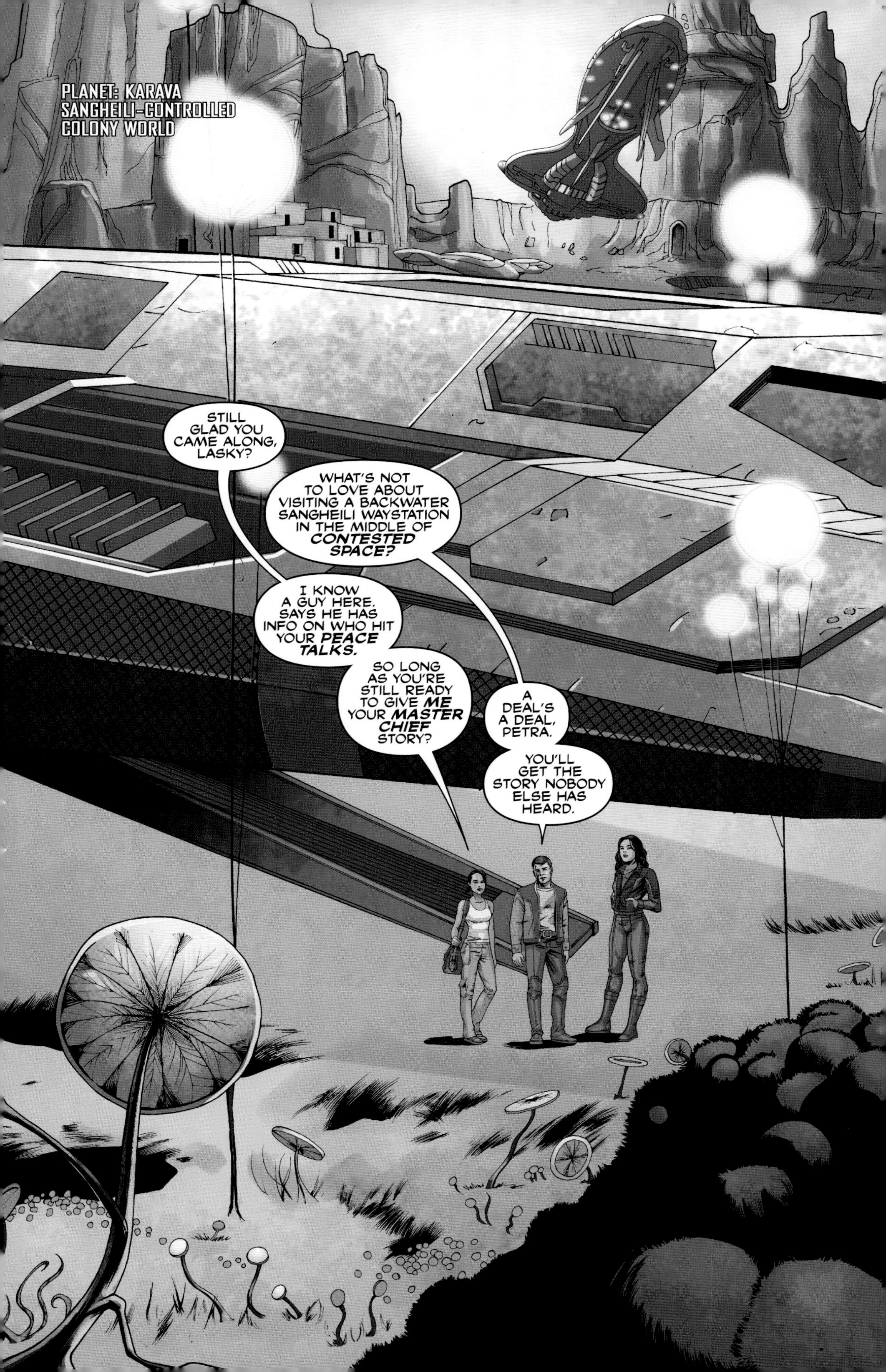
PLANET: KARAVA
SANGHEILI-CONTROLLED
COLONY WORLD
STILL GLAD YOU CAME ALONG, LASKY?
WHAT'S NOT TO LOVE ABOUT VISITING A BACKWATER SANGHEILI WAYSTATION IN THE MIDDLE OF CONTESTED SPACE?
I KNOW A GUY HERE. SAYS HE HAS INFO ON WHO HIT YOUR PEACE TALKS.
SO LONG AS YOU'RE STILL READY TO GIVE ME YOUR MASTER CHIEF STORY?
A DEAL'S A DEAL, PETRA.
YOU'LL GET THE STORY NOBODY ELSE HAS HEARD.

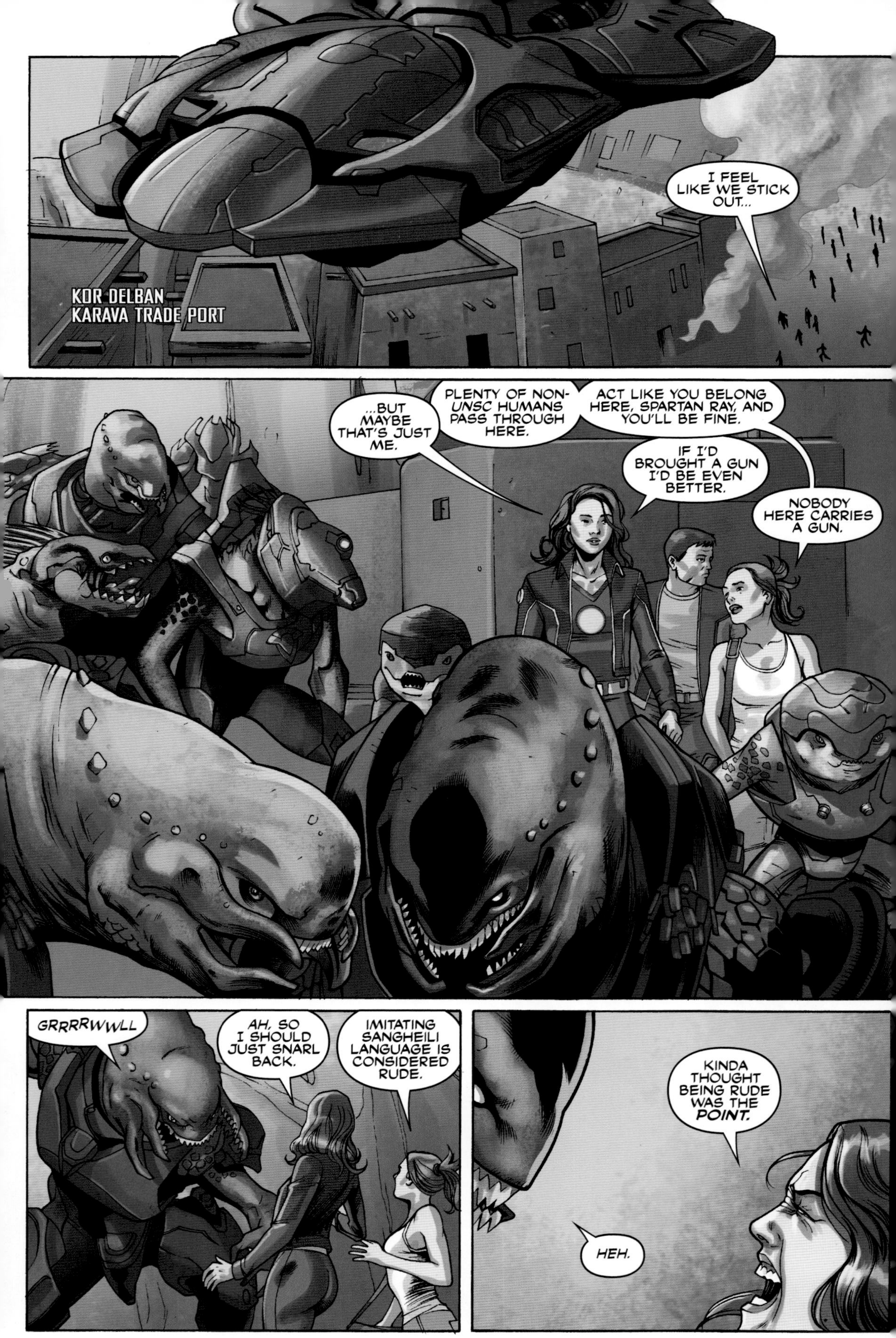
KOR DELBAN
KARAVA TRADE PORT
I FEEL LIKE WE STICK OUT...
...BUT MAYBE THAT'S JUST ME.
PLENTY OF NON-UNSC HUMANS PASS THROUGH HERE.
ACT LIKE YOU BELONG HERE, SPARTAN RAY, AND YOU'LL BE FINE.
IF I'D BROUGHT A GUN I'D BE EVEN BETTER.
NOBODY HERE CARRIES A GUN.
GRRRRWWLL
AH, SO I SHOULD JUST SNARL BACK.
IMITATING SANGHEILI LANGUAGE IS CONSIDERED RUDE.
KINDA THOUGHT BEING RUDE WAS THE POINT.
HEH.

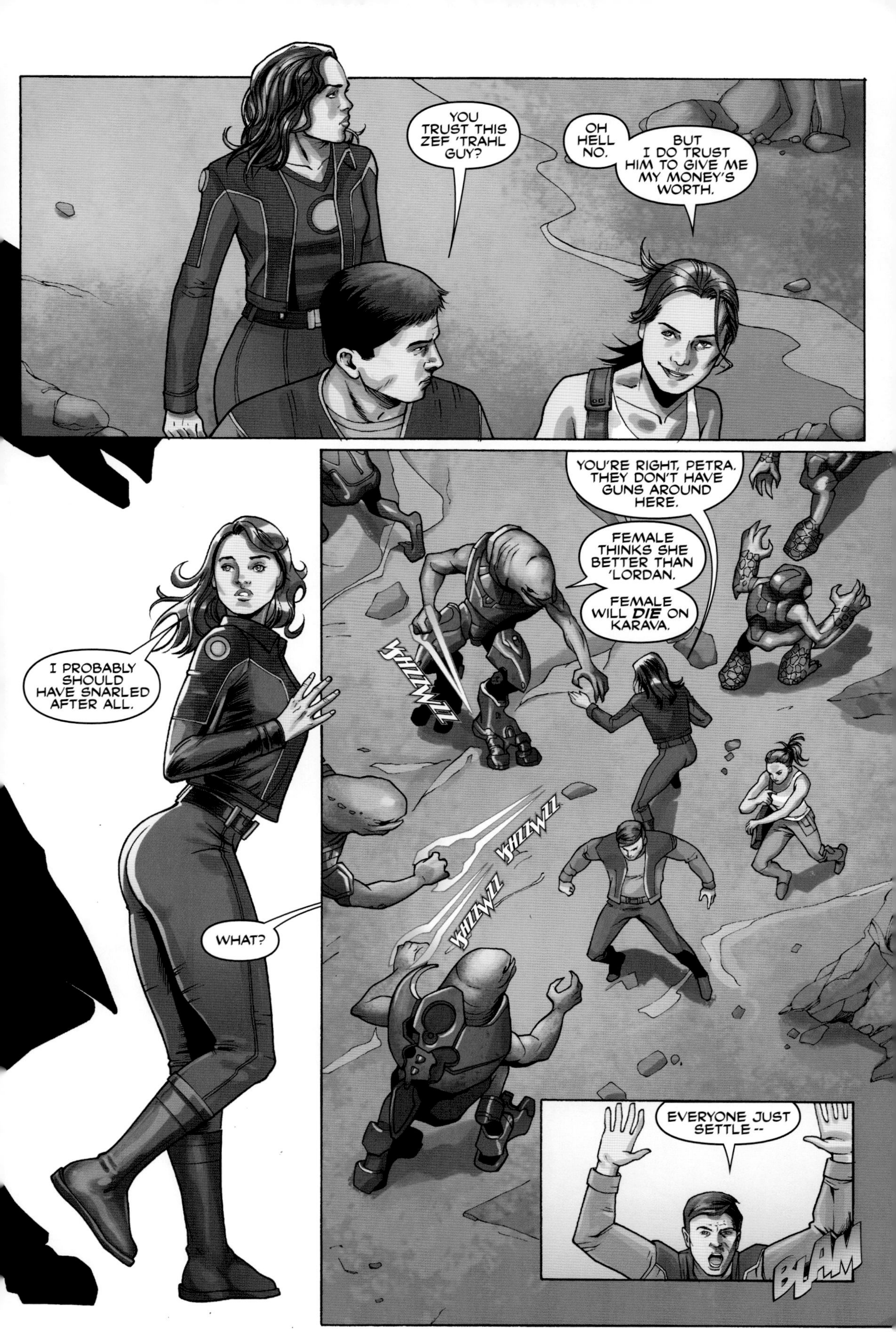
YOU TRUST THIS ZEF 'TRAHL GUY?
OH HELL NO.
BUT I DO TRUST HIM TO GIVE ME MY MONEY'S WORTH.
I PROBABLY SHOULD HAVE SNARLED AFTER ALL.
WHAT?
YOU'RE RIGHT, PETRA. THEY DON'T HAVE GUNS AROUND HERE.
FEMALE THINKS SHE BETTER THAN 'LORDAN.
FEMALE WILL DIE ON KARAVA.
WHIZWZZ
WHIZWZZ
WHIZWZZ
EVERYONE JUST SETTLE --
BLAM

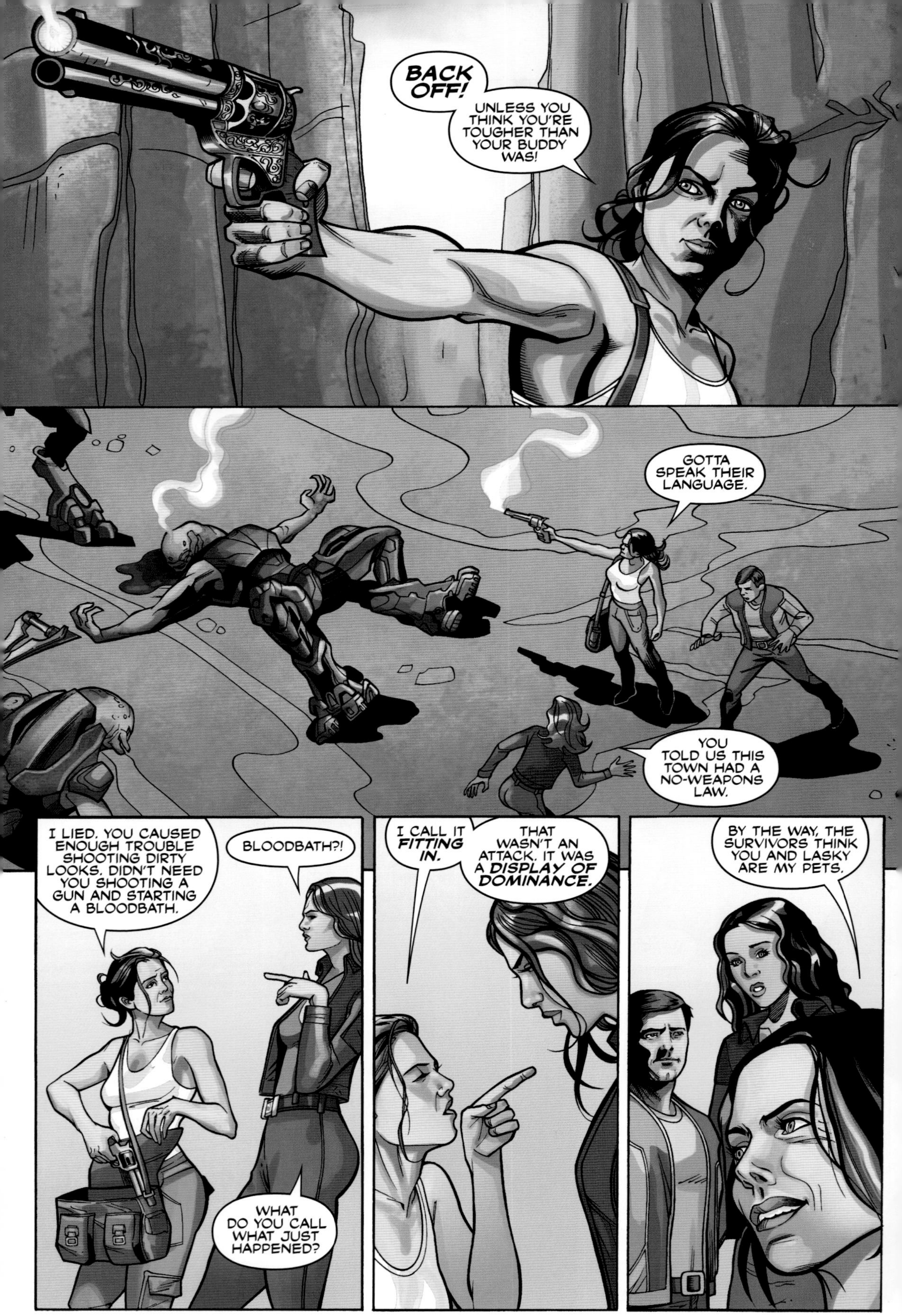
BACK OFF!
UNLESS YOU THINK YOU'RE TOUGHER THAN YOUR BUDDY WAS!
GOTTA SPEAK THEIR LANGUAGE.
YOU TOLD US THIS TOWN HAD A NO-WEAPONS LAW.
I LIED. YOU CAUSED ENOUGH TROUBLE SHOOTING DIRTY LOOKS. DIDN'T NEED YOU SHOOTING A GUN AND STARTING A BLOODBATH.
BLOODBATH?!
WHAT DO YOU CALL WHAT JUST HAPPENED?
I CALL IT FITTING IN.
THAT WASN'T AN ATTACK. IT WAS A DISPLAY OF DOMINANCE.
BY THE WAY, THE SURVIVORS THINK YOU AND LASKY ARE MY PETS.

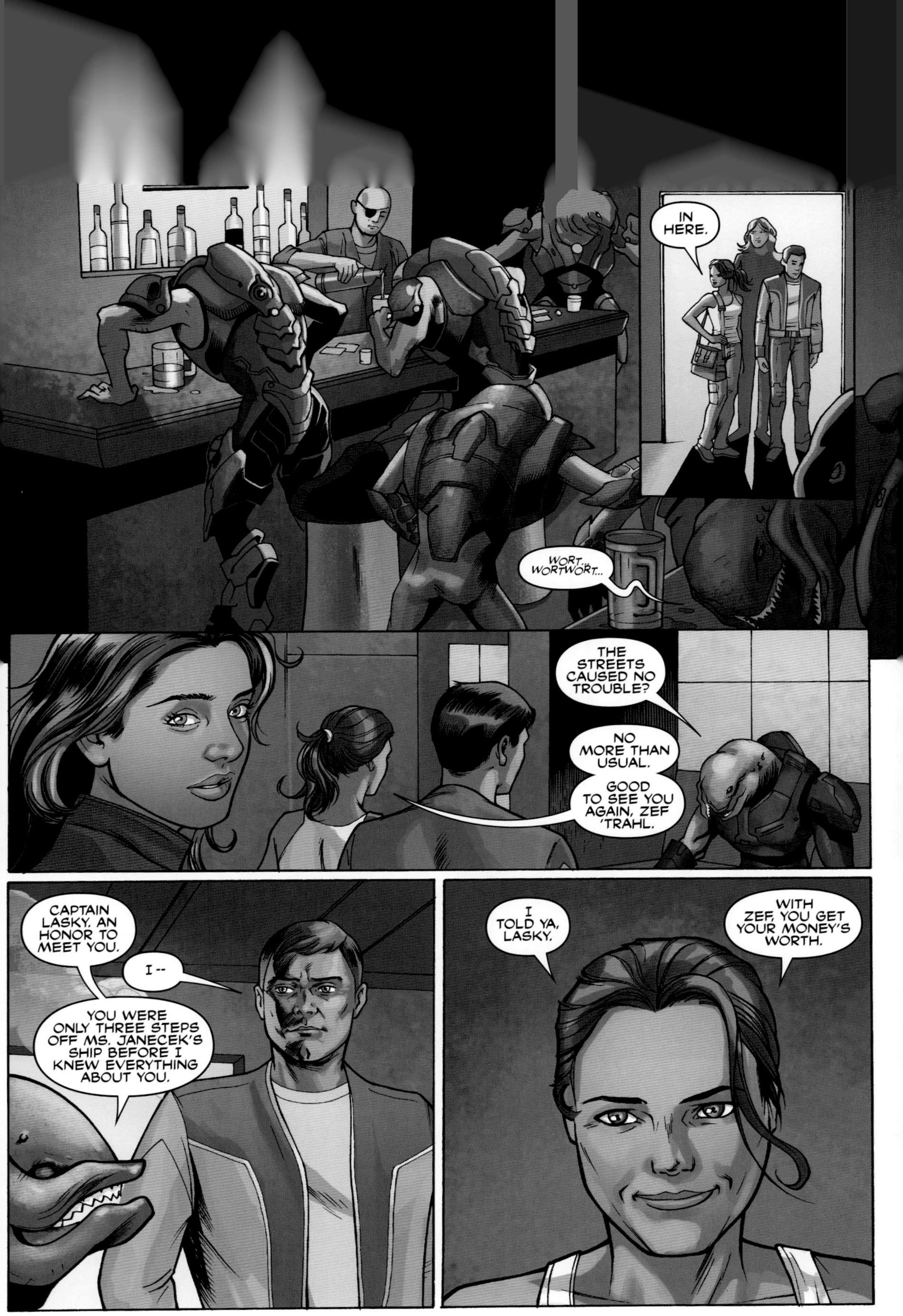
IN HERE.
WORT... WORTWORT...
THE STREETS CAUSED NO TROUBLE?
NO MORE THAN USUAL.
GOOD TO SEE YOU AGAIN, ZEF 'TRAHL.
CAPTAIN LASKY. AN HONOR TO MEET YOU.
I --
YOU WERE ONLY THREE STEPS OFF MS. JANECEK'S SHIP BEFORE I KNEW EVERYTHING ABOUT YOU.
I TOLD YA, LASKY.
WITH ZEF, YOU GET YOUR MONEY'S WORTH.

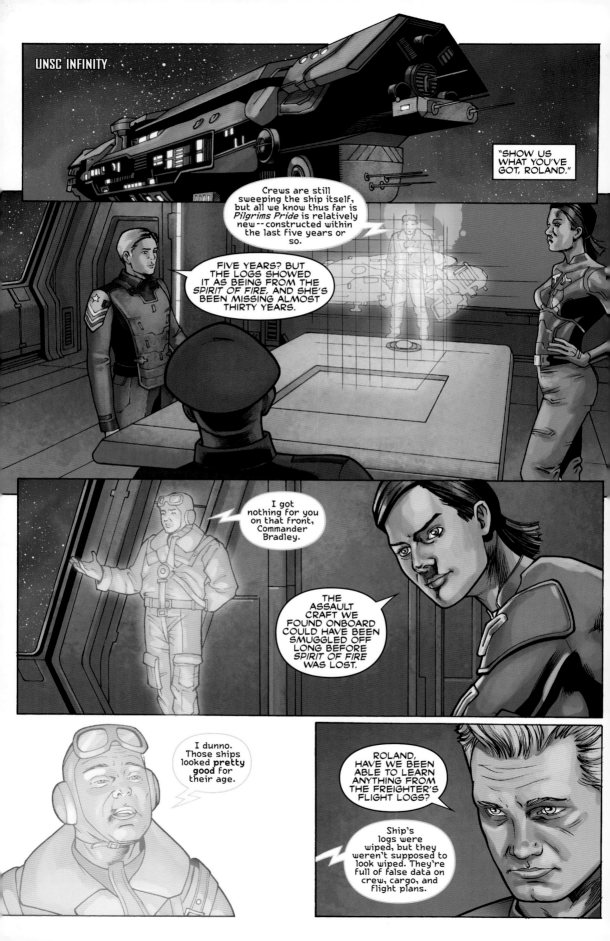

UNSC INFINITY

"SHOW US WHAT YOU'VE GOT, ROLAND."

Crews are still sweeping the ship itself, but all we know thus far is *Pilgrims Pride* is relatively new -- constructed within the last five years or so.

FIVE YEARS? BUT THE LOGS SHOWED IT AS BEING FROM THE *SPIRIT OF FIRE*, AND SHE'S BEEN MISSING ALMOST THIRTY YEARS.

I got nothing for you on that front, Commander Bradley.

THE ASSAULT CRAFT WE FOUND ONBOARD COULD HAVE BEEN SMUGGLED OFF LONG BEFORE *SPIRIT OF FIRE* WAS LOST.

I dunno. Those ships looked **pretty good** for their age.

ROLAND, HAVE WE BEEN ABLE TO LEARN ANYTHING FROM THE FREIGHTER'S FLIGHT LOGS?

Ship's logs were wiped, but they weren't supposed to look wiped. They're full of false data on crew, cargo, and flight plans.

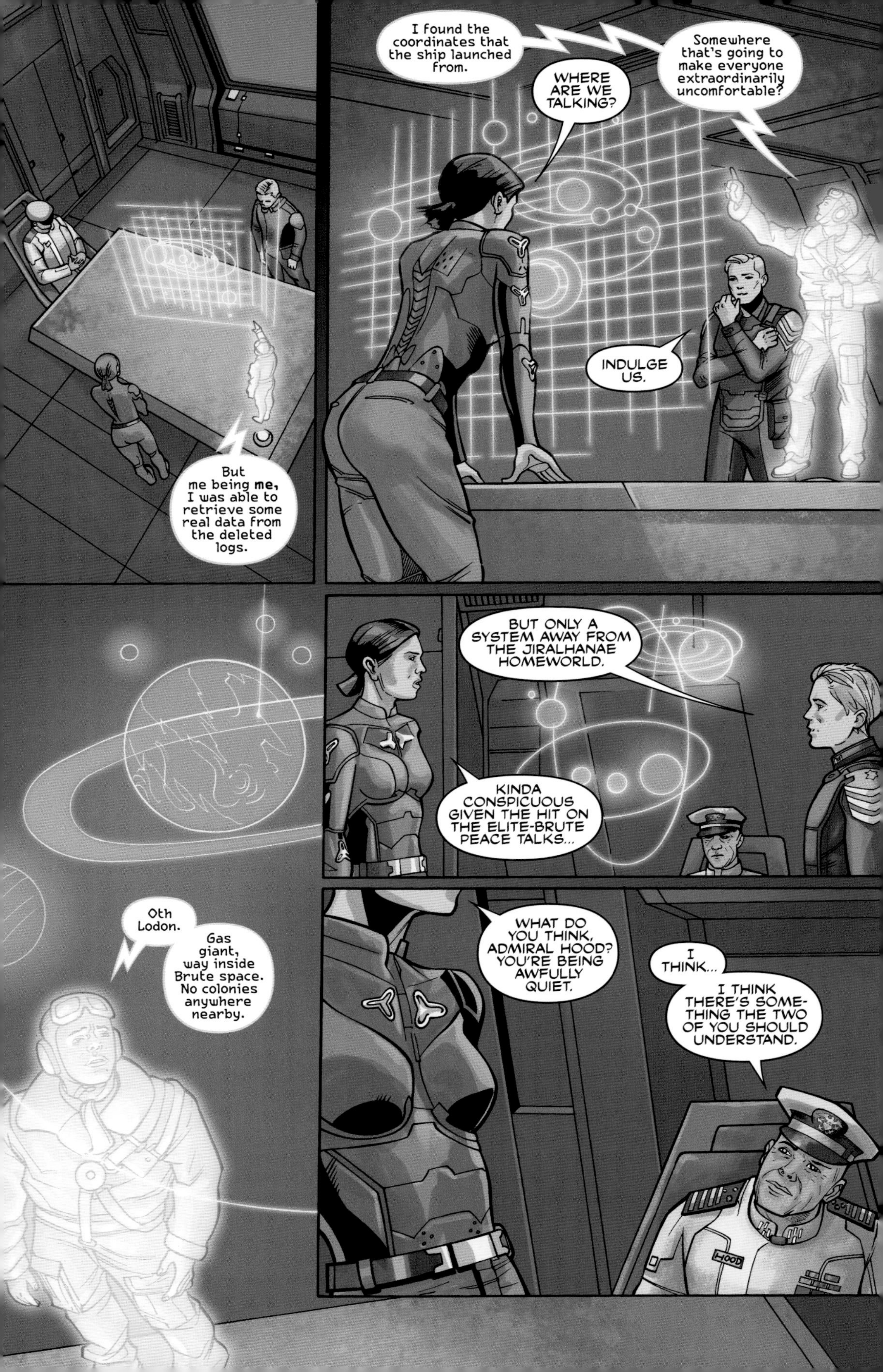

But me being me, I was able to retrieve some real data from the deleted logs.
I found the coordinates that the ship launched from.
Somewhere that's going to make everyone extraordinarily uncomfortable?
WHERE ARE WE TALKING?
INDULGE US.
Oth Lodon.
Gas giant, way inside Brute space. No colonies anywhere nearby.
BUT ONLY A SYSTEM AWAY FROM THE JIRALHANAE HOMEWORLD.
KINDA CONSPICUOUS GIVEN THE HIT ON THE ELITE-BRUTE PEACE TALKS...
WHAT DO YOU THINK, ADMIRAL HOOD? YOU'RE BEING AWFULLY QUIET.
I THINK...
I THINK THERE'S SOME-THING THE TWO OF YOU SHOULD UNDERSTAND.
HOOD

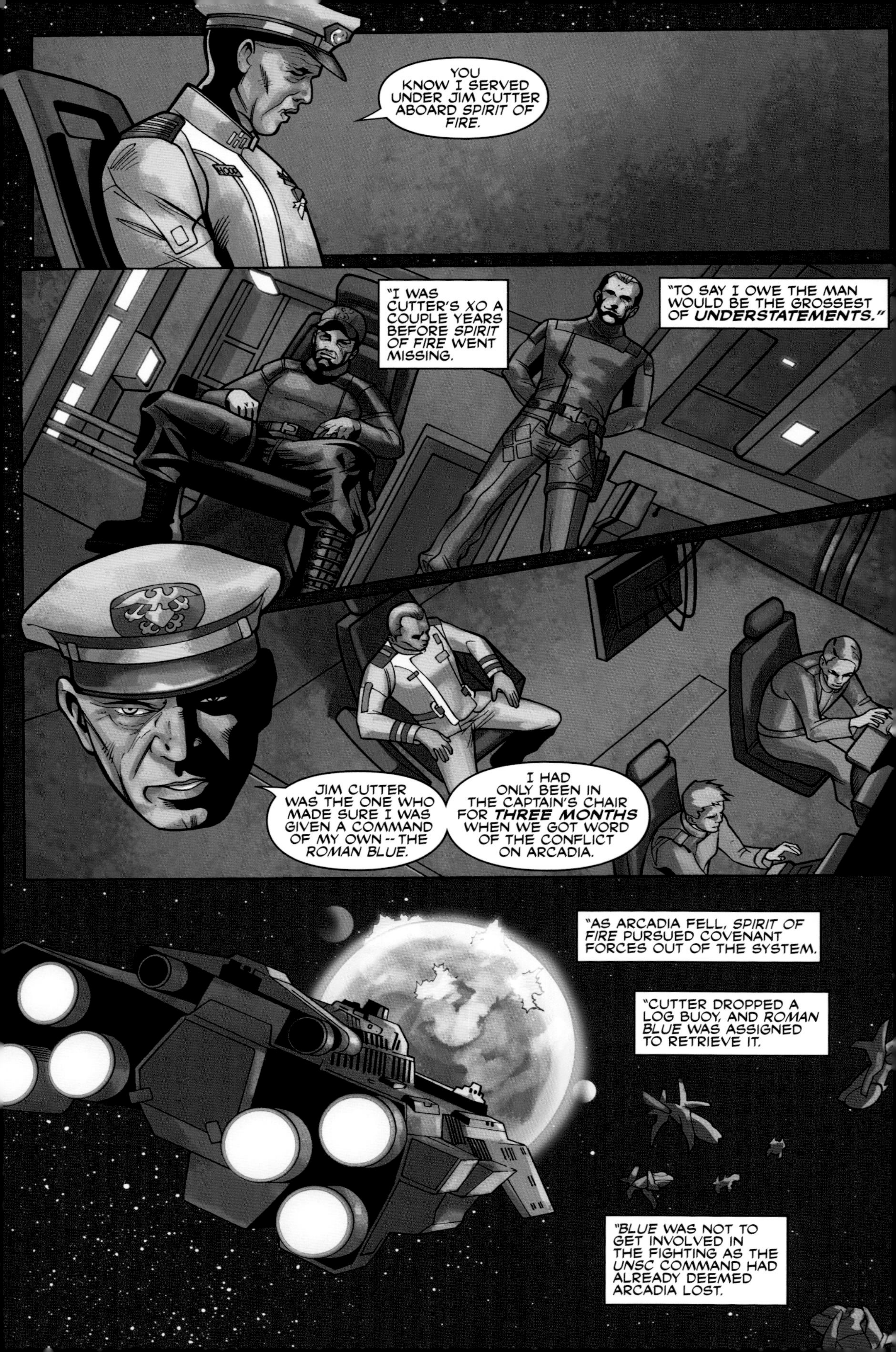
YOU KNOW I SERVED UNDER JIM CUTTER ABOARD *SPIRIT OF FIRE.*
"I WAS CUTTER'S *XO* A COUPLE YEARS BEFORE *SPIRIT OF FIRE* WENT MISSING.
"TO SAY I OWE THE MAN WOULD BE THE GROSSEST OF ***UNDERSTATEMENTS."***
JIM CUTTER WAS THE ONE WHO MADE SURE I WAS GIVEN A COMMAND OF MY OWN -- THE *ROMAN BLUE.*
I HAD ONLY BEEN IN THE CAPTAIN'S CHAIR FOR ***THREE MONTHS*** WHEN WE GOT WORD OF THE CONFLICT ON ARCADIA.
"AS ARCADIA FELL, *SPIRIT OF FIRE* PURSUED COVENANT FORCES OUT OF THE SYSTEM.
"CUTTER DROPPED A LOG BUOY, AND *ROMAN BLUE* WAS ASSIGNED TO RETRIEVE IT.
"*BLUE* WAS NOT TO GET INVOLVED IN THE FIGHTING AS THE *UNSC* COMMAND HAD ALREADY DEEMED ARCADIA LOST.

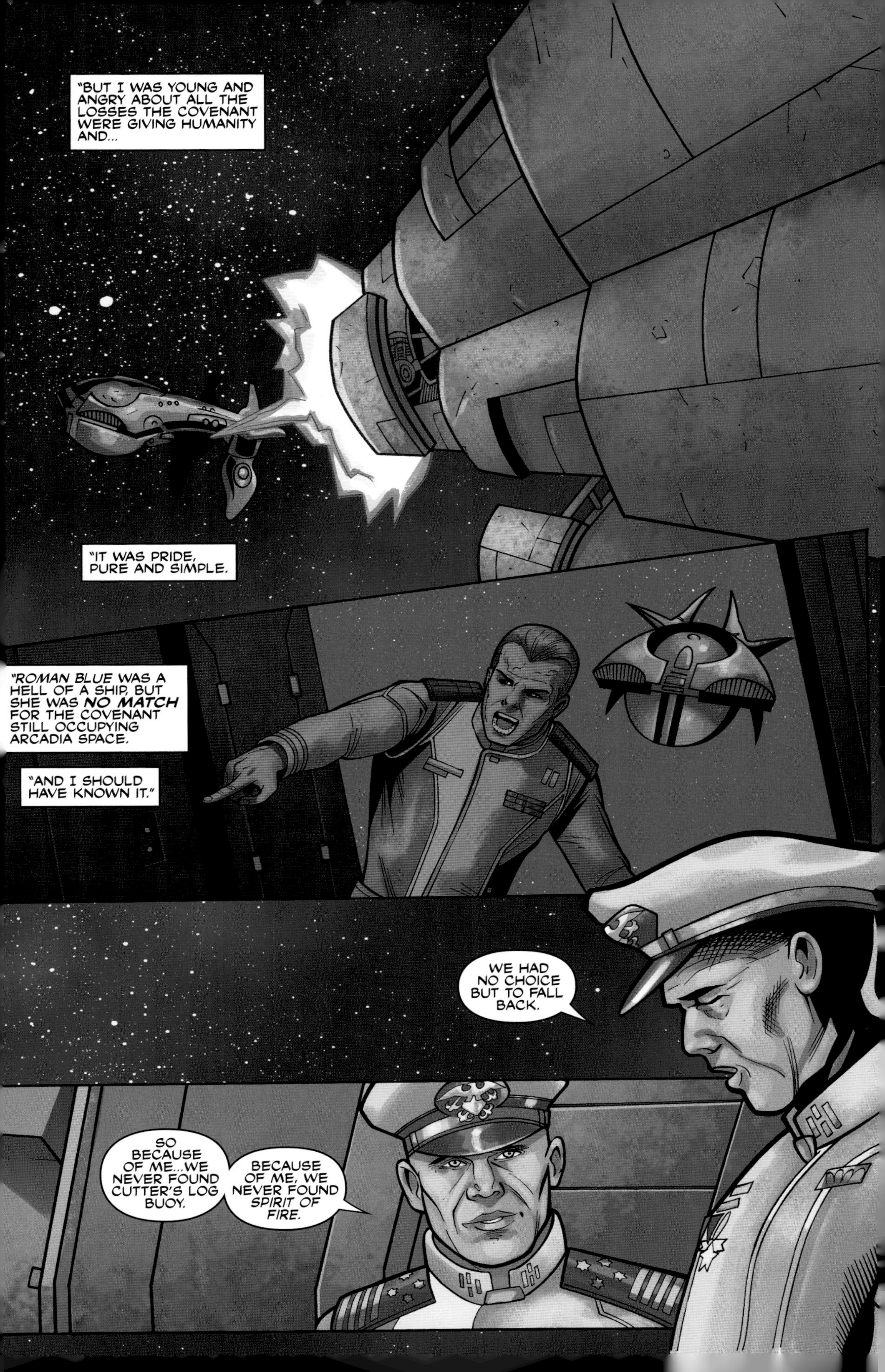
"BUT I WAS YOUNG AND ANGRY ABOUT ALL THE LOSSES THE COVENANT WERE GIVING HUMANITY AND...
"IT WAS PRIDE, PURE AND SIMPLE.
"ROMAN BLUE WAS A HELL OF A SHIP, BUT SHE WAS NO MATCH FOR THE COVENANT STILL OCCUPYING ARCADIA SPACE.
"AND I SHOULD HAVE KNOWN IT."
WE HAD NO CHOICE BUT TO FALL BACK.
SO BECAUSE OF ME...WE NEVER FOUND CUTTER'S LOG BUOY.
BECAUSE OF ME, WE NEVER FOUND SPIRIT OF FIRE.

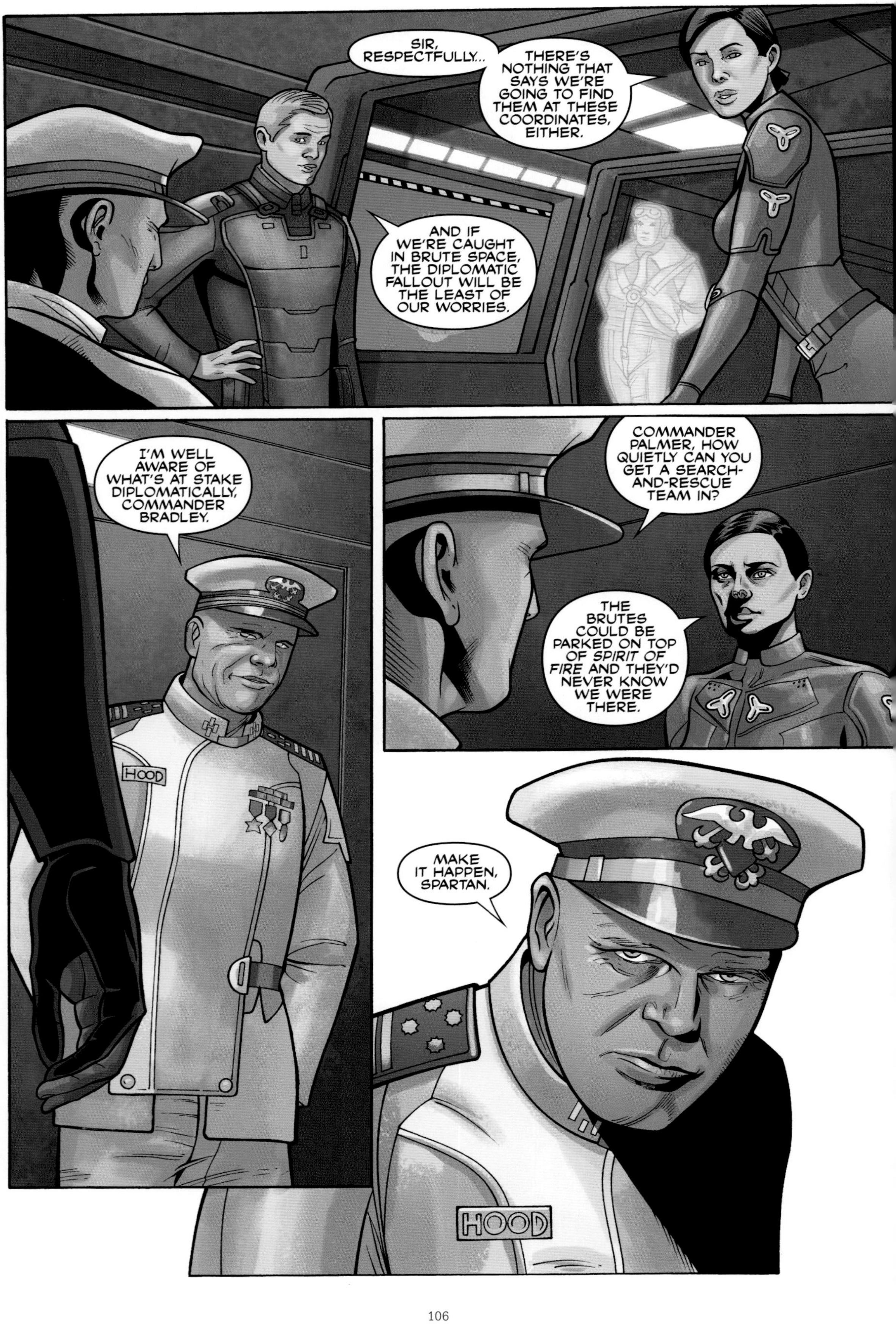
SIR, RESPECTFULLY...
THERE'S NOTHING THAT SAYS WE'RE GOING TO FIND THEM AT THESE COORDINATES, EITHER.
AND IF WE'RE CAUGHT IN BRUTE SPACE, THE DIPLOMATIC FALLOUT WILL BE THE LEAST OF OUR WORRIES.
I'M WELL AWARE OF WHAT'S AT STAKE DIPLOMATICALLY, COMMANDER BRADLEY.
HOOD
COMMANDER PALMER, HOW QUIETLY CAN YOU GET A SEARCH-AND-RESCUE TEAM IN?
THE BRUTES COULD BE PARKED ON TOP OF *SPIRIT OF FIRE* AND THEY'D NEVER KNOW WE WERE THERE.
MAKE IT HAPPEN, SPARTAN.
HOOD

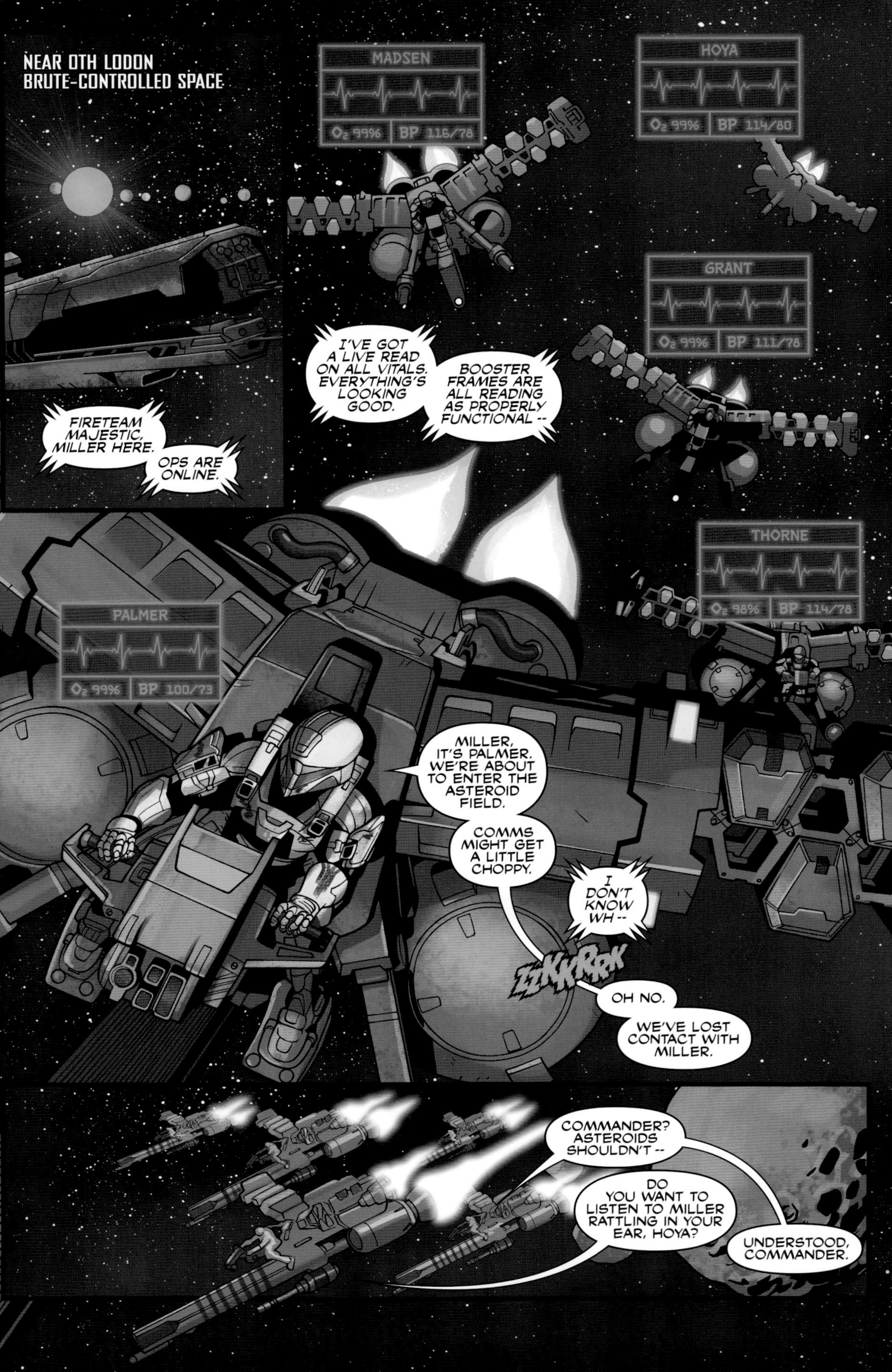
NEAR OTH LODON
BRUTE-CONTROLLED SPACE
FIRETEAM MAJESTIC, MILLER HERE.
OPS ARE ONLINE.
MADSEN
O₂ 99% BP 116/78
HOYA
O₂ 99% BP 114/80
I'VE GOT A LIVE READ ON ALL VITALS. EVERYTHING'S LOOKING GOOD.
BOOSTER FRAMES ARE ALL READING AS PROPERLY FUNCTIONAL --
GRANT
O₂ 99% BP 111/78
THORNE
O₂ 98% BP 114/78
PALMER
O₂ 99% BP 100/73
MILLER, IT'S PALMER. WE'RE ABOUT TO ENTER THE ASTEROID FIELD.
COMMS MIGHT GET A LITTLE CHOPPY.
I DON'T KNOW WH --
ZZKKRRK
OH NO.
WE'VE LOST CONTACT WITH MILLER.
COMMANDER? ASTEROIDS SHOULDN'T --
DO YOU WANT TO LISTEN TO MILLER RATTLING IN YOUR EAR, HOYA?
UNDERSTOOD, COMMANDER.

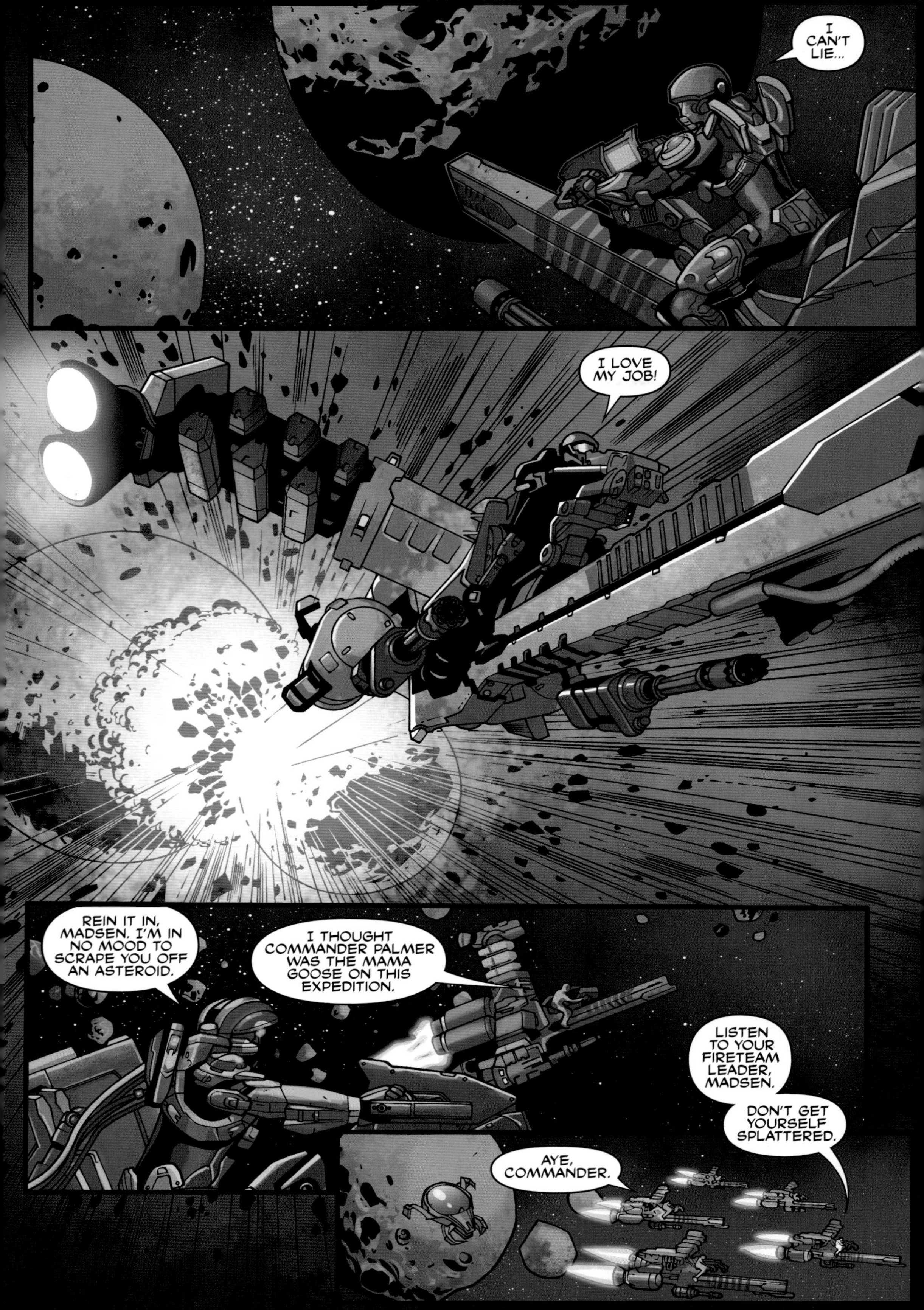
I CAN'T LIE...
I LOVE MY JOB!
REIN IT IN, MADSEN. I'M IN NO MOOD TO SCRAPE YOU OFF AN ASTEROID.
I THOUGHT COMMANDER PALMER WAS THE MAMA GOOSE ON THIS EXPEDITION.
LISTEN TO YOUR FIRETEAM LEADER, MADSEN.
DON'T GET YOURSELF SPLATTERED.
AYE, COMMANDER.

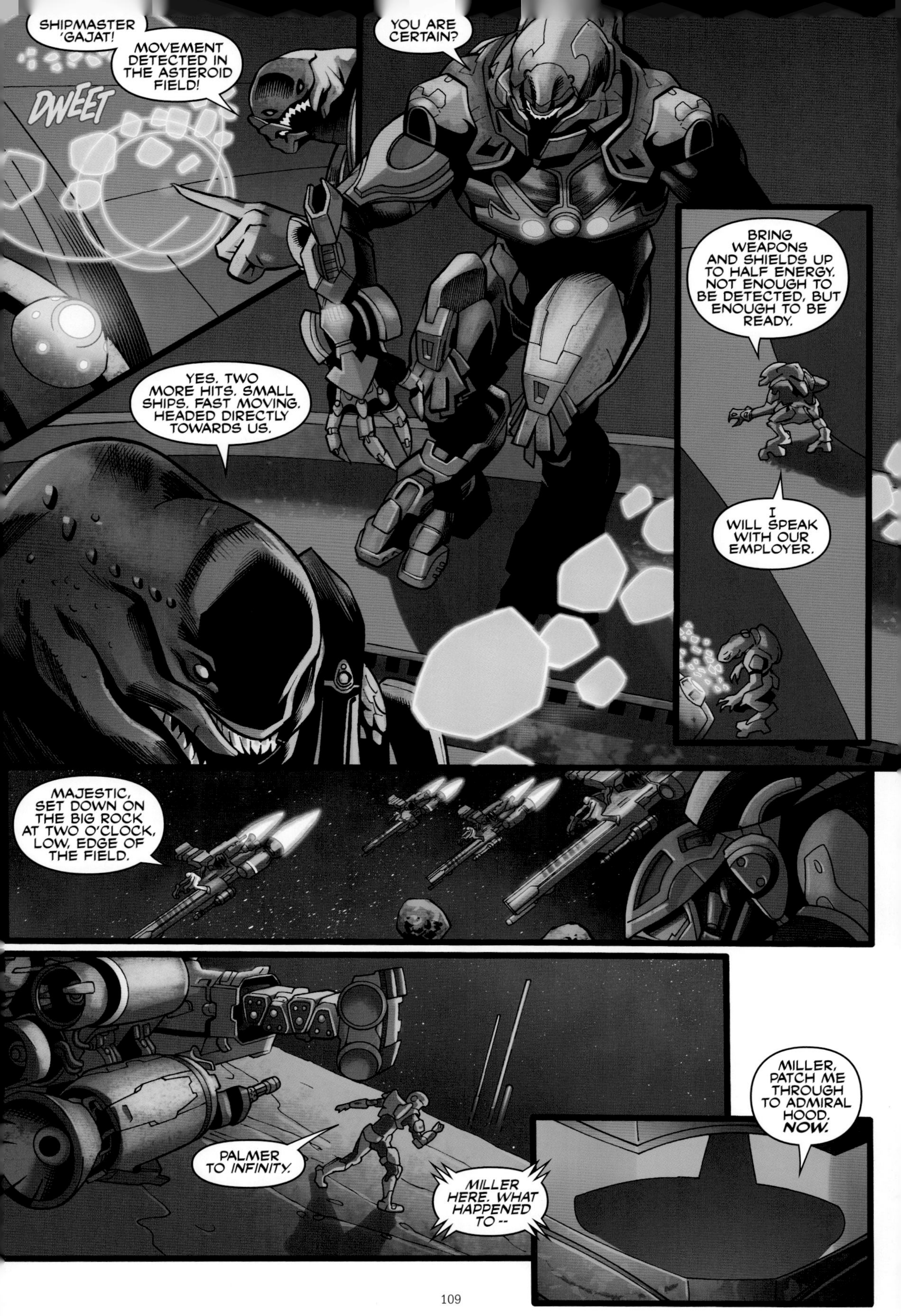
SHIPMASTER 'GAJAT!
MOVEMENT DETECTED IN THE ASTEROID FIELD!
DWEET
YOU ARE CERTAIN?
YES. TWO MORE HITS. SMALL SHIPS. FAST MOVING. HEADED DIRECTLY TOWARDS US.
BRING WEAPONS AND SHIELDS UP TO HALF ENERGY. NOT ENOUGH TO BE DETECTED, BUT ENOUGH TO BE READY.
I WILL SPEAK WITH OUR EMPLOYER.
MAJESTIC, SET DOWN ON THE BIG ROCK AT TWO O'CLOCK, LOW, EDGE OF THE FIELD.
PALMER TO *INFINITY.*
MILLER HERE. WHAT HAPPENED TO --
MILLER, PATCH ME THROUGH TO ADMIRAL HOOD. ***NOW.***

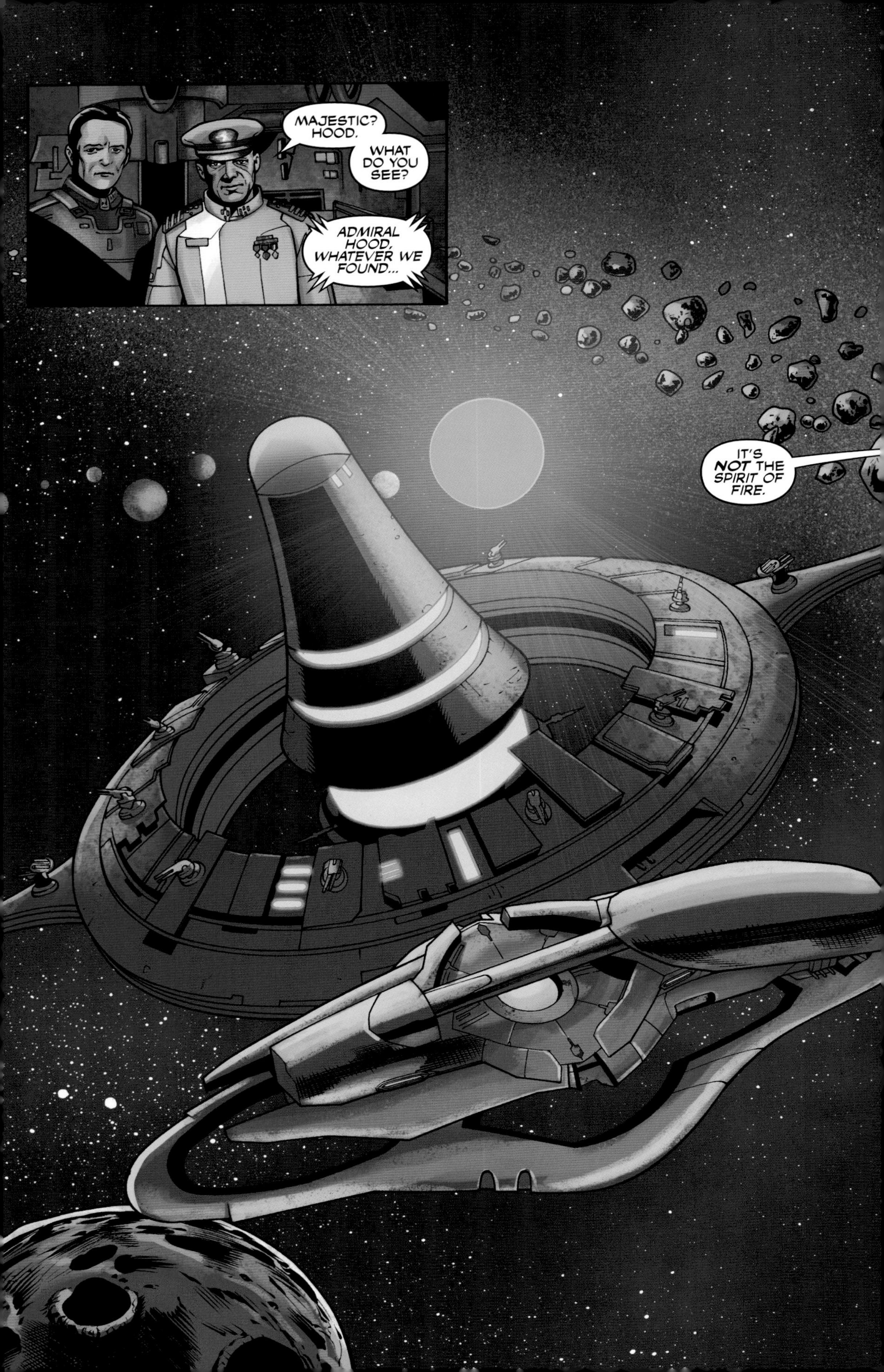

MAJESTIC? HOOD.
WHAT DO YOU SEE?
ADMIRAL HOOD, WHATEVER WE FOUND...
IT'S NOT THE SPIRIT OF FIRE.

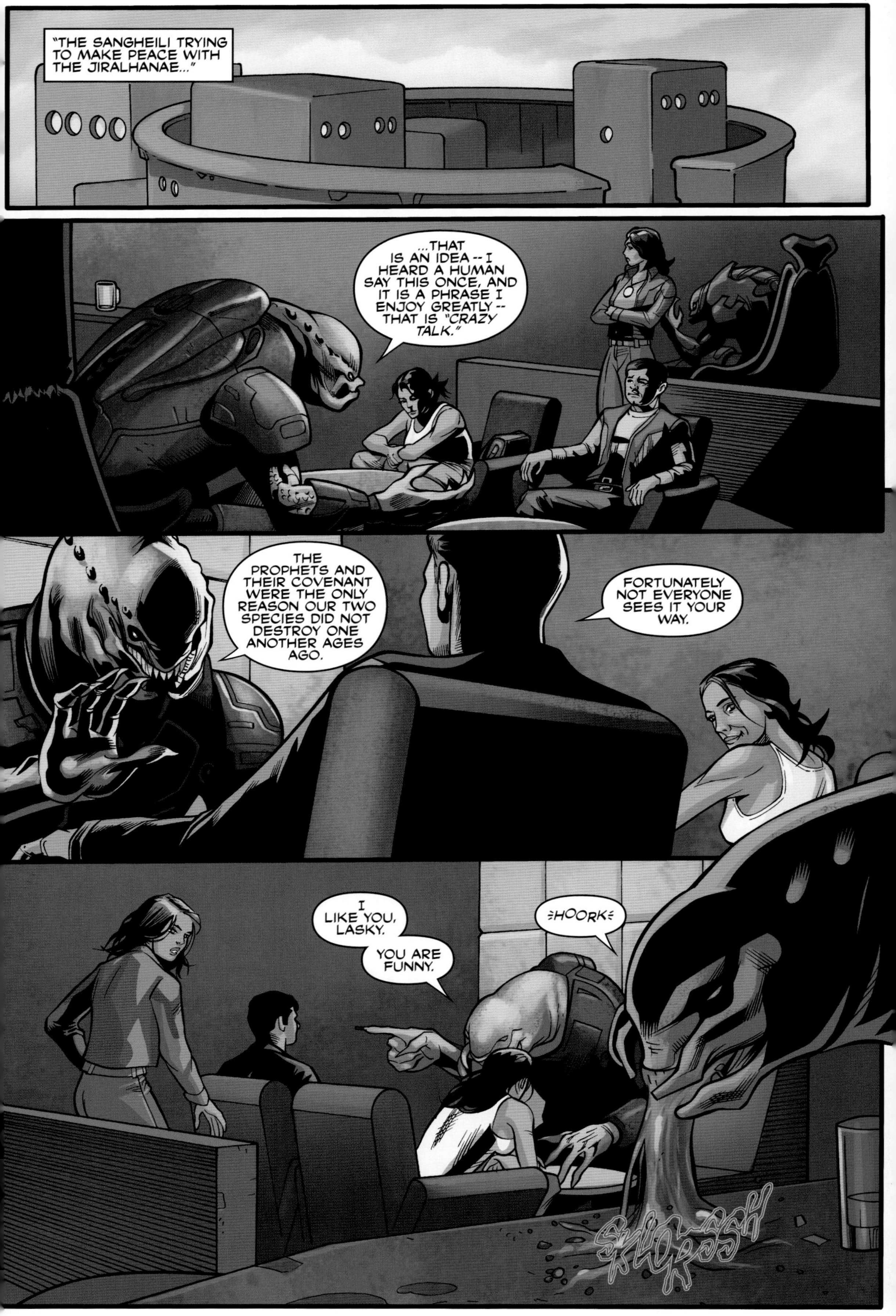
"THE SANGHEILI TRYING TO MAKE PEACE WITH THE JIRALHANAE..."
...THAT IS AN IDEA -- I HEARD A HUMAN SAY THIS ONCE, AND IT IS A PHRASE I ENJOY GREATLY -- THAT IS "CRAZY TALK."
THE PROPHETS AND THEIR COVENANT WERE THE ONLY REASON OUR TWO SPECIES DID NOT DESTROY ONE ANOTHER AGES AGO.
FORTUNATELY NOT EVERYONE SEES IT YOUR WAY.
I LIKE YOU, LASKY.
YOU ARE FUNNY.
HOORK
SHLORSSH

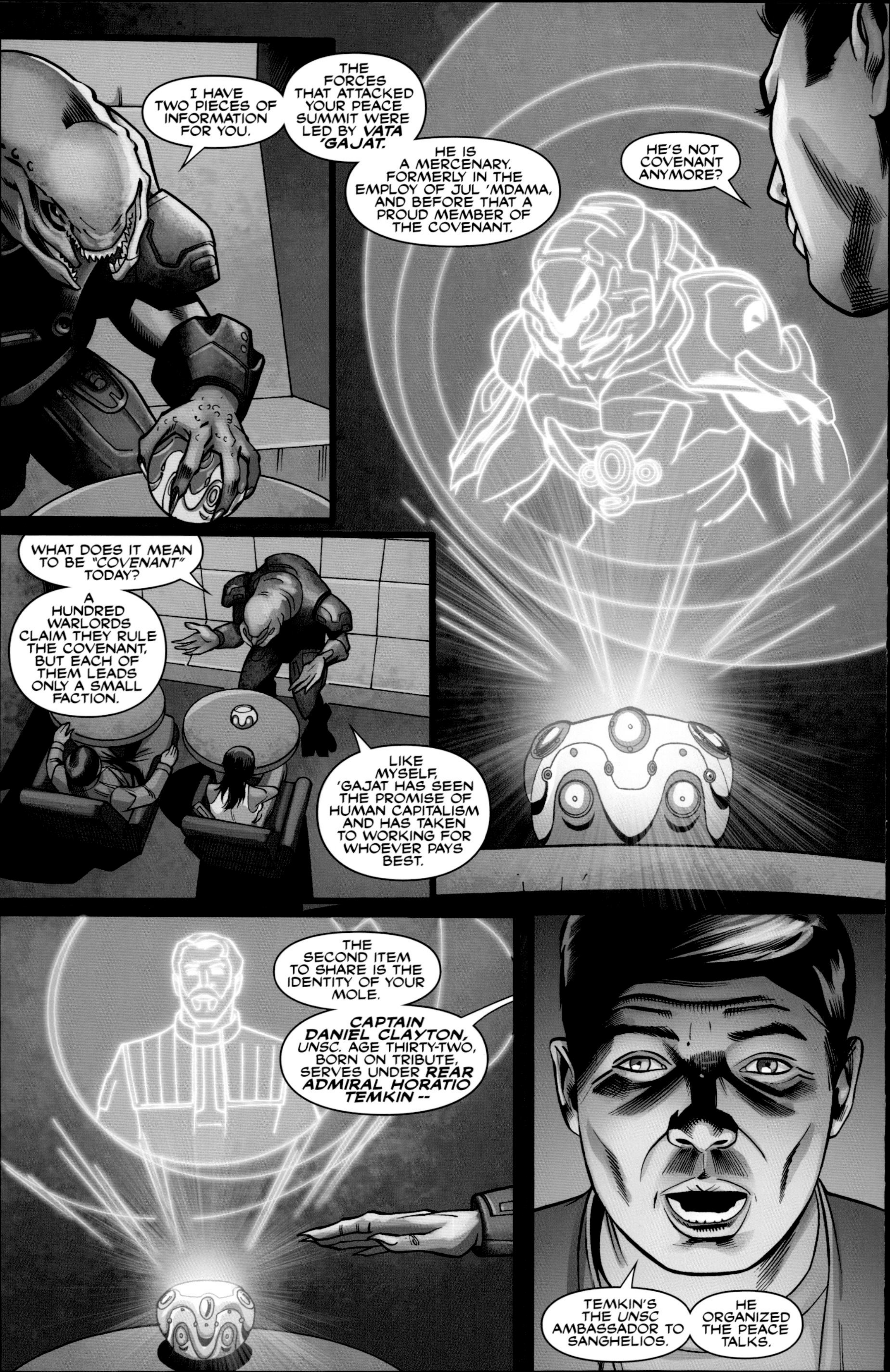
I HAVE TWO PIECES OF INFORMATION FOR YOU.
THE FORCES THAT ATTACKED YOUR PEACE SUMMIT WERE LED BY *VATA 'GAJAT.*
HE IS A MERCENARY. FORMERLY IN THE EMPLOY OF JUL 'MDAMA, AND BEFORE THAT A PROUD MEMBER OF THE COVENANT.
HE'S NOT COVENANT ANYMORE?
WHAT DOES IT MEAN TO BE *"COVENANT"* TODAY?
A HUNDRED WARLORDS CLAIM THEY RULE THE COVENANT, BUT EACH OF THEM LEADS ONLY A SMALL FACTION.
LIKE MYSELF, 'GAJAT HAS SEEN THE PROMISE OF HUMAN CAPITALISM AND HAS TAKEN TO WORKING FOR WHOEVER PAYS BEST.
THE SECOND ITEM TO SHARE IS THE IDENTITY OF YOUR MOLE.
CAPTAIN DANIEL CLAYTON, *UNSC.* AGE THIRTY-TWO, BORN ON TRIBUTE, SERVES UNDER ***REAR ADMIRAL HORATIO TEMKIN --***
TEMKIN'S THE *UNSC* AMBASSADOR TO SANGHELIOS.
HE ORGANIZED THE PEACE TALKS.

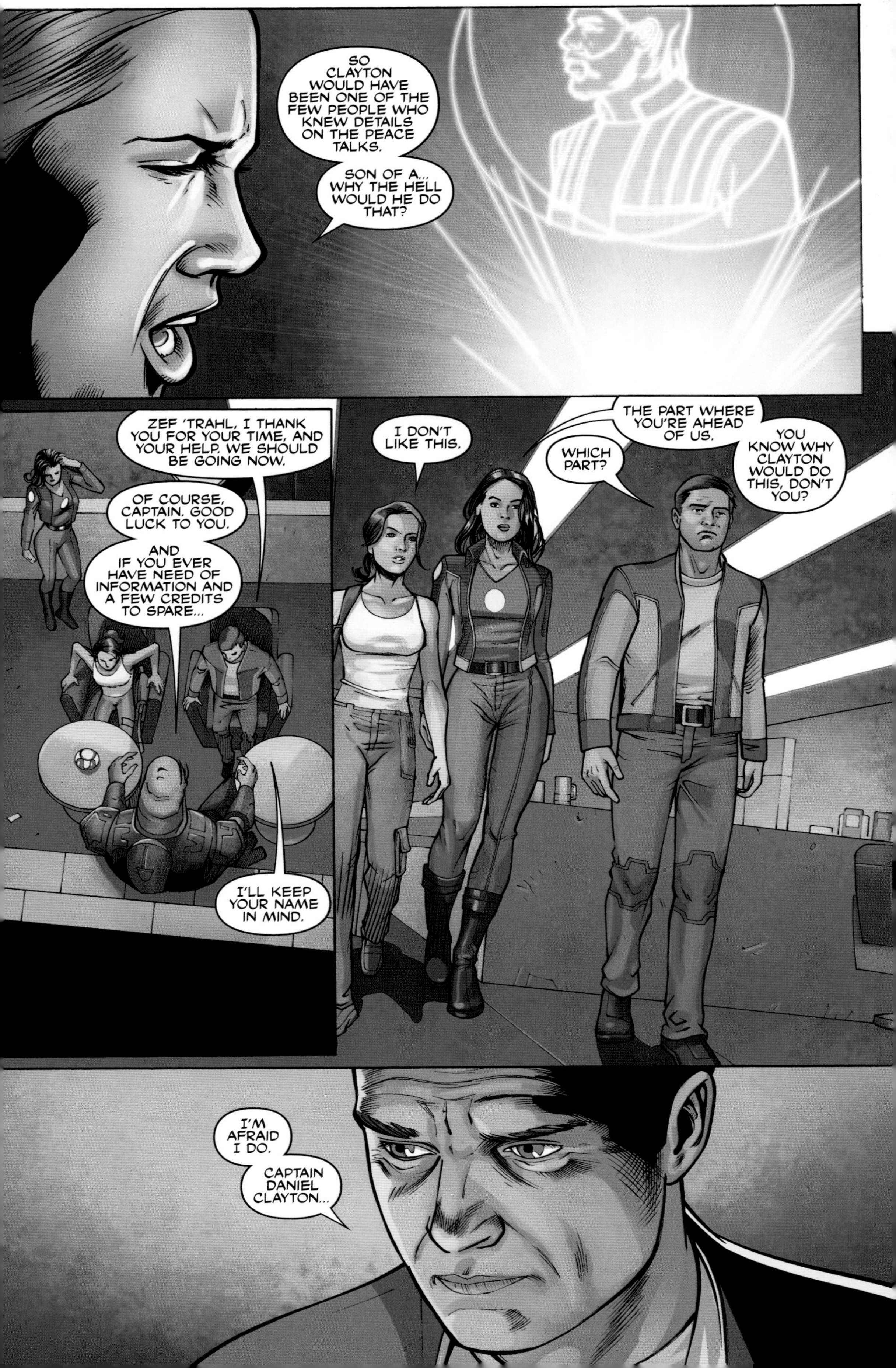
SO CLAYTON WOULD HAVE BEEN ONE OF THE FEW PEOPLE WHO KNEW DETAILS ON THE PEACE TALKS.
SON OF A... WHY THE HELL WOULD HE DO THAT?
ZEF 'TRAHL, I THANK YOU FOR YOUR TIME, AND YOUR HELP. WE SHOULD BE GOING NOW.
OF COURSE, CAPTAIN. GOOD LUCK TO YOU.
AND IF YOU EVER HAVE NEED OF INFORMATION AND A FEW CREDITS TO SPARE...
I'LL KEEP YOUR NAME IN MIND.
I DON'T LIKE THIS.
WHICH PART?
THE PART WHERE YOU'RE AHEAD OF US.
YOU KNOW WHY CLAYTON WOULD DO THIS, DON'T YOU?
I'M AFRAID I DO.
CAPTAIN DANIEL CLAYTON...

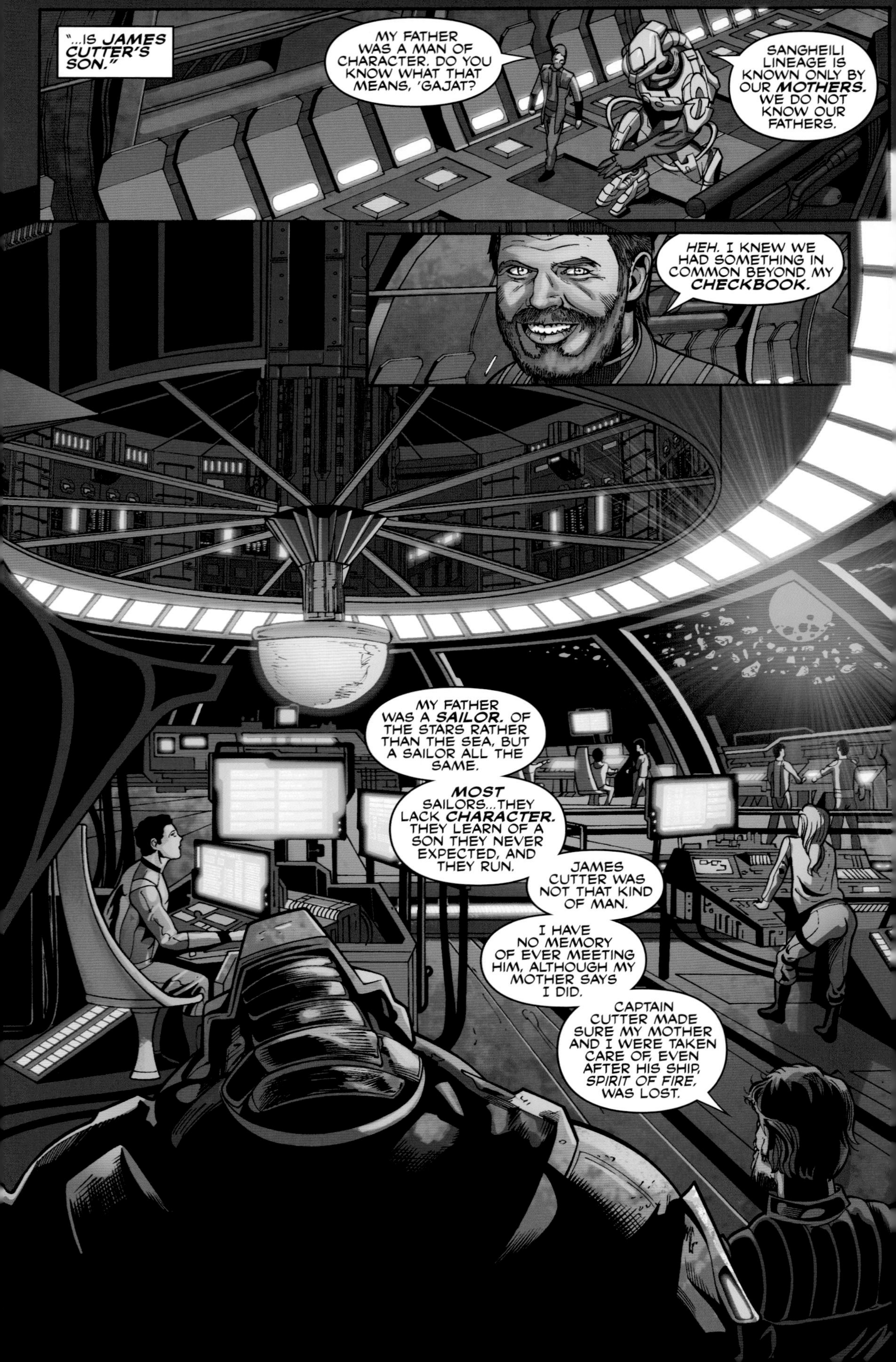
"...IS JAMES CUTTER'S SON."
MY FATHER WAS A MAN OF CHARACTER. DO YOU KNOW WHAT THAT MEANS, 'GAJAT?
SANGHEILI LINEAGE IS KNOWN ONLY BY OUR MOTHERS. WE DO NOT KNOW OUR FATHERS.
HEH. I KNEW WE HAD SOMETHING IN COMMON BEYOND MY CHECKBOOK.
MY FATHER WAS A SAILOR. OF THE STARS RATHER THAN THE SEA, BUT A SAILOR ALL THE SAME.
MOST SAILORS...THEY LACK CHARACTER. THEY LEARN OF A SON THEY NEVER EXPECTED, AND THEY RUN.
JAMES CUTTER WAS NOT THAT KIND OF MAN.
I HAVE NO MEMORY OF EVER MEETING HIM, ALTHOUGH MY MOTHER SAYS I DID.
CAPTAIN CUTTER MADE SURE MY MOTHER AND I WERE TAKEN CARE OF, EVEN AFTER HIS SHIP, SPIRIT OF FIRE, WAS LOST.

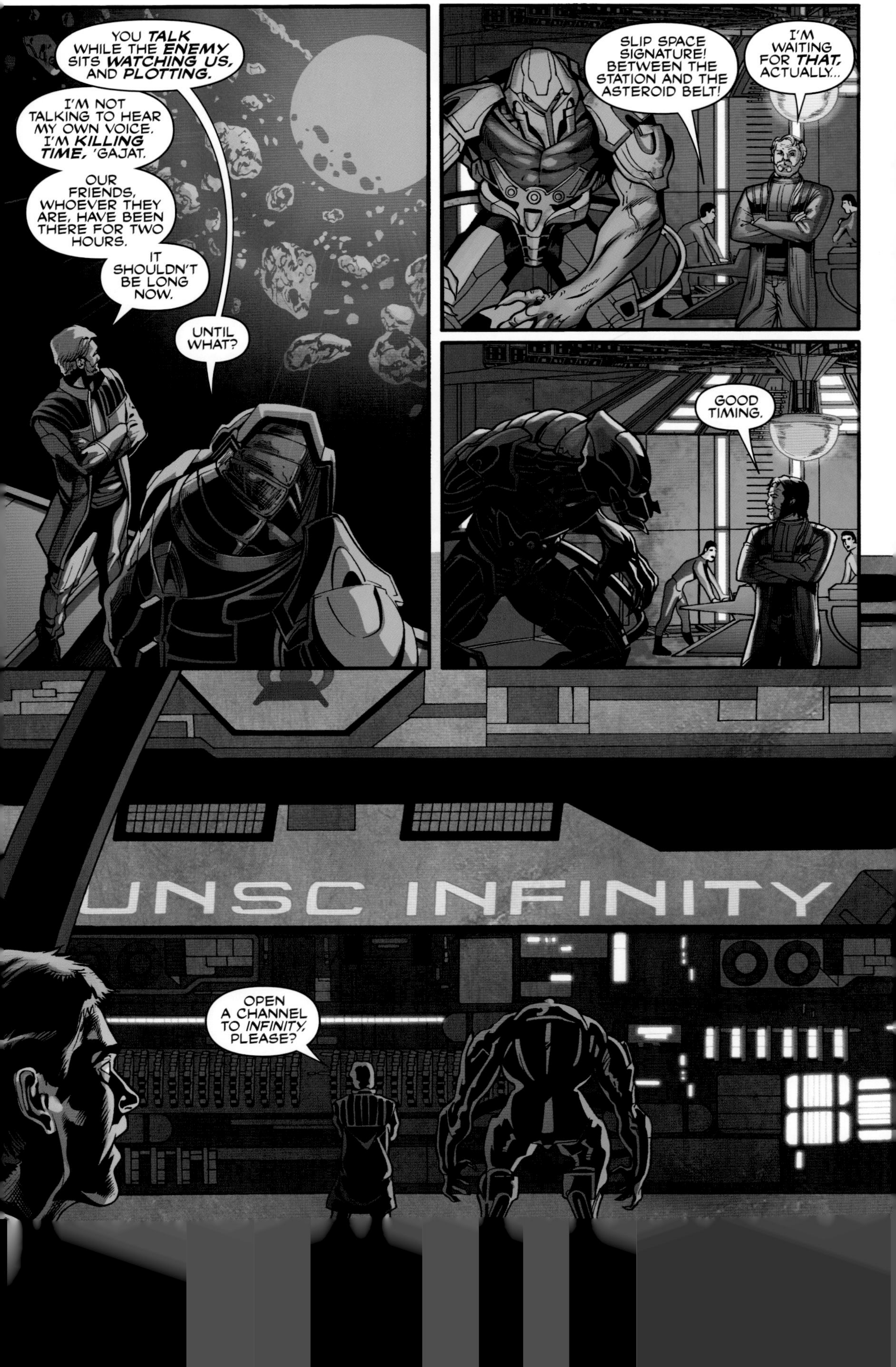
YOU TALK WHILE THE ENEMY SITS WATCHING US, AND PLOTTING.
I'M NOT TALKING TO HEAR MY OWN VOICE. I'M KILLING TIME, 'GAJAT.
OUR FRIENDS, WHOEVER THEY ARE, HAVE BEEN THERE FOR TWO HOURS.
IT SHOULDN'T BE LONG NOW.
UNTIL WHAT?
SLIP SPACE SIGNATURE! BETWEEN THE STATION AND THE ASTEROID BELT!
I'M WAITING FOR THAT, ACTUALLY...
GOOD TIMING.
UNSC INFINITY
OPEN A CHANNEL TO INFINITY, PLEASE?

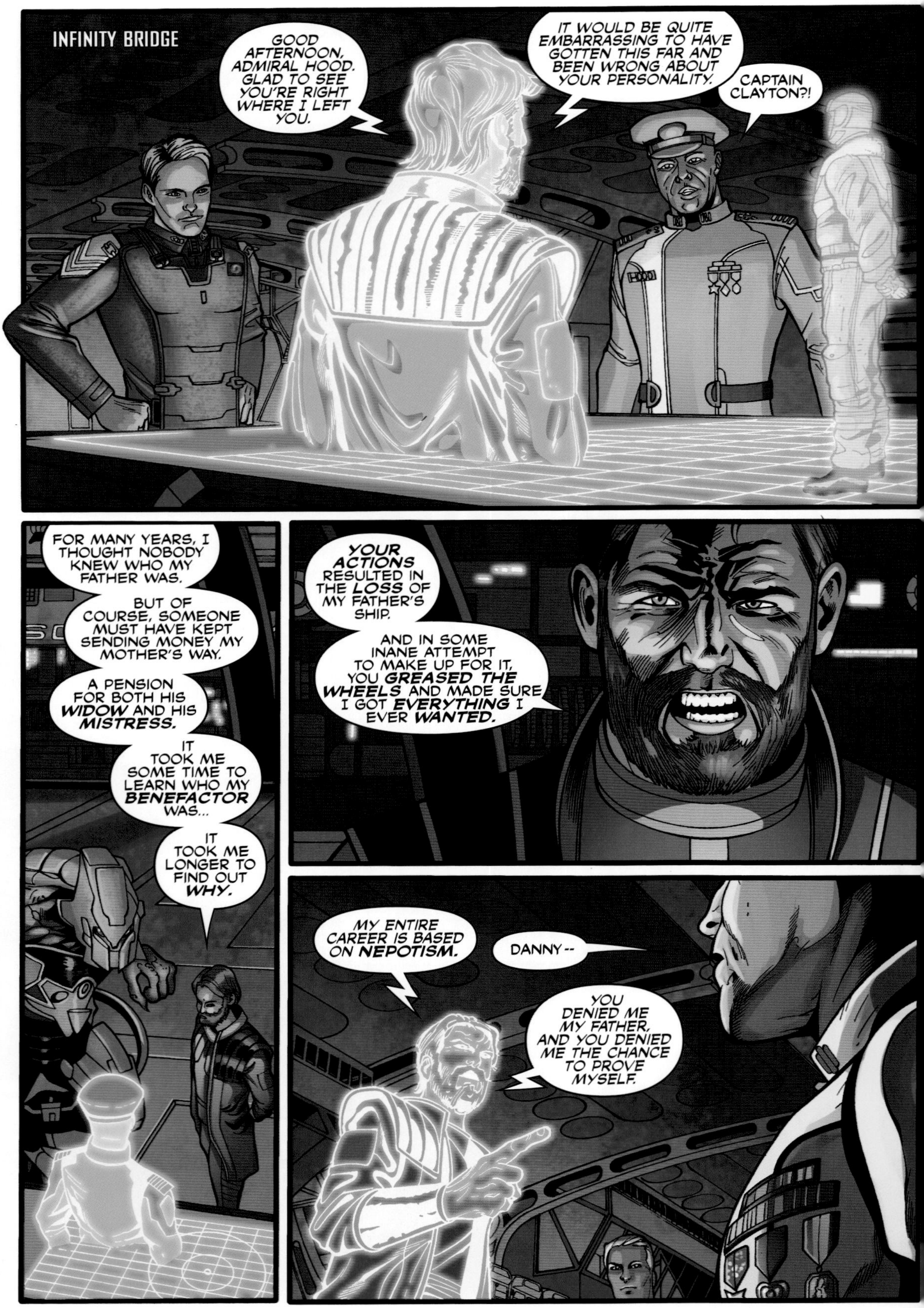
INFINITY BRIDGE
GOOD AFTERNOON, ADMIRAL HOOD. GLAD TO SEE YOU'RE RIGHT WHERE I LEFT YOU.
IT WOULD BE QUITE EMBARRASSING TO HAVE GOTTEN THIS FAR AND BEEN WRONG ABOUT YOUR PERSONALITY.
CAPTAIN CLAYTON?!
FOR MANY YEARS, I THOUGHT NOBODY KNEW WHO MY FATHER WAS.
BUT OF COURSE, SOMEONE MUST HAVE KEPT SENDING MONEY MY MOTHER'S WAY.
A PENSION FOR BOTH HIS WIDOW AND HIS MISTRESS.
IT TOOK ME SOME TIME TO LEARN WHO MY BENEFACTOR WAS...
IT TOOK ME LONGER TO FIND OUT WHY.
YOUR ACTIONS RESULTED IN THE LOSS OF MY FATHER'S SHIP.
AND IN SOME INANE ATTEMPT TO MAKE UP FOR IT, YOU GREASED THE WHEELS AND MADE SURE I GOT EVERYTHING I EVER WANTED.
MY ENTIRE CAREER IS BASED ON NEPOTISM.
DANNY --
YOU DENIED ME MY FATHER, AND YOU DENIED ME THE CHANCE TO PROVE MYSELF.

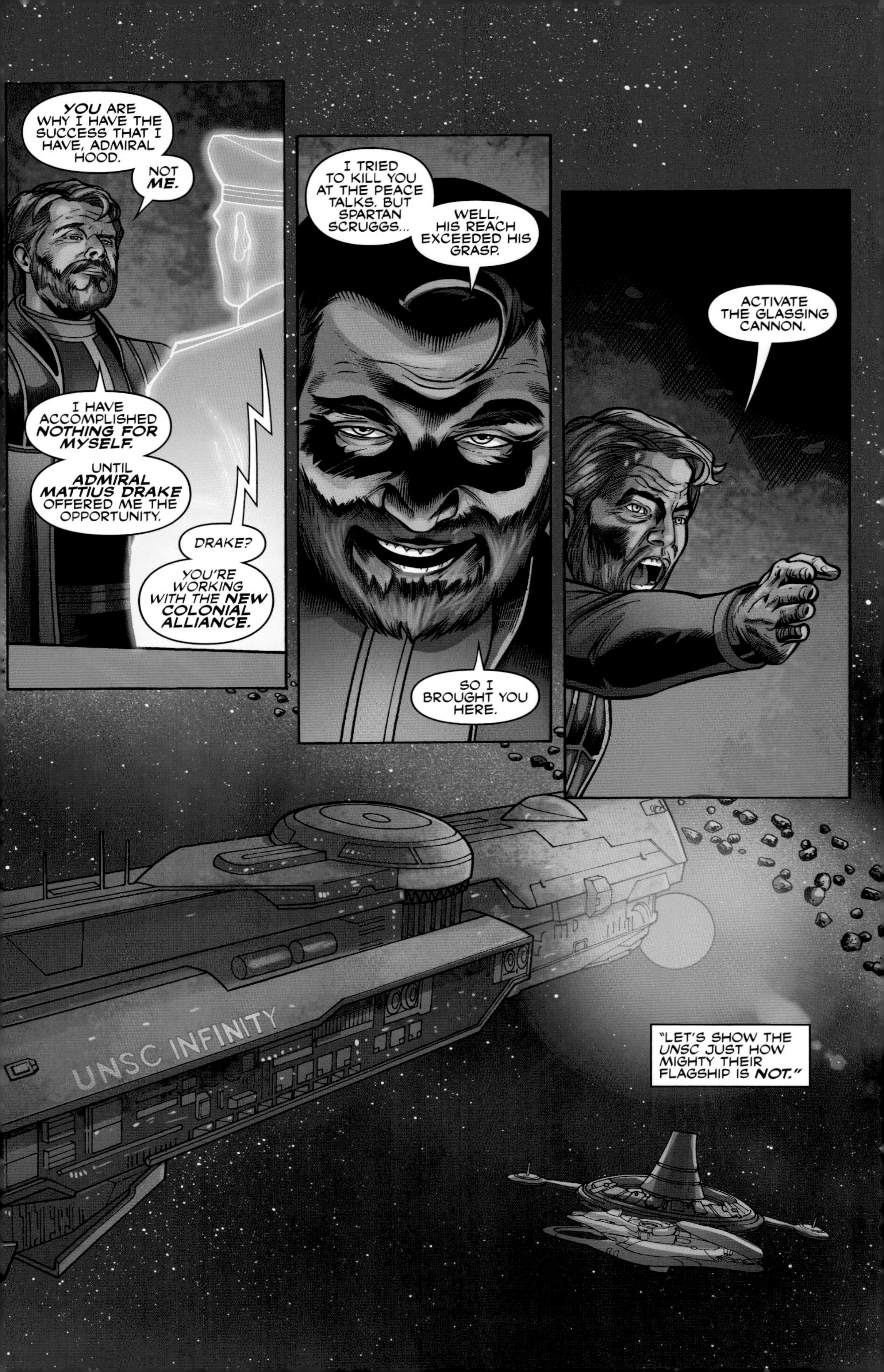
YOU ARE WHY I HAVE THE SUCCESS THAT I HAVE, ADMIRAL HOOD.
NOT ME.
I HAVE ACCOMPLISHED NOTHING FOR MYSELF.
UNTIL ADMIRAL MATTIUS DRAKE OFFERED ME THE OPPORTUNITY.
DRAKE?
YOU'RE WORKING WITH THE NEW COLONIAL ALLIANCE.
I TRIED TO KILL YOU AT THE PEACE TALKS. BUT SPARTAN SCRUGGS...
WELL, HIS REACH EXCEEDED HIS GRASP.
SO I BROUGHT YOU HERE.
ACTIVATE THE GLASSING CANNON.
UNSC INFINITY
"LET'S SHOW THE UNSC JUST HOW MIGHTY THEIR FLAGSHIP IS NOT."

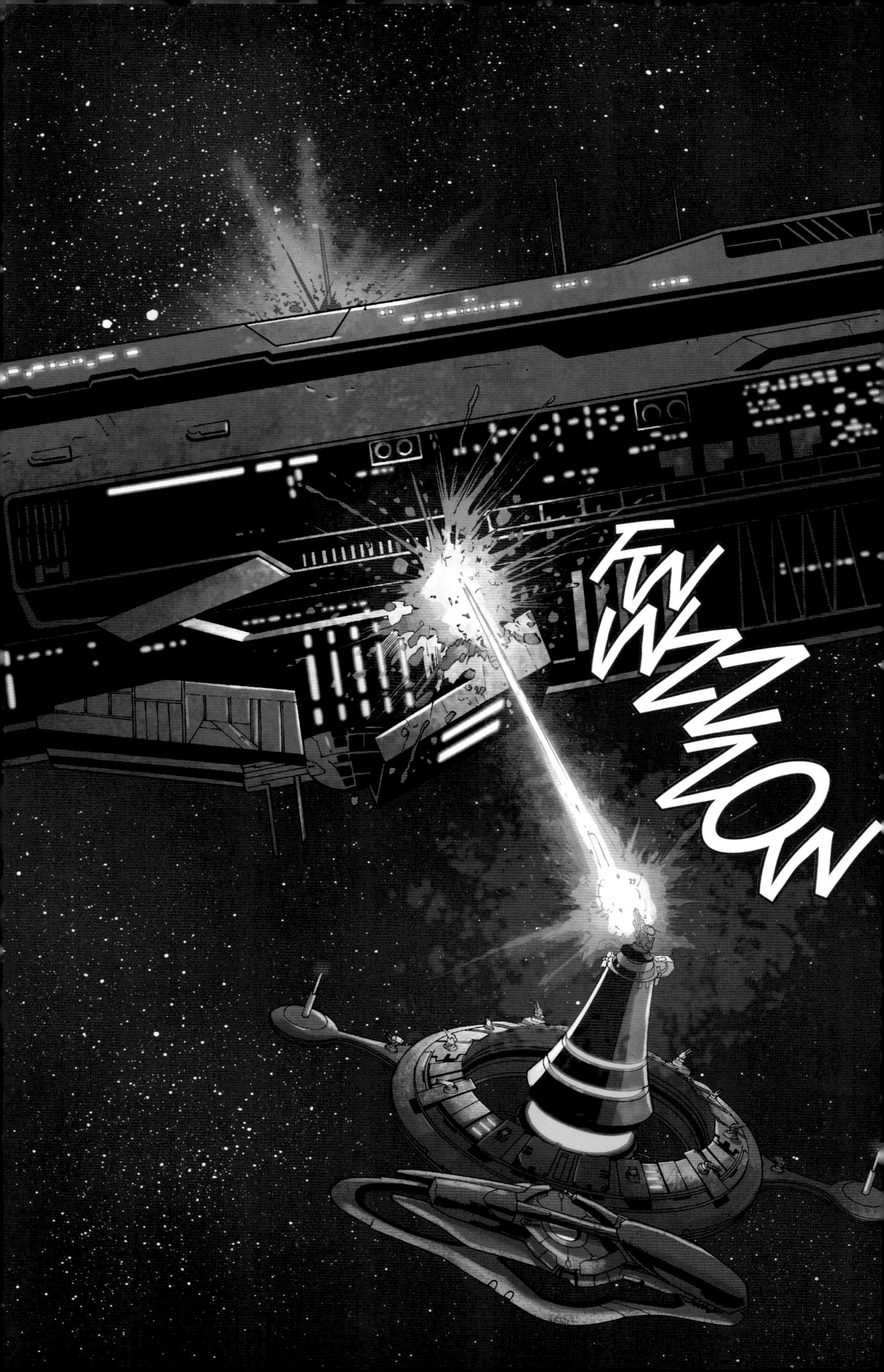
FWWWOW

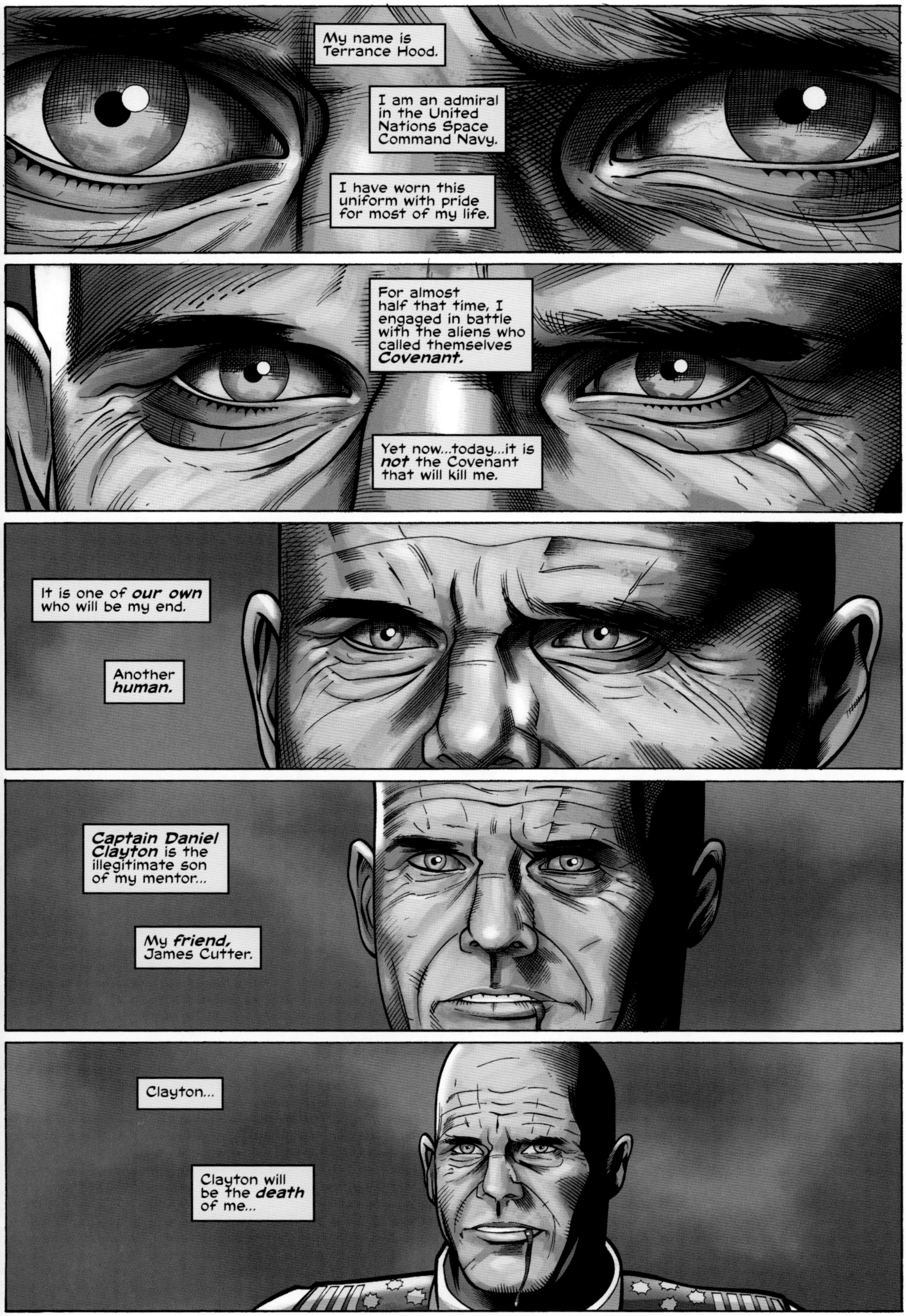
My name is Terrance Hood.
I am an admiral in the United Nations Space Command Navy.
I have worn this uniform with pride for most of my life.
For almost half that time, I engaged in battle with the aliens who called themselves *Covenant.*
Yet now...today...it is *not* the Covenant that will kill me.
It is one of *our own* who will be my end.
Another *human.*
Captain Daniel Clayton is the illegitimate son of my mentor...
My *friend,* James Cutter.
Clayton...
Clayton will be the *death* of me...

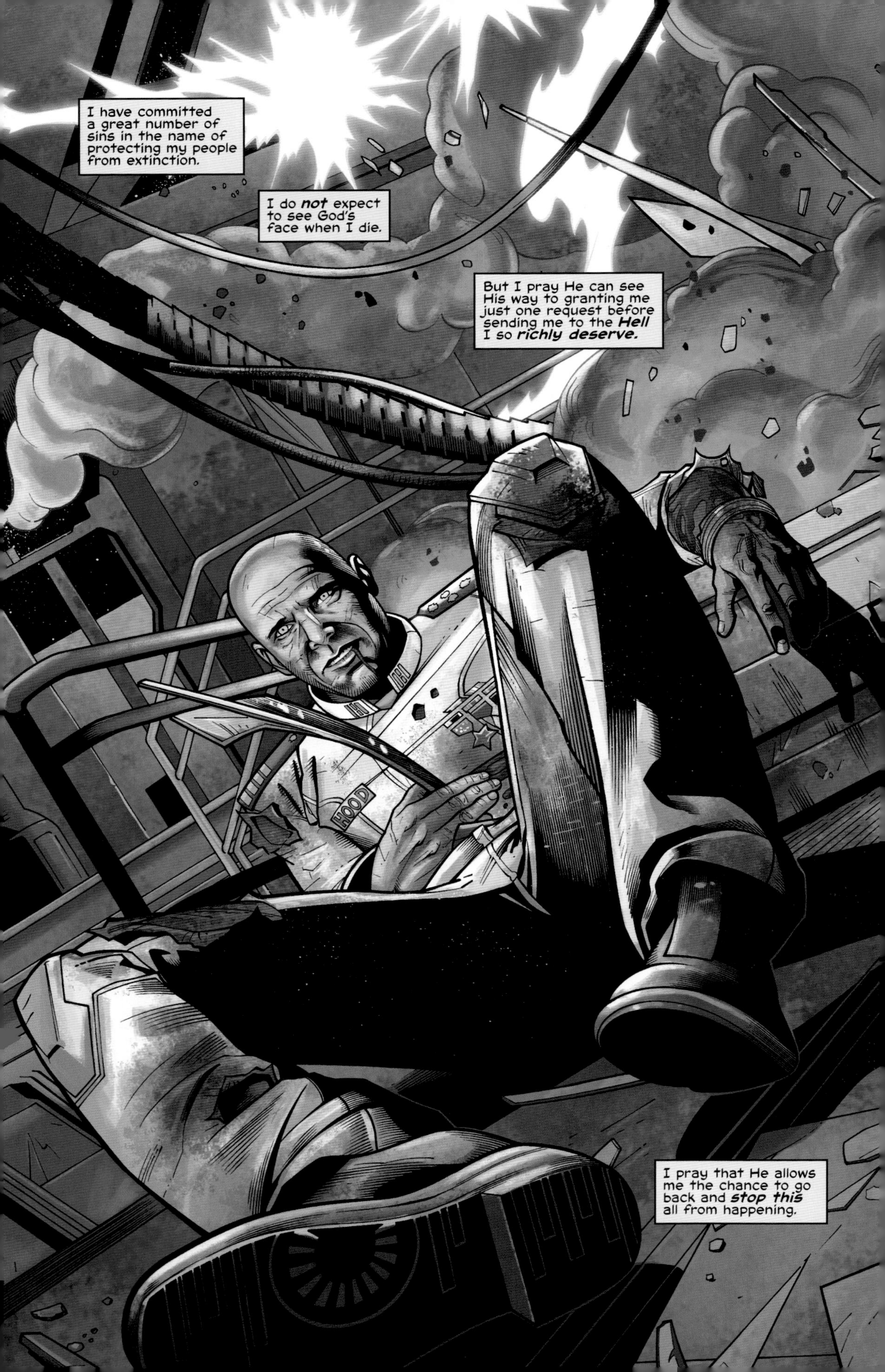
I have committed a great number of sins in the name of protecting my people from extinction.
I do *not* expect to see God's face when I die.
But I pray He can see His way to granting me just one request before sending me to the *Hell* I so *richly deserve.*
I pray that He allows me the chance to go back and *stop this* all from happening.
HOOD

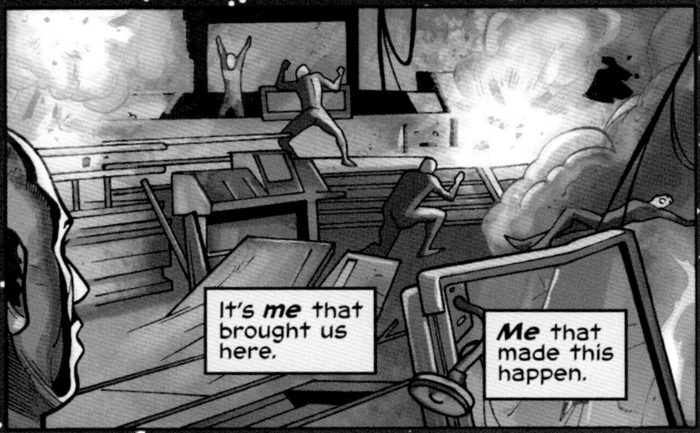
It's *me* that brought us here.
Me that made this happen.

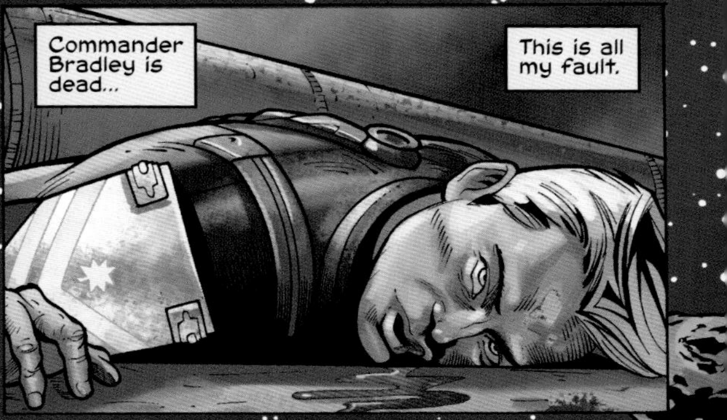
Commander Bradley is dead...
This is all my fault.

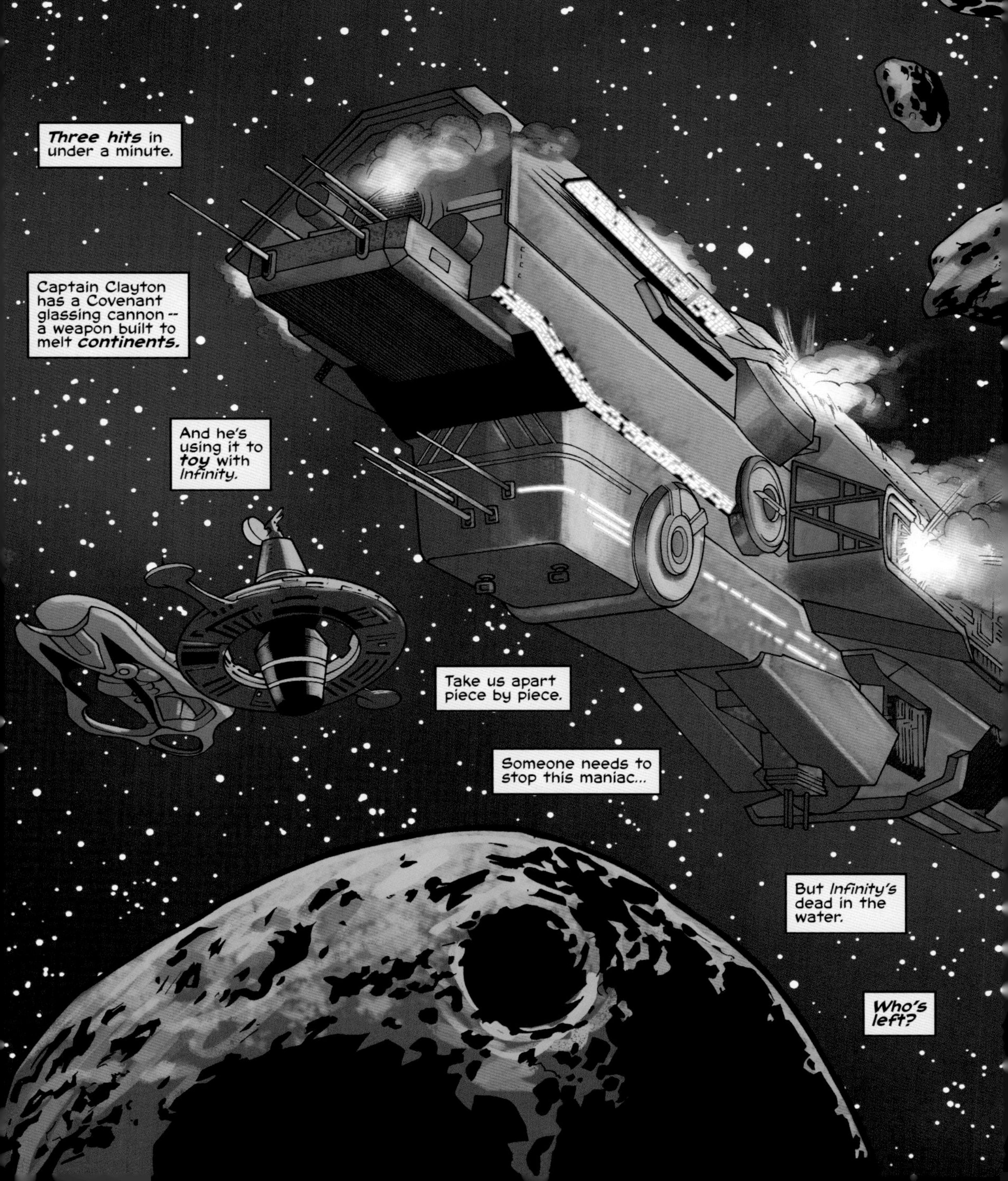
Three hits in under a minute.
Captain Clayton has a Covenant glassing cannon -- a weapon built to melt *continents.*
And he's using it to *toy* with *Infinity.*
Take us apart piece by piece.
Someone needs to stop this maniac...
But *Infinity's* dead in the water.
Who's left?

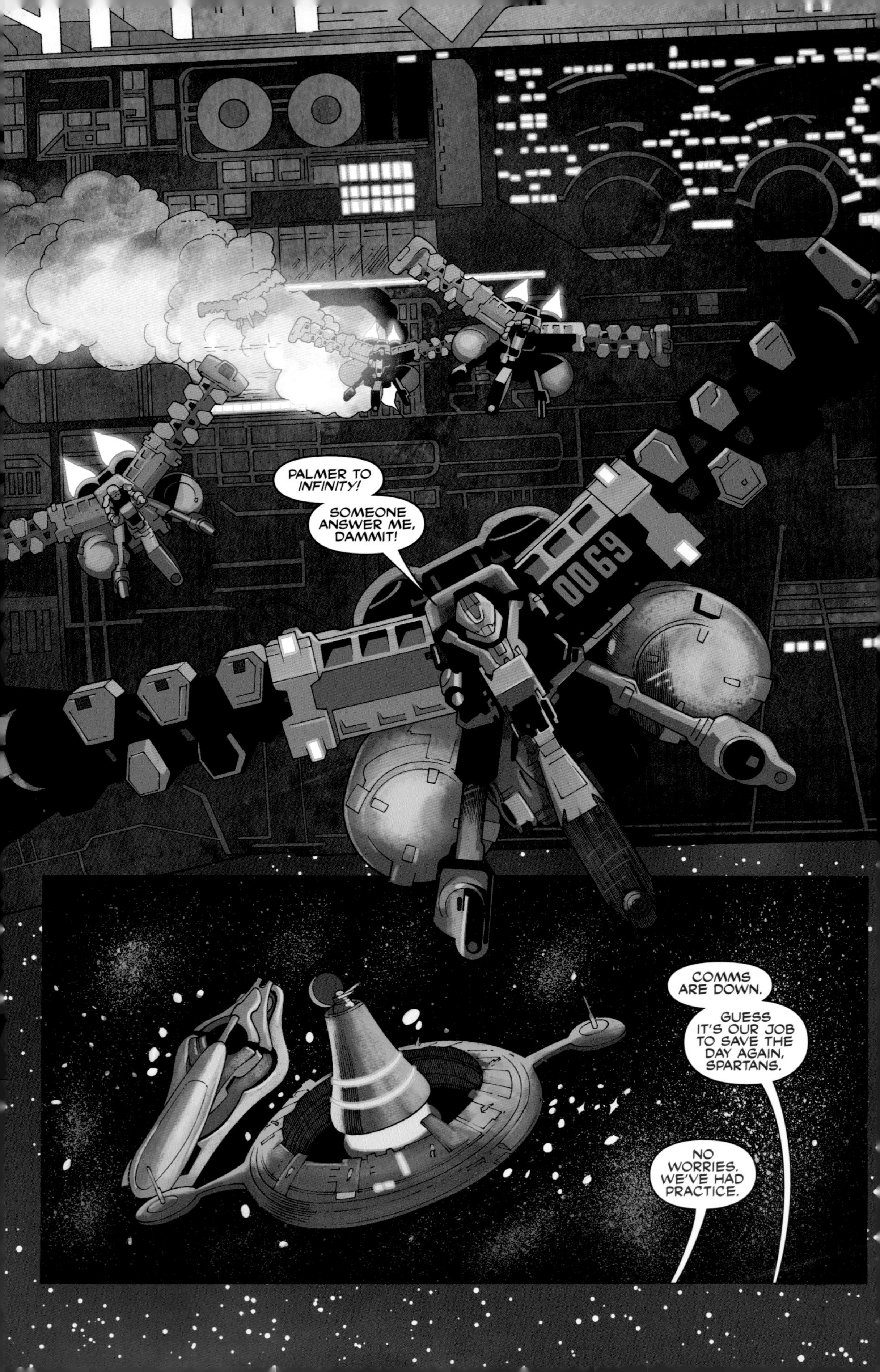
PALMER TO INFINITY!
SOMEONE ANSWER ME, DAMMIT!
COMMS ARE DOWN.
GUESS IT'S OUR JOB TO SAVE THE DAY AGAIN, SPARTANS.
NO WORRIES. WE'VE HAD PRACTICE.

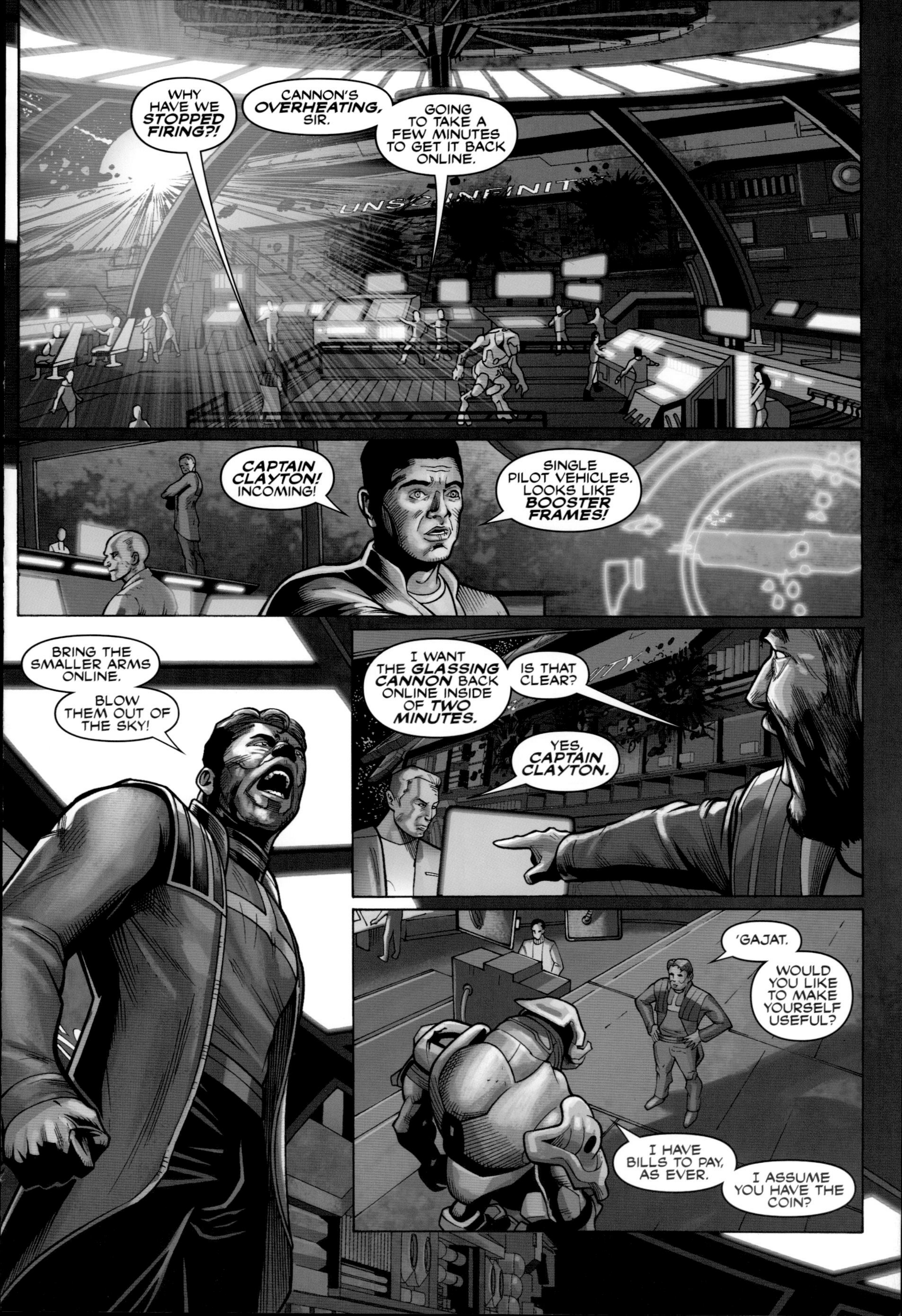

WHY HAVE WE STOPPED FIRING?!
CANNON'S OVERHEATING, SIR.
GOING TO TAKE A FEW MINUTES TO GET IT BACK ONLINE.
UNSC INFINITY
CAPTAIN CLAYTON! INCOMING!
SINGLE PILOT VEHICLES. LOOKS LIKE BOOSTER FRAMES!
BRING THE SMALLER ARMS ONLINE.
BLOW THEM OUT OF THE SKY!
I WANT THE GLASSING CANNON BACK ONLINE INSIDE OF TWO MINUTES.
IS THAT CLEAR?
YES, CAPTAIN CLAYTON.
'GAJAT.
WOULD YOU LIKE TO MAKE YOURSELF USEFUL?
I HAVE BILLS TO PAY, AS EVER.
I ASSUME YOU HAVE THE COIN?

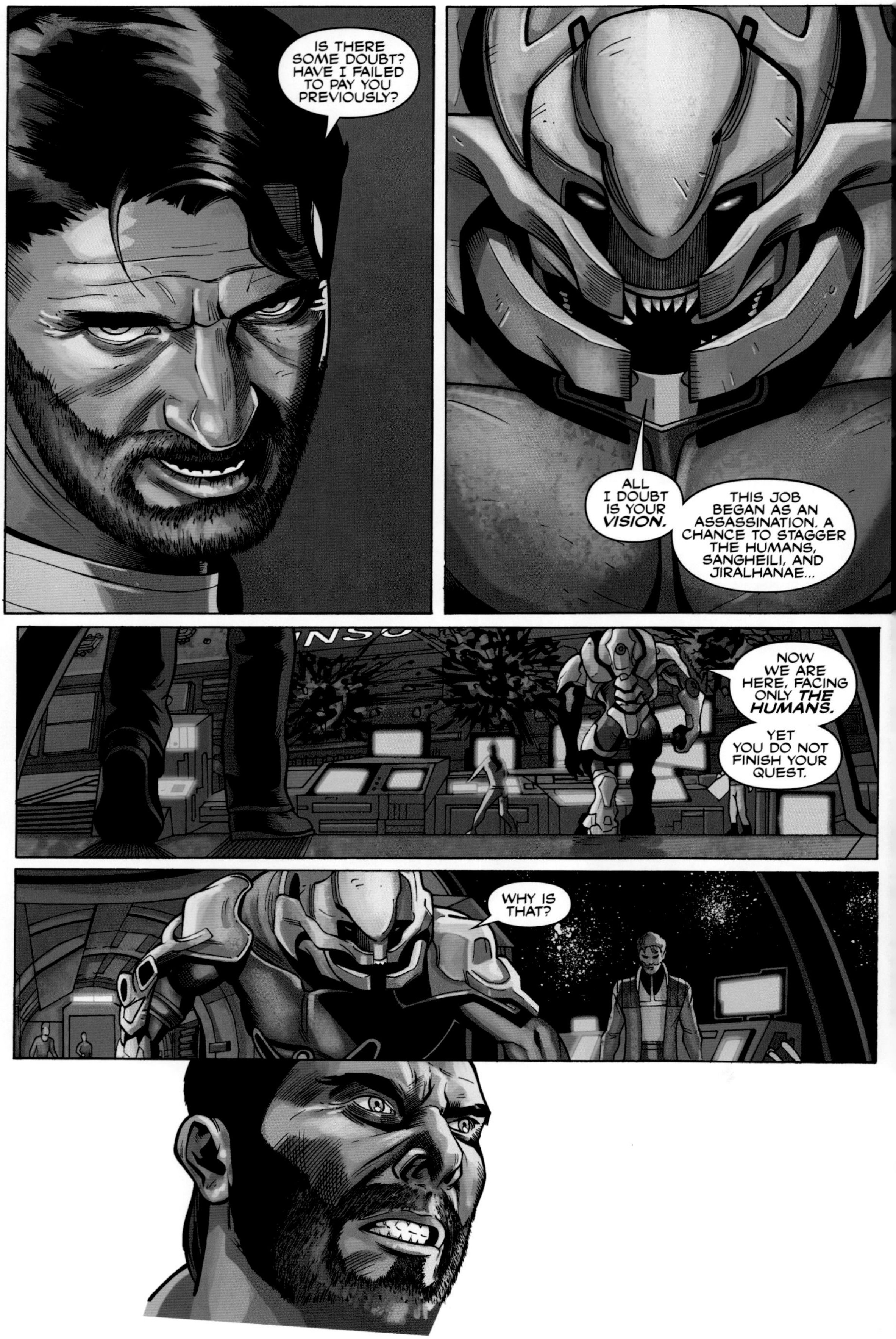
IS THERE SOME DOUBT? HAVE I FAILED TO PAY YOU PREVIOUSLY?
ALL I DOUBT IS YOUR *VISION.*
THIS JOB BEGAN AS AN ASSASSINATION. A CHANCE TO STAGGER THE HUMANS, SANGHEILI, AND JIRALHANAE...
NOW WE ARE HERE, FACING ONLY *THE HUMANS.*
YET YOU DO NOT FINISH YOUR QUEST.
WHY IS THAT?

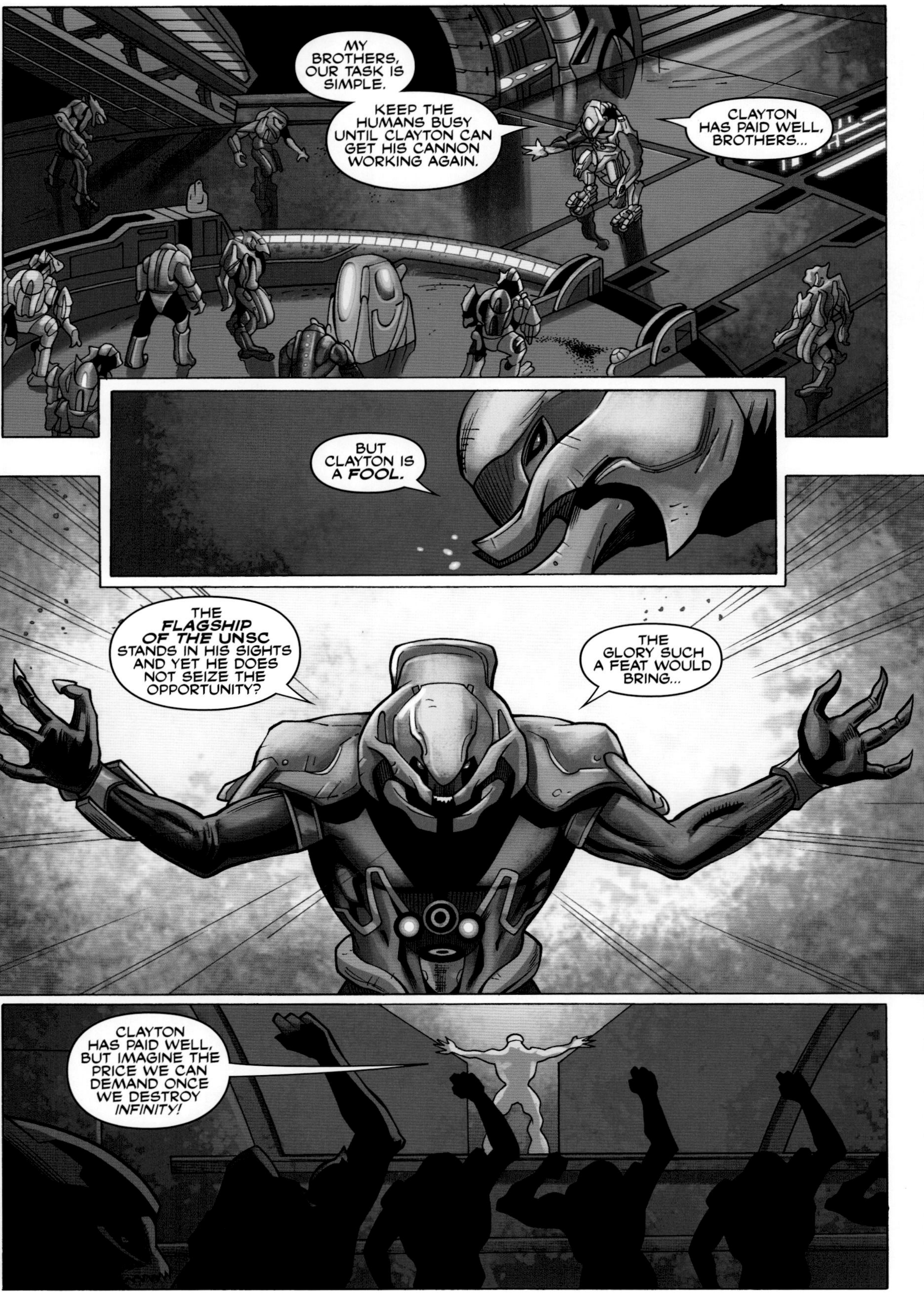
MY BROTHERS, OUR TASK IS SIMPLE.
KEEP THE HUMANS BUSY UNTIL CLAYTON CAN GET HIS CANNON WORKING AGAIN.
CLAYTON HAS PAID WELL, BROTHERS...
BUT CLAYTON IS A *FOOL.*
THE ***FLAGSHIP OF THE*** **UNSC** STANDS IN HIS SIGHTS AND YET HE DOES NOT SEIZE THE OPPORTUNITY?
THE GLORY SUCH A FEAT WOULD BRING...
CLAYTON HAS PAID WELL, BUT IMAGINE THE PRICE WE CAN DEMAND ONCE WE DESTROY *INFINITY!*

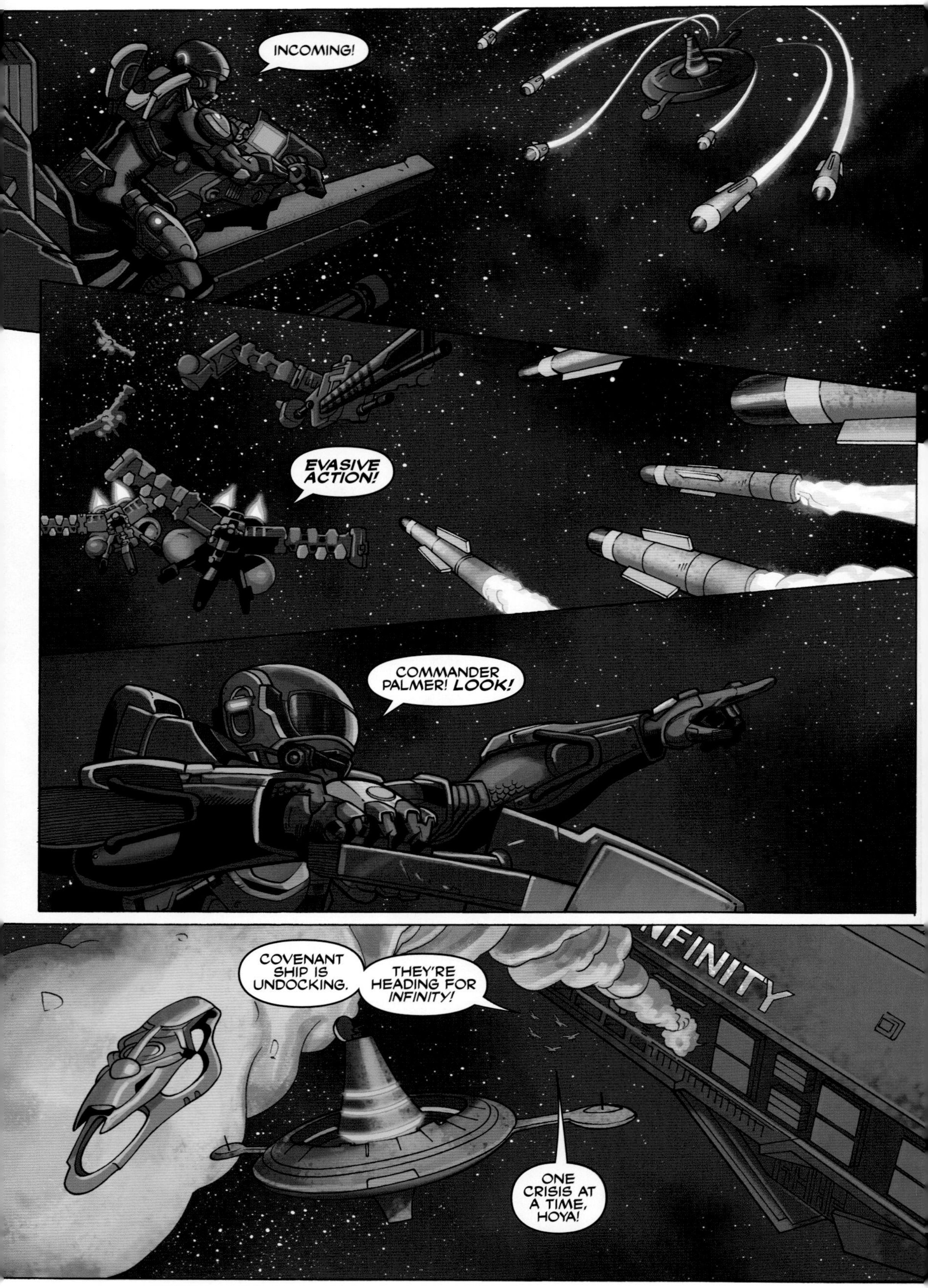
INCOMING!
EVASIVE ACTION!
COMMANDER PALMER! LOOK!
COVENANT SHIP IS UNDOCKING.
THEY'RE HEADING FOR INFINITY!
ONE CRISIS AT A TIME, HOYA!
INFINITY

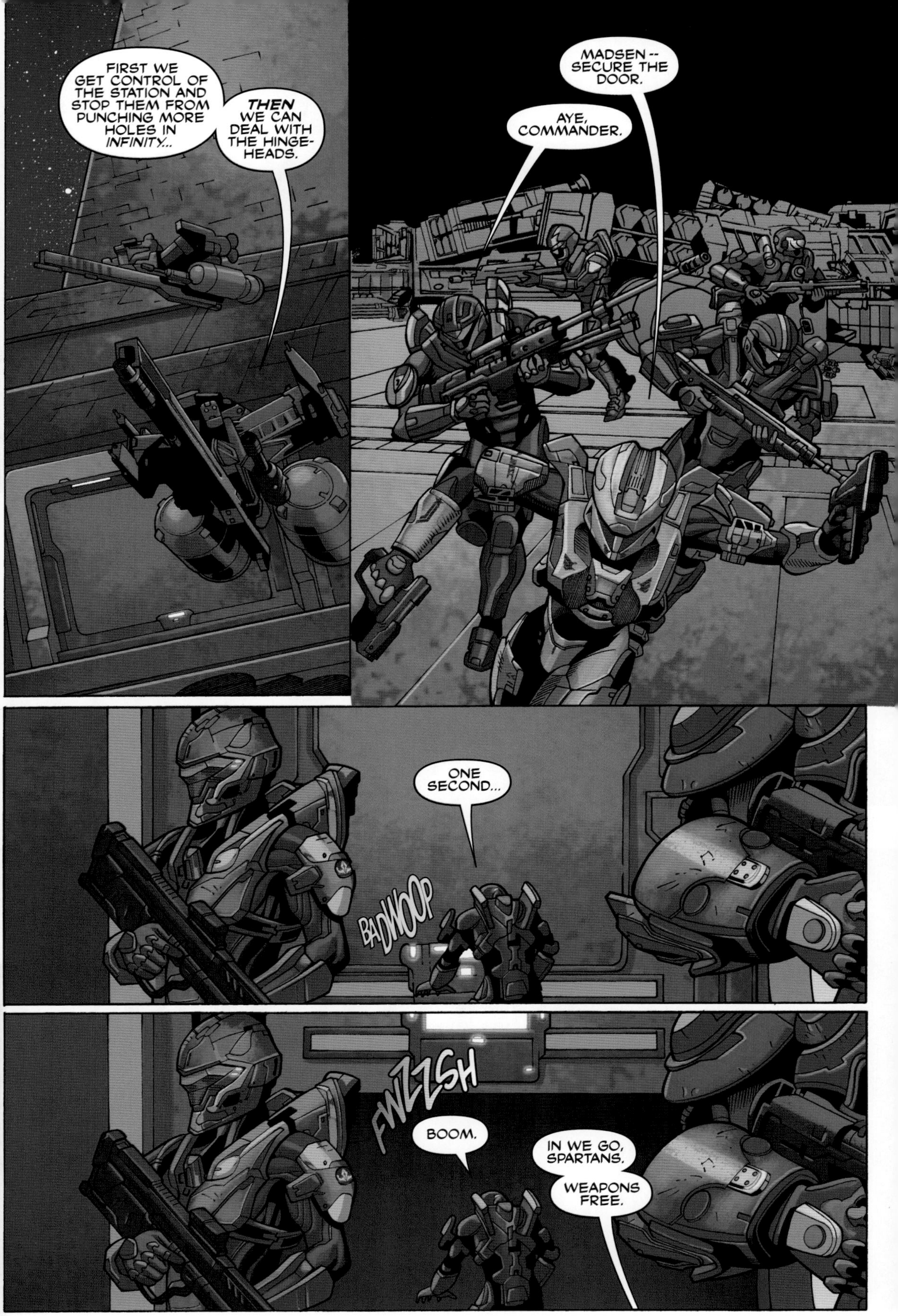
FIRST WE GET CONTROL OF THE STATION AND STOP THEM FROM PUNCHING MORE HOLES IN *INFINITY*...
THEN WE CAN DEAL WITH THE HINGE-HEADS.
MADSEN -- SECURE THE DOOR.
AYE, COMMANDER.
ONE SECOND...
BADWOOP
FWZZSH
BOOM.
IN WE GO, SPARTANS.
WEAPONS FREE.

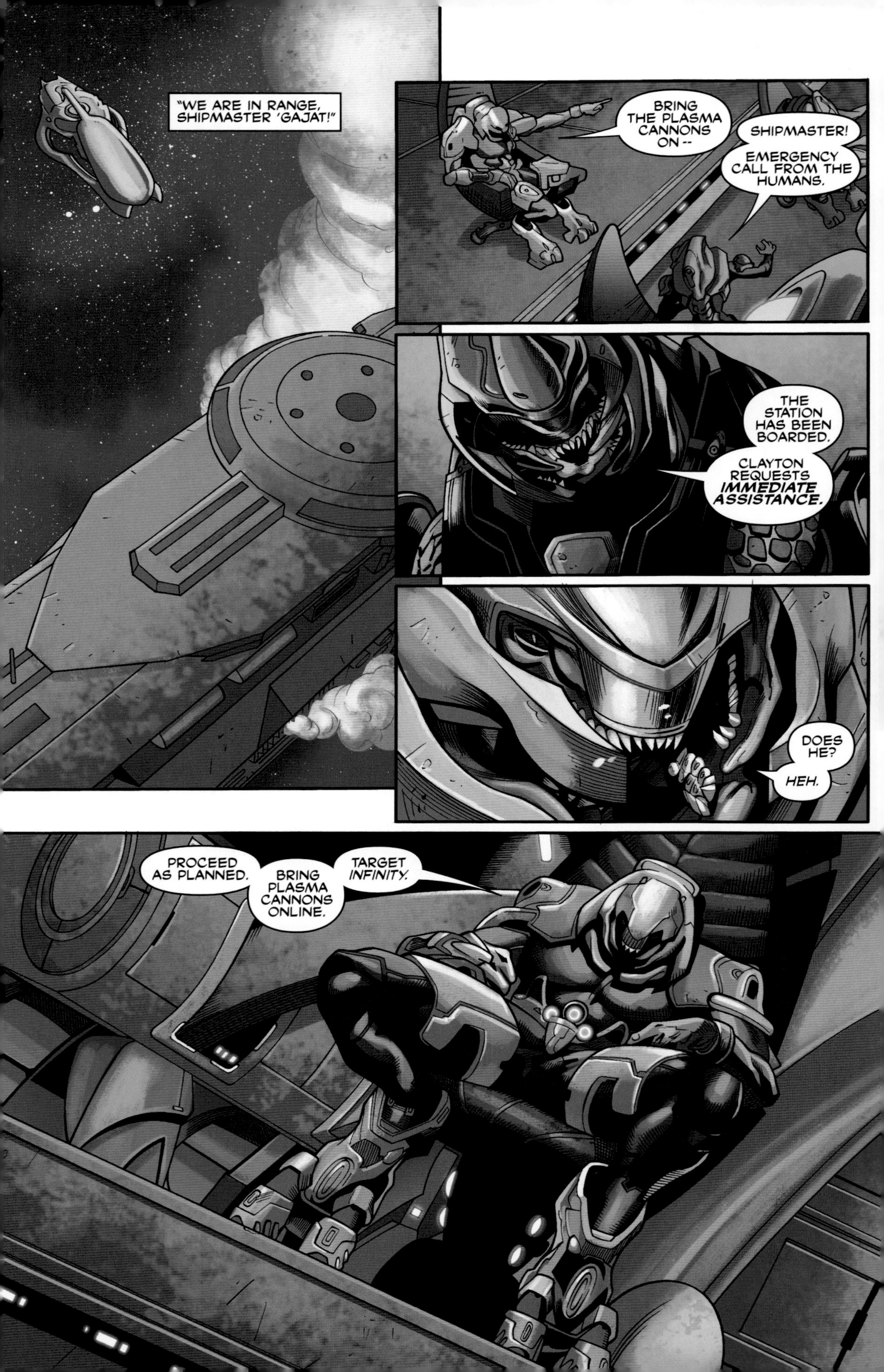
"WE ARE IN RANGE, SHIPMASTER 'GAJAT!"
BRING THE PLASMA CANNONS ON --
SHIPMASTER!
EMERGENCY CALL FROM THE HUMANS.
THE STATION HAS BEEN BOARDED.
CLAYTON REQUESTS *IMMEDIATE ASSISTANCE.*
DOES HE?
HEH.
PROCEED AS PLANNED.
BRING PLASMA CANNONS ONLINE.
TARGET *INFINITY.*

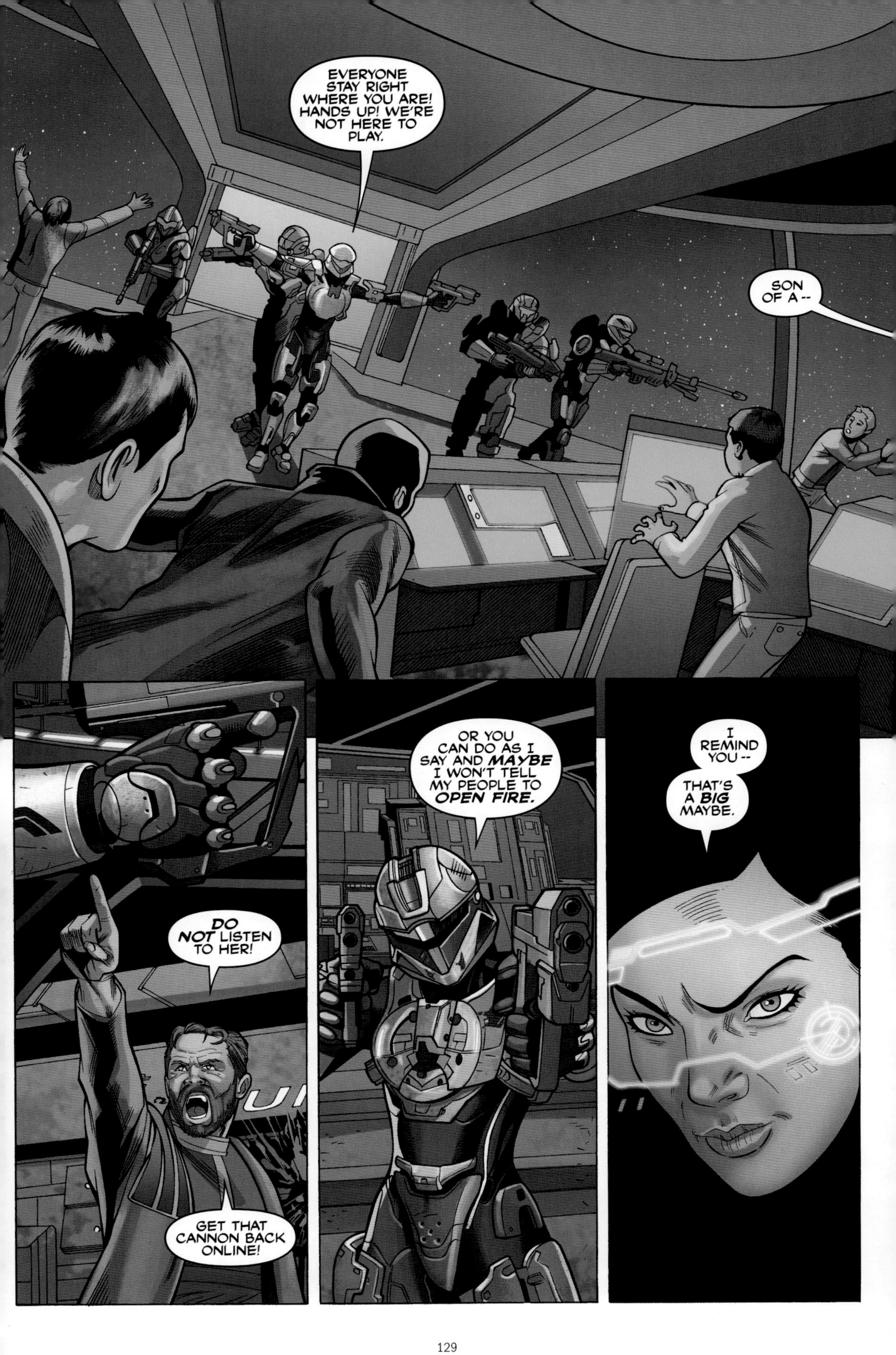
EVERYONE STAY RIGHT WHERE YOU ARE! HANDS UP! WE'RE NOT HERE TO PLAY.
SON OF A --
DO NOT LISTEN TO HER!
GET THAT CANNON BACK ONLINE!
OR YOU CAN DO AS I SAY AND MAYBE I WON'T TELL MY PEOPLE TO OPEN FIRE.
I REMIND YOU --
THAT'S A BIG MAYBE.

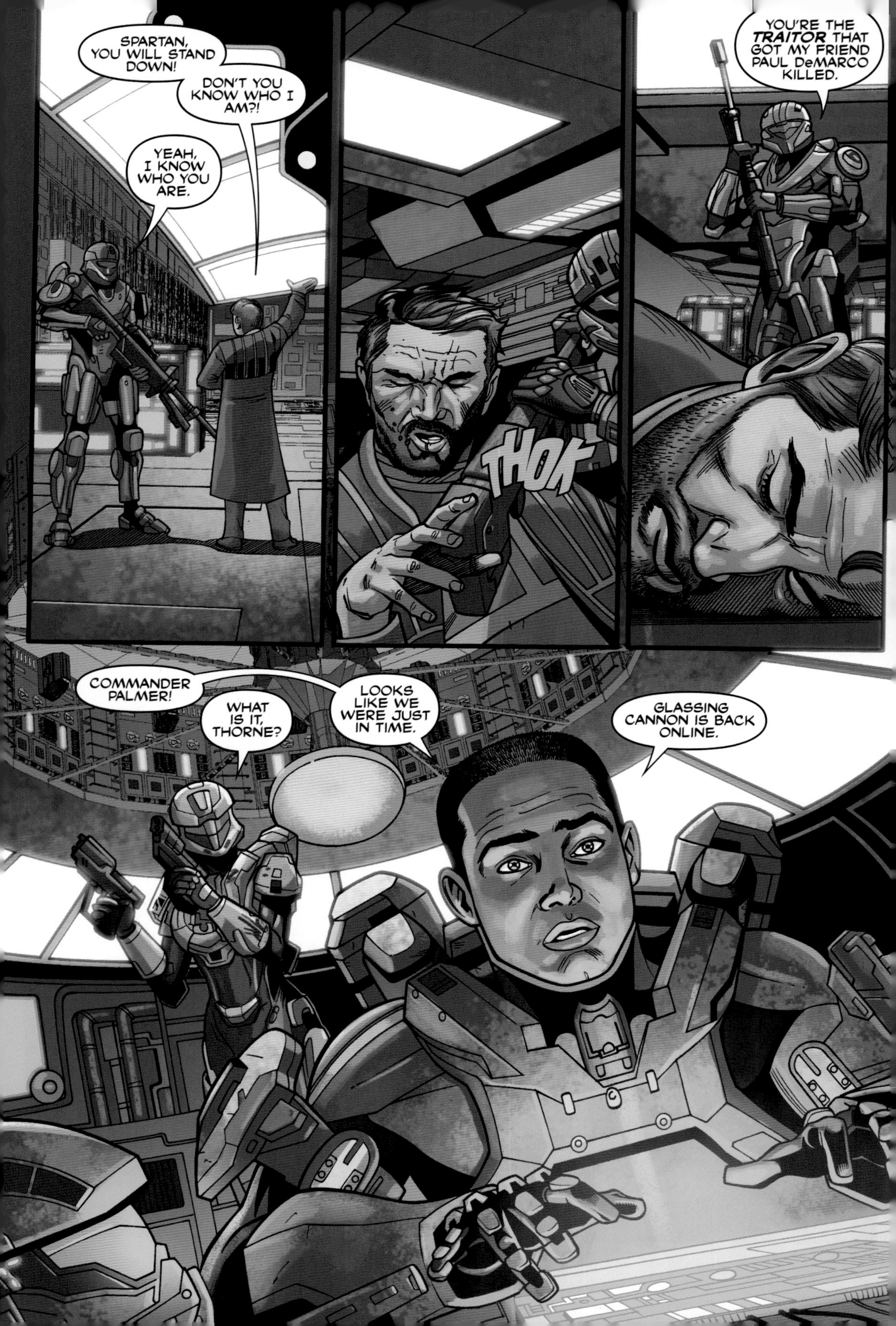
SPARTAN, YOU WILL STAND DOWN!
DON'T YOU KNOW WHO I AM?!
YEAH, I KNOW WHO YOU ARE.
THOK
YOU'RE THE TRAITOR THAT GOT MY FRIEND PAUL DeMARCO KILLED.
COMMANDER PALMER!
WHAT IS IT, THORNE?
LOOKS LIKE WE WERE JUST IN TIME.
GLASSING CANNON IS BACK ONLINE.

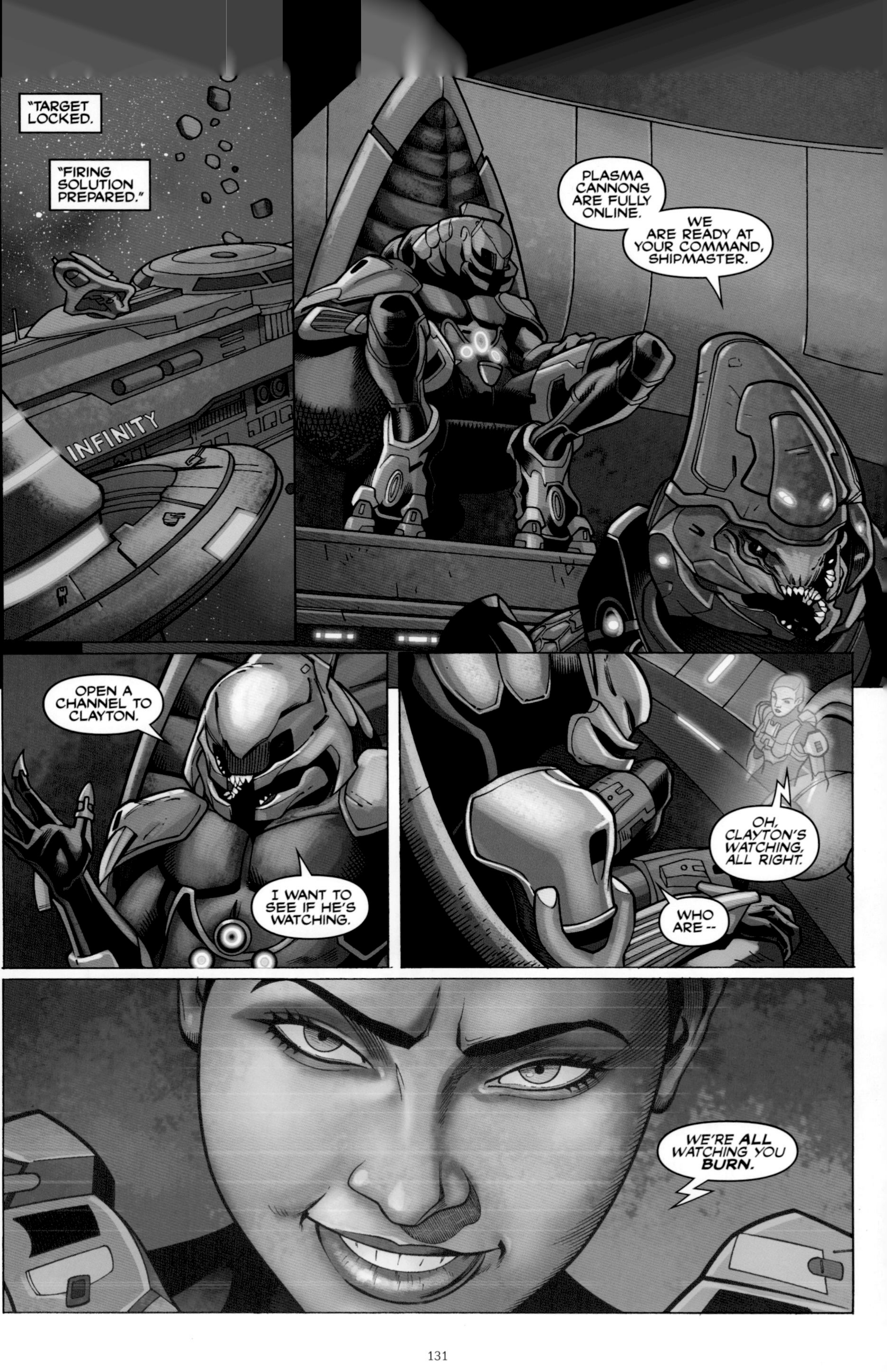
"TARGET LOCKED.
"FIRING SOLUTION PREPARED."
INFINITY
PLASMA CANNONS ARE FULLY ONLINE.
WE ARE READY AT YOUR COMMAND, SHIPMASTER.
OPEN A CHANNEL TO CLAYTON.
I WANT TO SEE IF HE'S WATCHING.
OH, CLAYTON'S WATCHING, ALL RIGHT.
WHO ARE --
WE'RE **ALL** WATCHING YOU **BURN.**

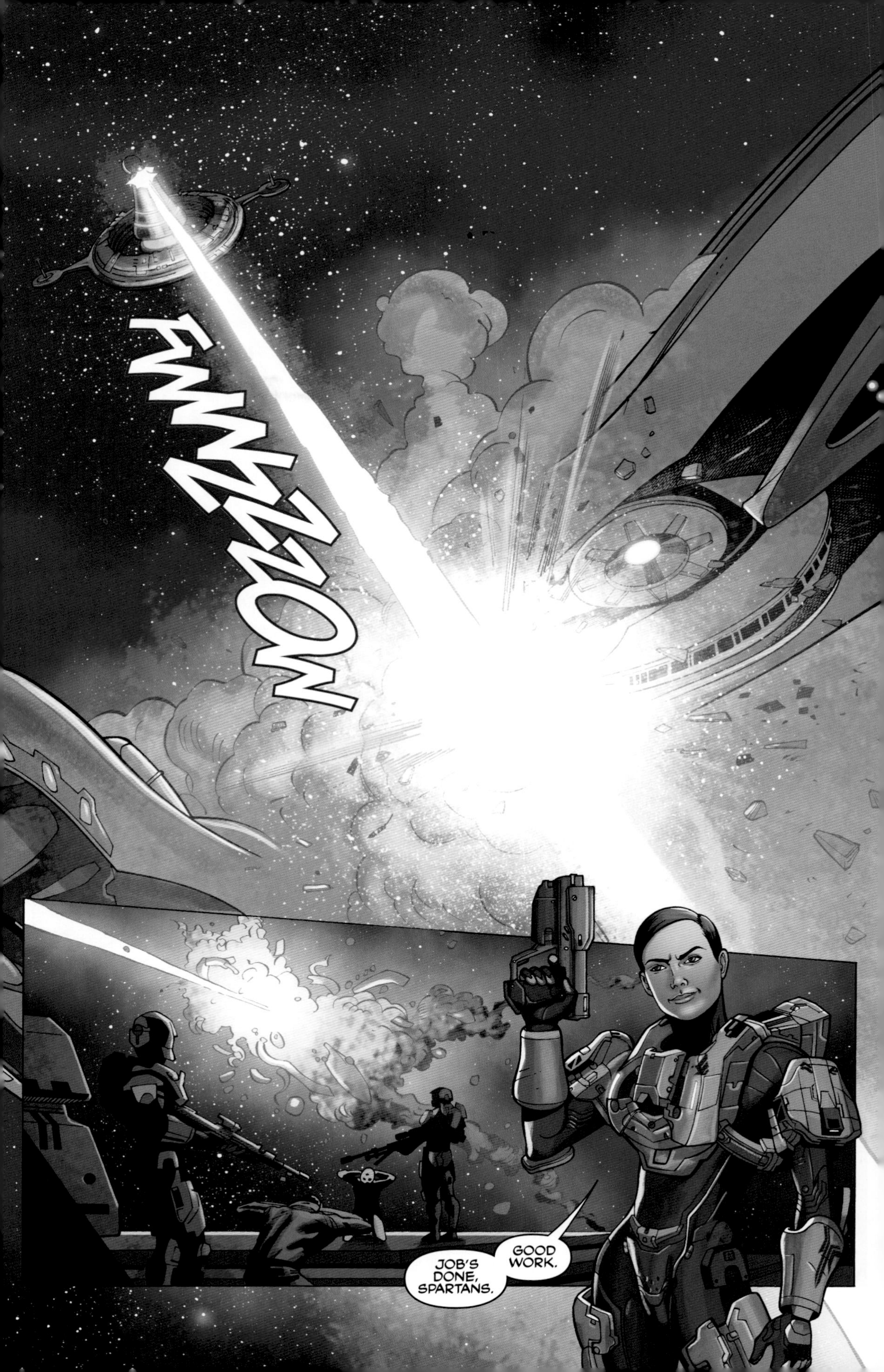
FWAZZOW
JOB'S DONE, SPARTANS.
GOOD WORK.

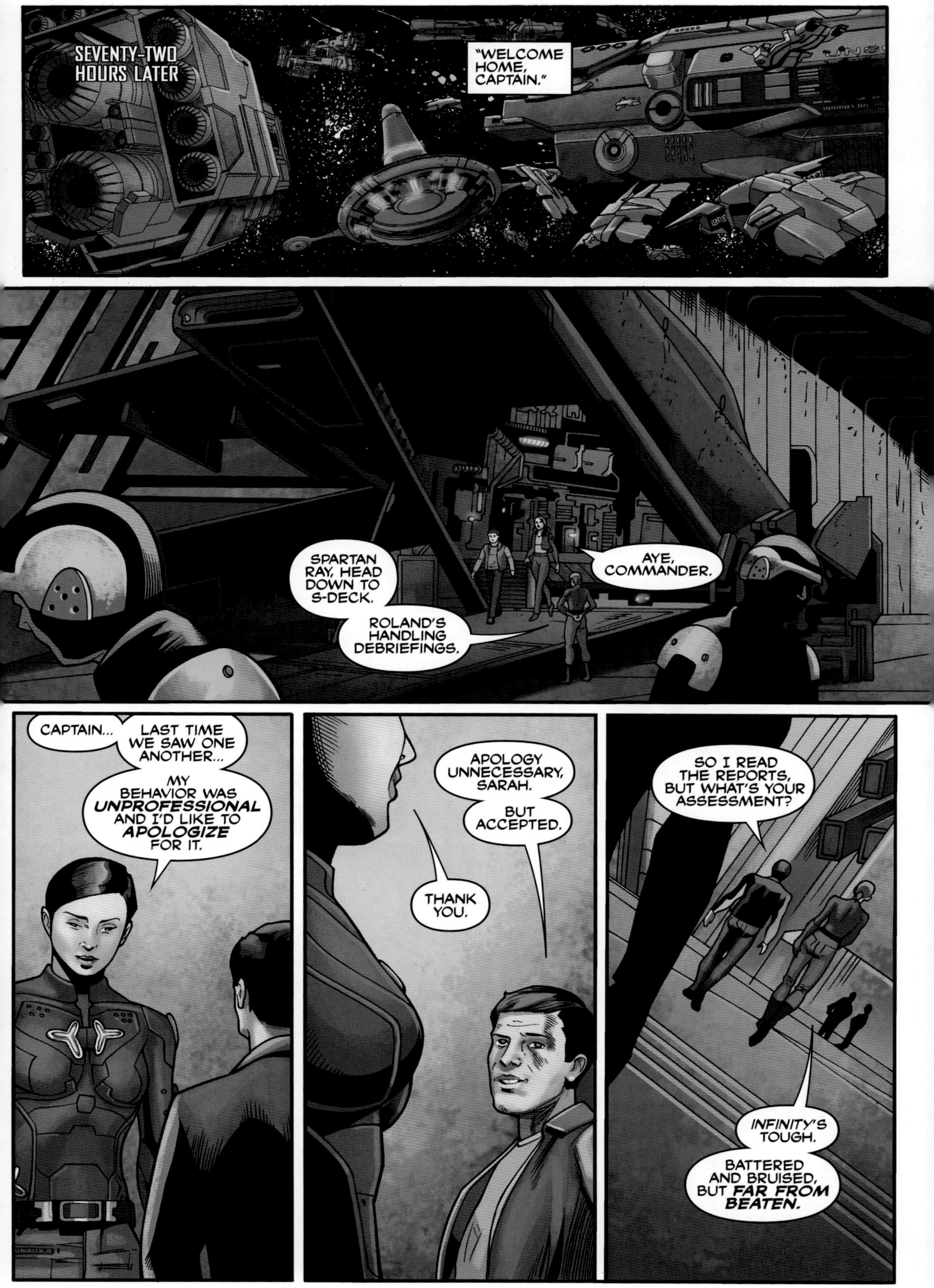
SEVENTY-TWO HOURS LATER
"WELCOME HOME, CAPTAIN."
SPARTAN RAY, HEAD DOWN TO S-DECK.
ROLAND'S HANDLING DEBRIEFINGS.
AYE, COMMANDER.
CAPTAIN...
LAST TIME WE SAW ONE ANOTHER...
MY BEHAVIOR WAS UNPROFESSIONAL AND I'D LIKE TO APOLOGIZE FOR IT.
THANK YOU.
APOLOGY UNNECESSARY, SARAH.
BUT ACCEPTED.
SO I READ THE REPORTS, BUT WHAT'S YOUR ASSESSMENT?
INFINITY'S TOUGH.
BATTERED AND BRUISED, BUT FAR FROM BEATEN.

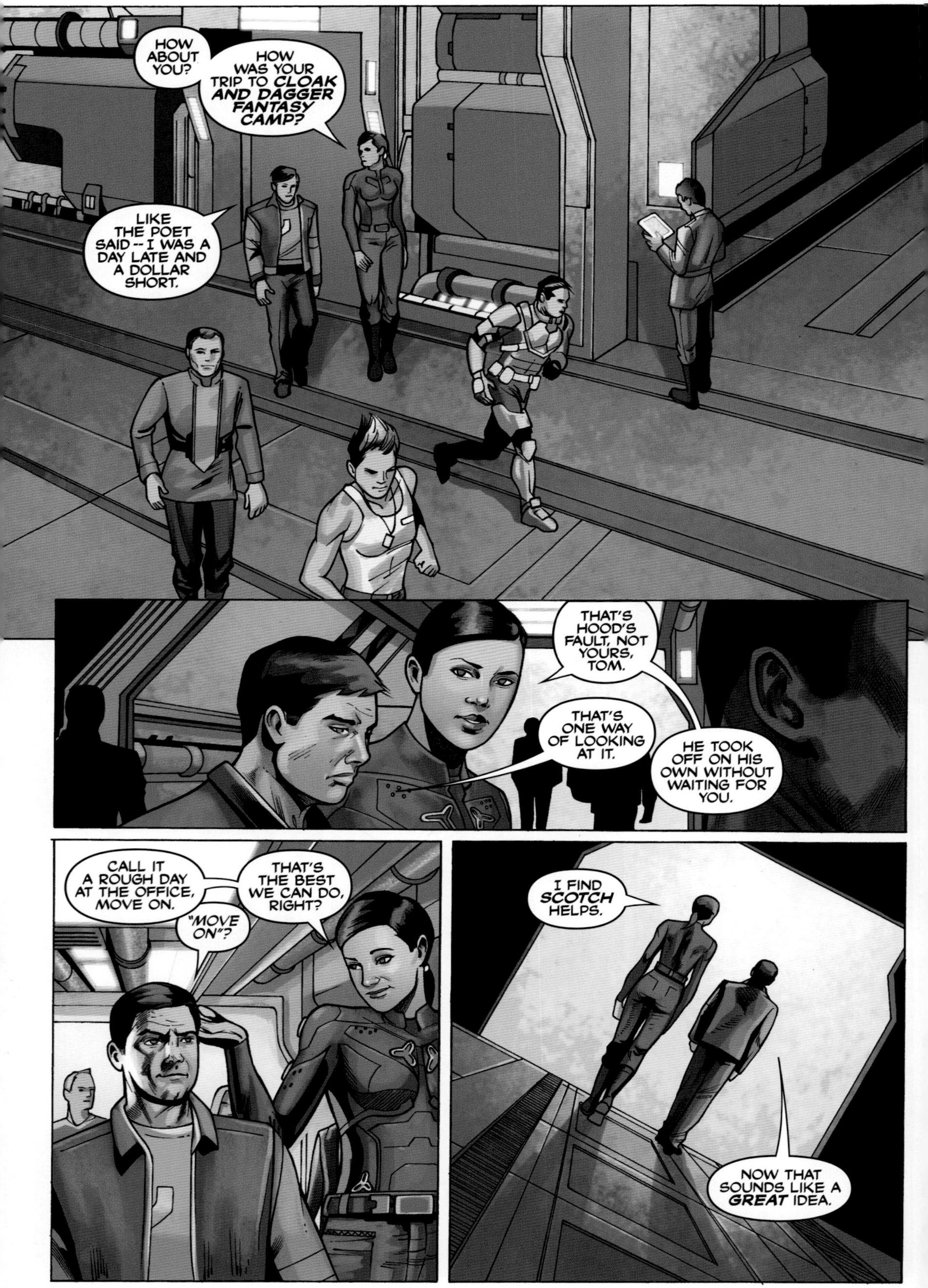
HOW WAS YOUR TRIP TO CLOAK AND DAGGER FANTASY CAMP?
HOW ABOUT YOU?
LIKE THE POET SAID -- I WAS A DAY LATE AND A DOLLAR SHORT.
THAT'S HOOD'S FAULT, NOT YOURS, TOM.
HE TOOK OFF ON HIS OWN WITHOUT WAITING FOR YOU.
THAT'S ONE WAY OF LOOKING AT IT.
CALL IT A ROUGH DAY AT THE OFFICE, MOVE ON.
"MOVE ON"?
THAT'S THE BEST WE CAN DO, RIGHT?
I FIND SCOTCH HELPS.
NOW THAT SOUNDS LIKE A GREAT IDEA.

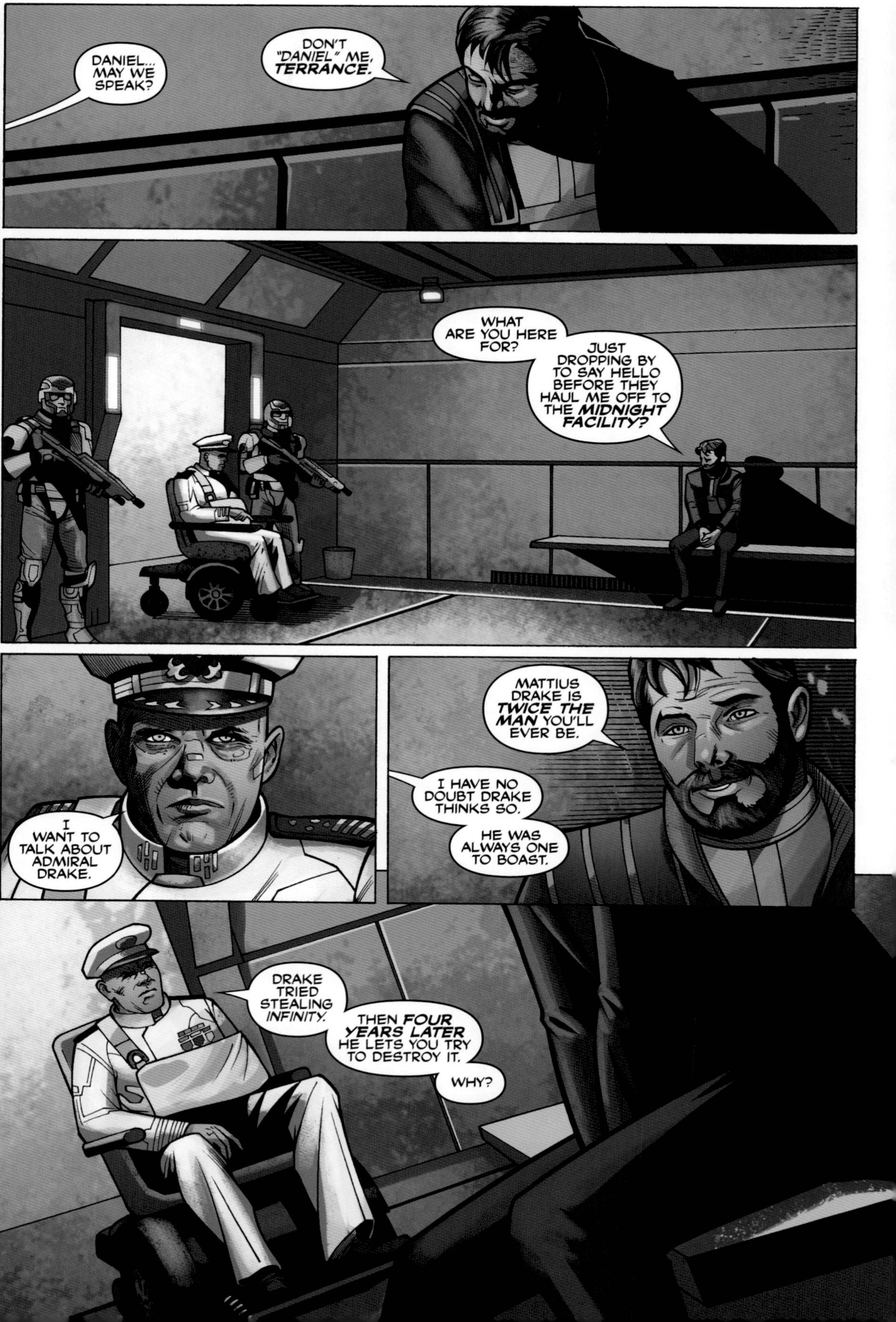
DANIEL... MAY WE SPEAK?
DON'T "DANIEL" ME, TERRANCE.
WHAT ARE YOU HERE FOR?
JUST DROPPING BY TO SAY HELLO BEFORE THEY HAUL ME OFF TO THE MIDNIGHT FACILITY?
I WANT TO TALK ABOUT ADMIRAL DRAKE.
MATTIUS DRAKE IS TWICE THE MAN YOU'LL EVER BE.
I HAVE NO DOUBT DRAKE THINKS SO.
HE WAS ALWAYS ONE TO BOAST.
DRAKE TRIED STEALING INFINITY.
THEN FOUR YEARS LATER HE LETS YOU TRY TO DESTROY IT.
WHY?

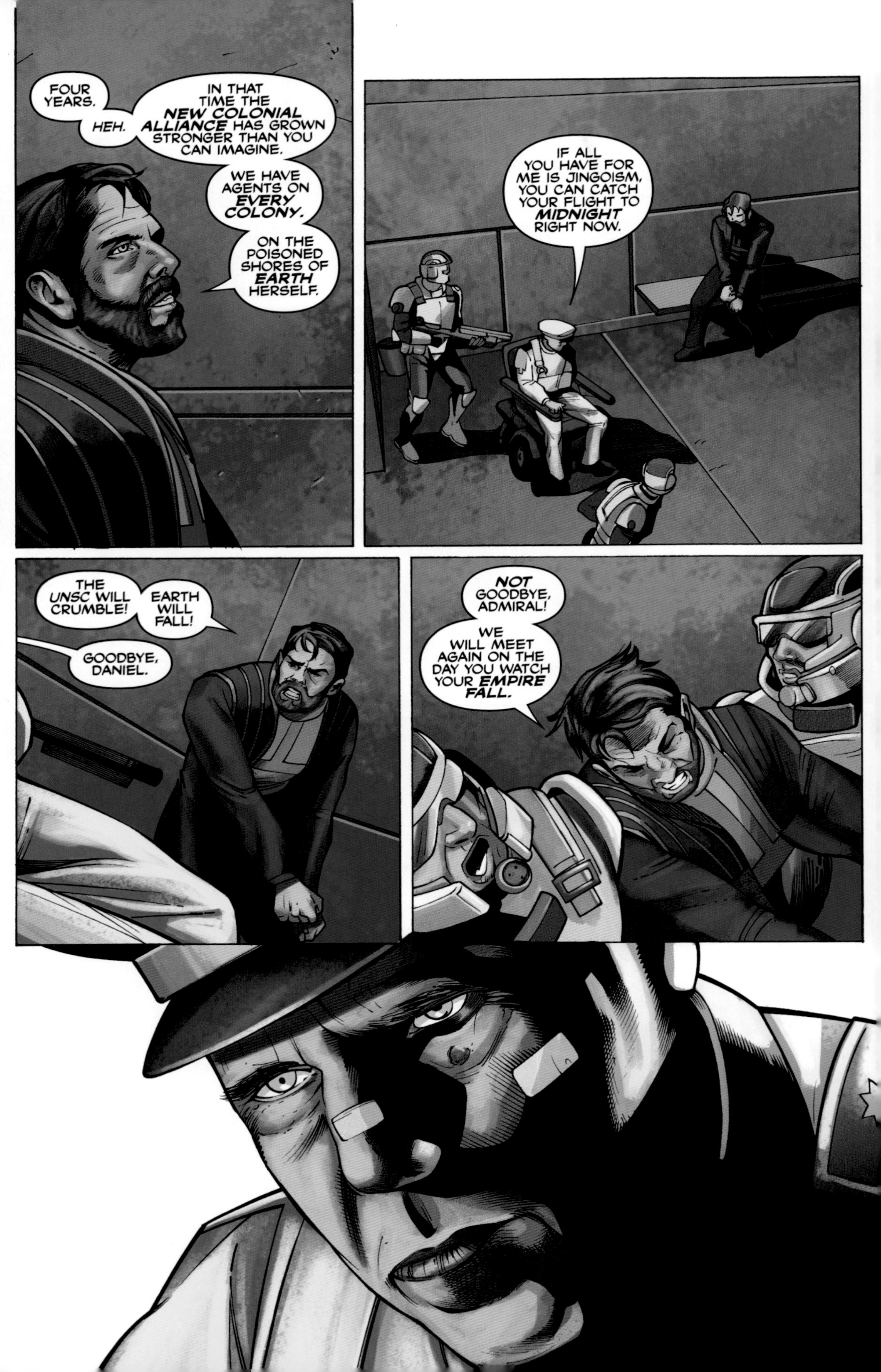
FOUR YEARS.
HEH.
IN THAT TIME THE NEW COLONIAL ALLIANCE HAS GROWN STRONGER THAN YOU CAN IMAGINE.
WE HAVE AGENTS ON EVERY COLONY.
ON THE POISONED SHORES OF EARTH HERSELF.
IF ALL YOU HAVE FOR ME IS JINGOISM, YOU CAN CATCH YOUR FLIGHT TO MIDNIGHT RIGHT NOW.
THE UNSC WILL CRUMBLE!
EARTH WILL FALL!
GOODBYE, DANIEL.
NOT GOODBYE, ADMIRAL!
WE WILL MEET AGAIN ON THE DAY YOU WATCH YOUR EMPIRE FALL.

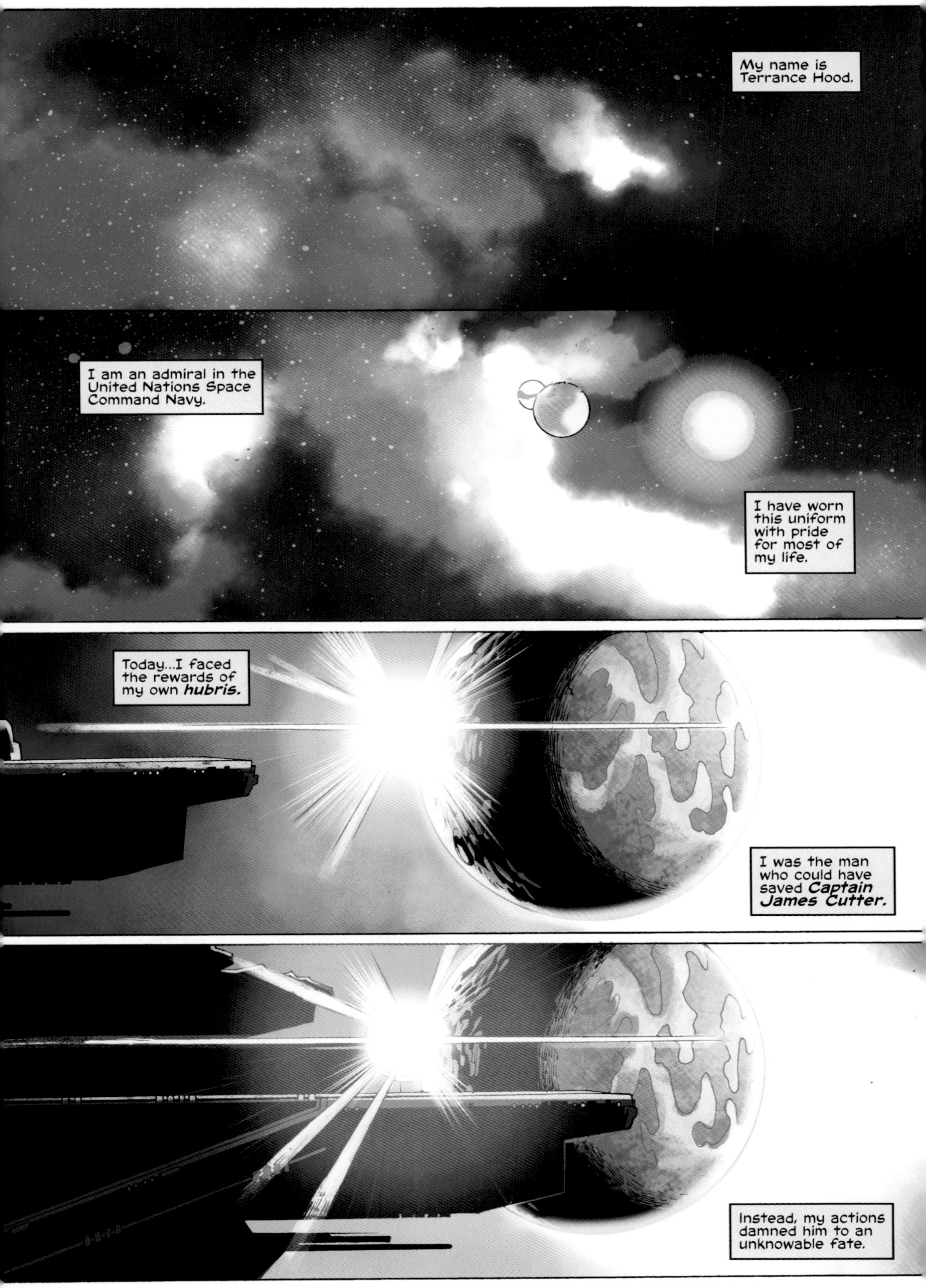
My name is Terrance Hood.
I am an admiral in the United Nations Space Command Navy.
I have worn this uniform with pride for most of my life.
Today...I faced the rewards of my own *hubris.*
I was the man who could have saved *Captain James Cutter.*
Instead, my actions damned him to an unknowable fate.

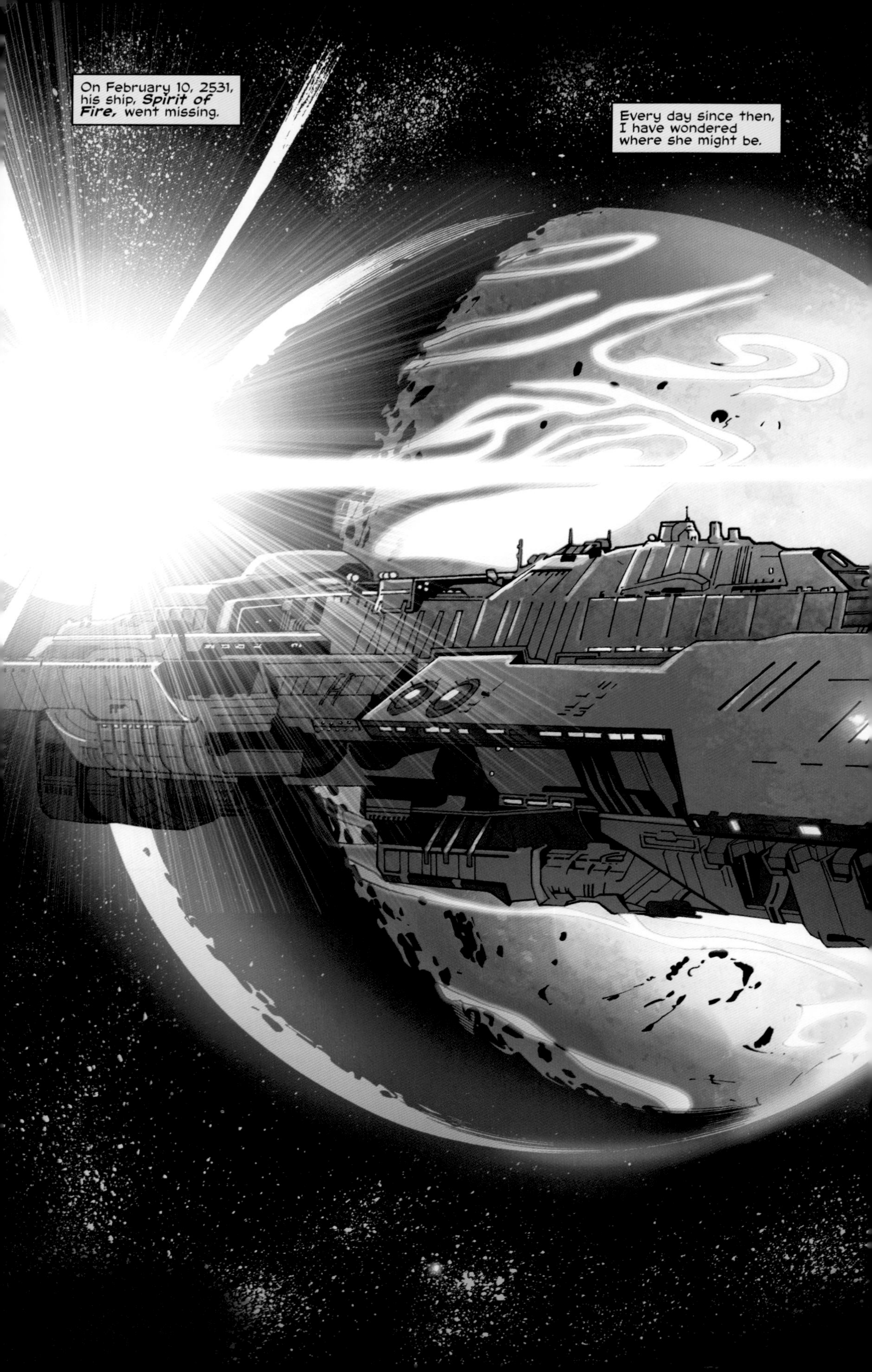
On February 10, 2531, his ship, ***Spirit of Fire,*** went missing.
Every day since then, I have wondered where she might be.

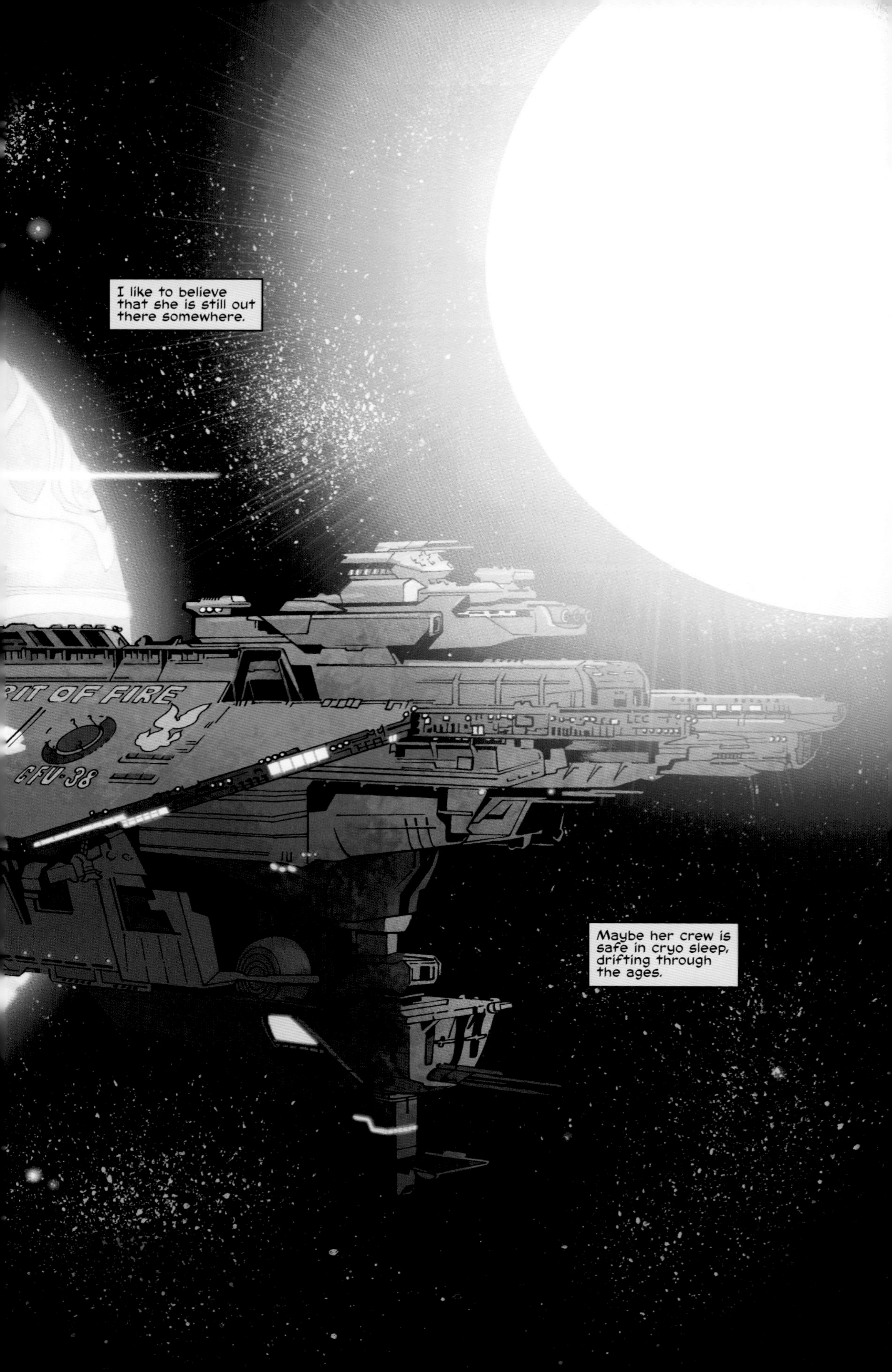
I like to believe that she is still out there somewhere.
RIT OF FIRE
CFV-38
Maybe her crew is safe in cryo sleep, drifting through the ages.

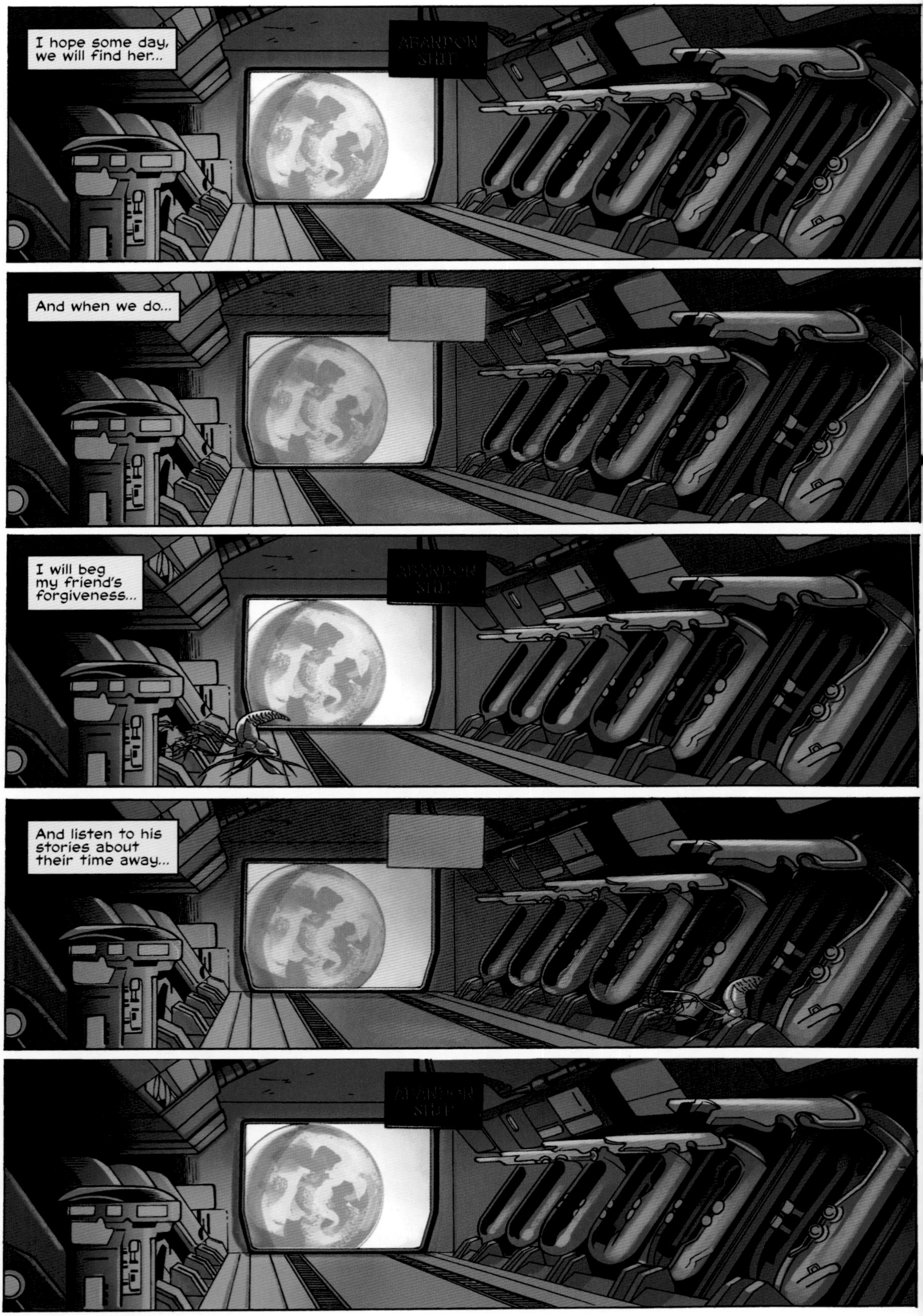
I hope some day, we will find her...
And when we do...
I will beg my friend's forgiveness...
And listen to his stories about their time away...

Illustration by Anthony Palumbo

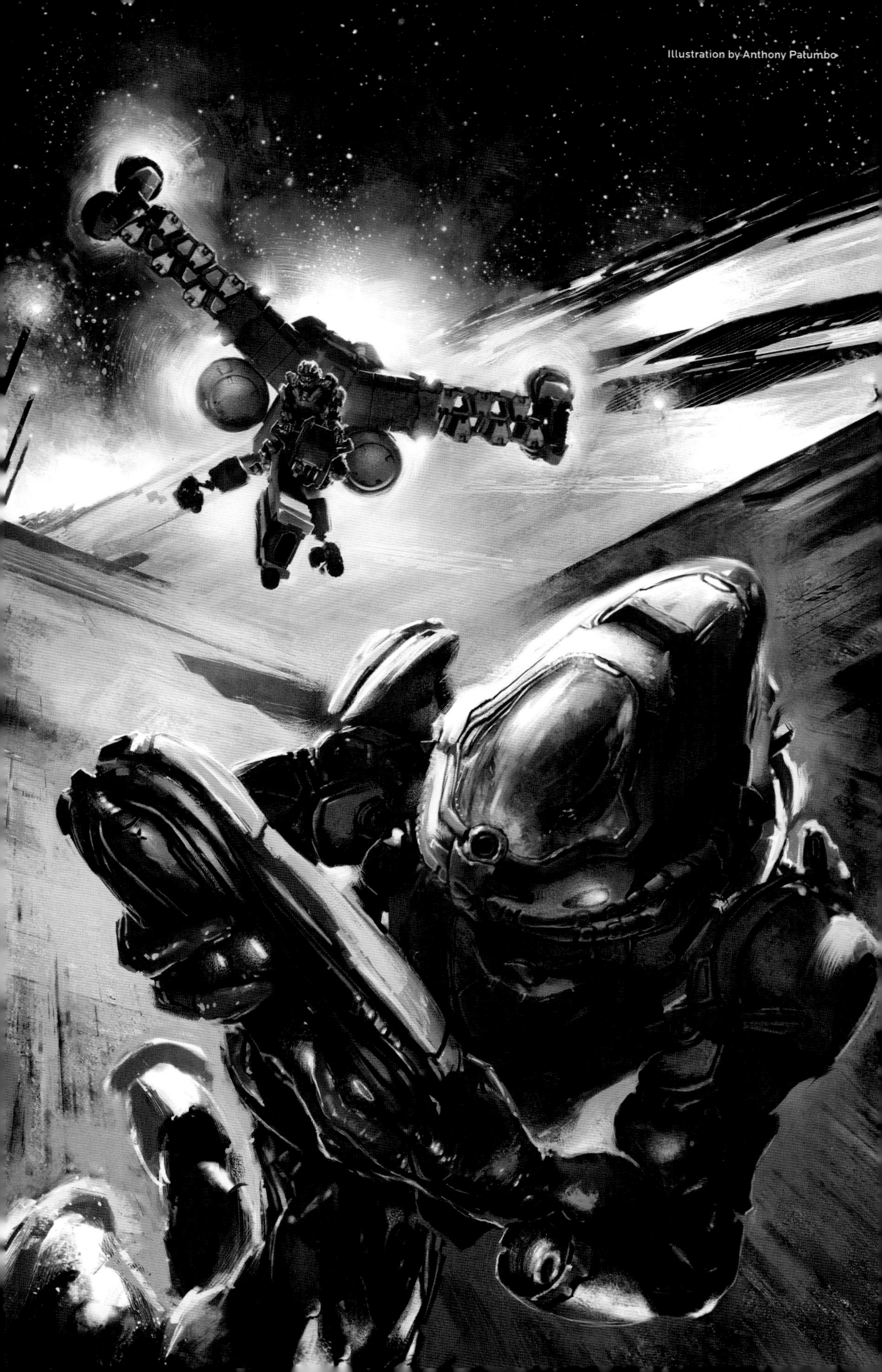

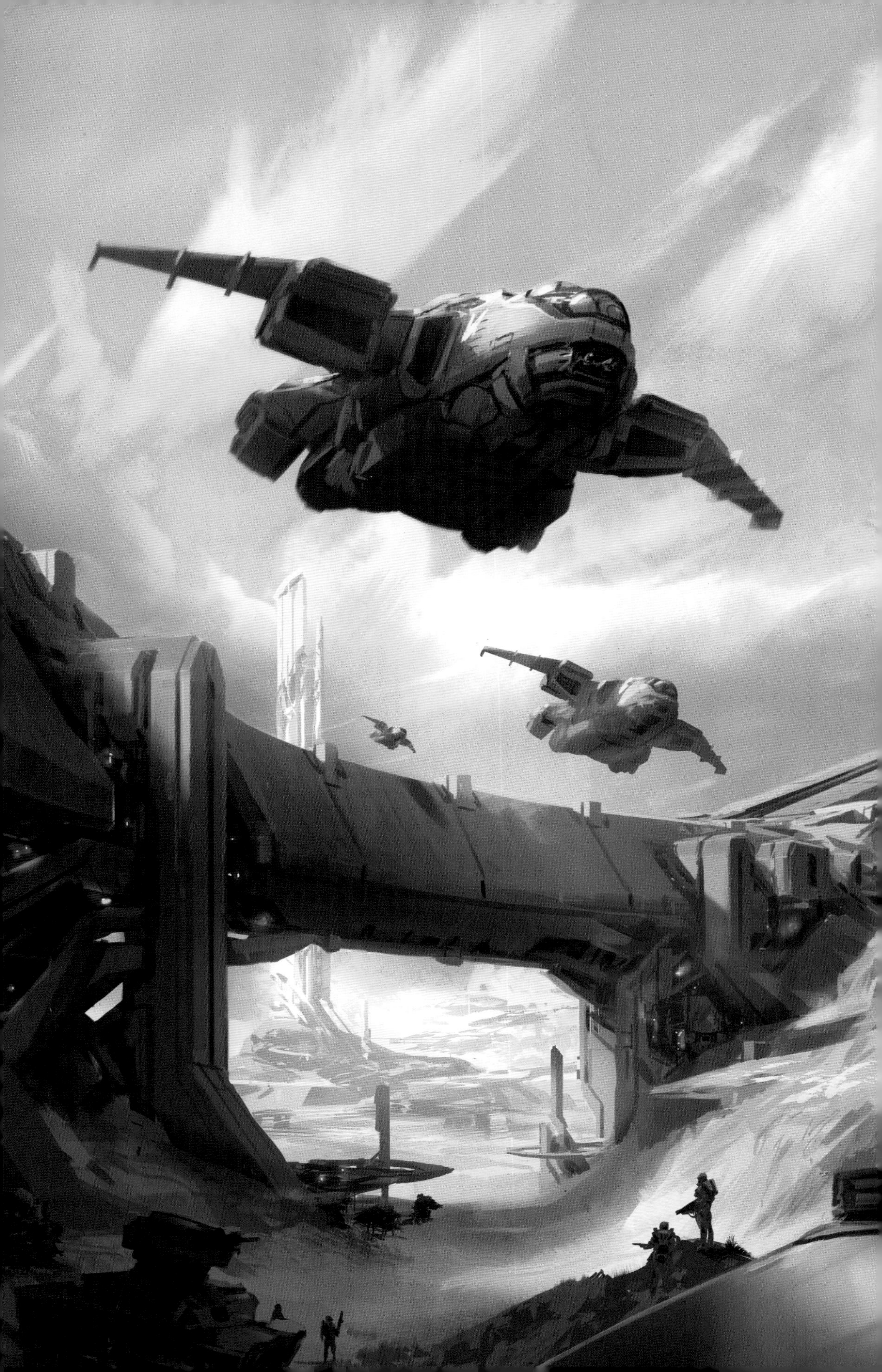

Illustration by Sparth

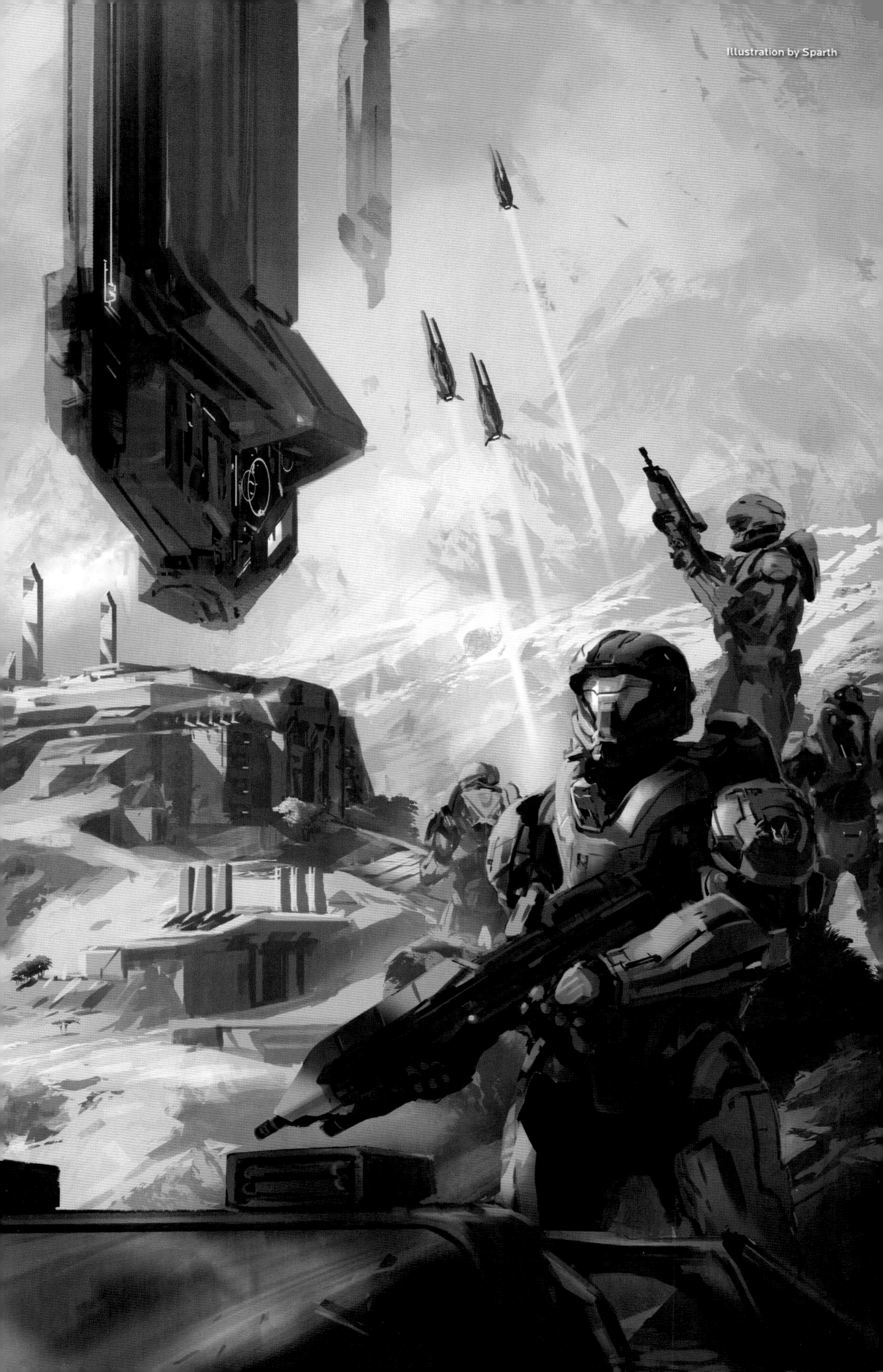

Illustration by Kenneth Scott

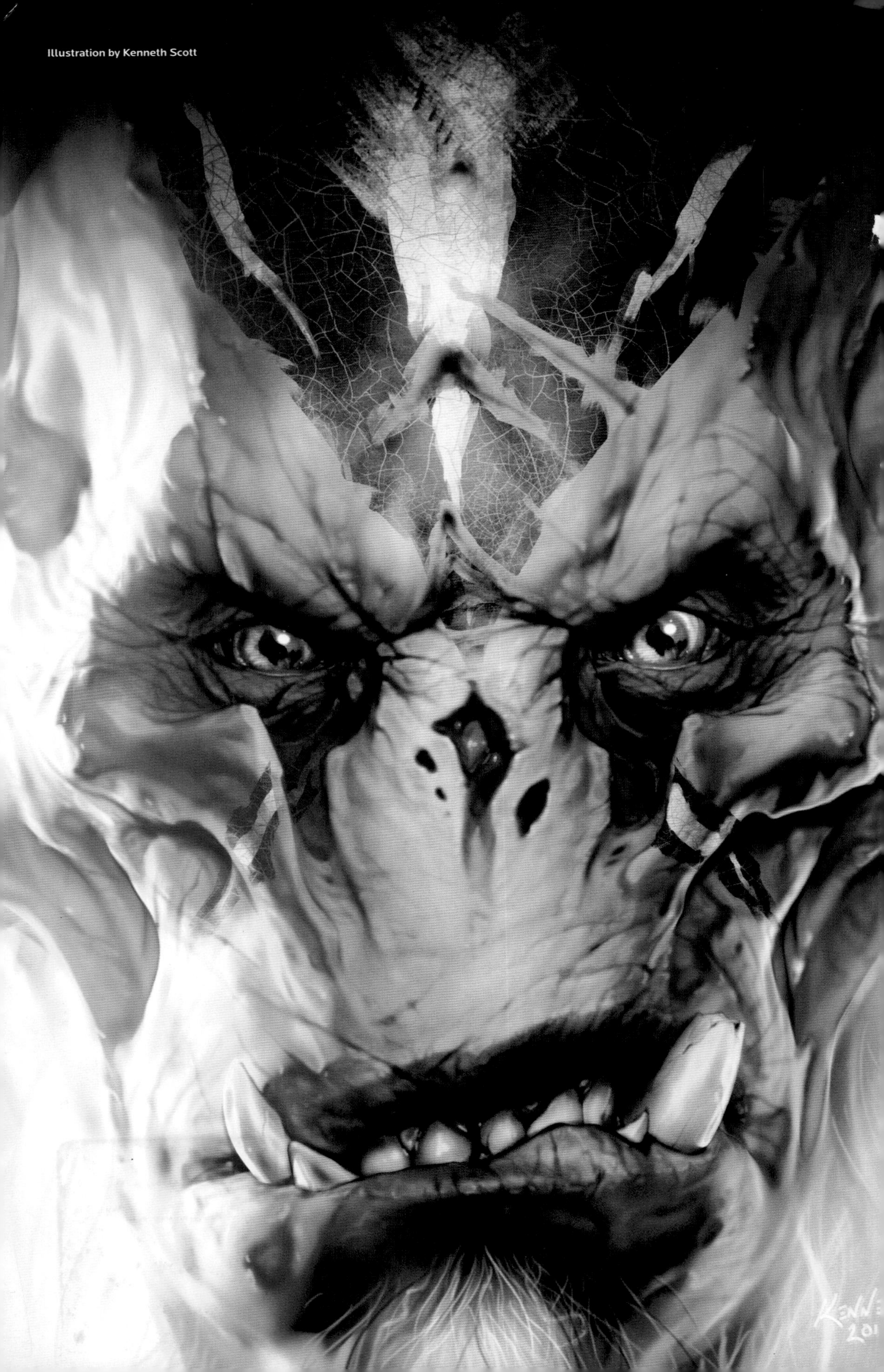